JAMES AVERY PRITCHARD

land Diary of

JAMES A. PRITCHARD

from Kentucky to California in

1849

With a biography of Captain James A. Pritchard by
HUGH PRITCHARD WILLIAMSON

Edited by

DALE L. MORGAN

With an introduction, bibliography, and a chart of travel by
all known diarists west across South Pass in 1849 and illustrated
with a portrait, and two unpublished maps of 1849
drawn by J. Goldsborough Bruff

FRED A. ROSENSTOCK

THE OLD WEST PUBLISHING COMPANY

MCMLIX

Library of Congress Card No. 59-9477

DESIGNED AND PRINTED BY LAWTON KENNEDY, SAN FRANCISCO

TO THAT *WEST*-BY-GOD VIRGINIAN

DAREL McCONKEY

Who, like James A. Pritchard in another century, has known
the lure and splendor of the continental spaces beyond the
Alleghenies, and who during nineteen years has been my friend.

DALE L. MORGAN

TABLE OF CONTENTS

Illustrations

INTRODUCTION

THE HEADLONG RUSH TO CALIFORNIA precipitated by James W. Marshall's find in the tail race of Sutter's mill at Coloma in January, 1848, affords one of the most compelling spectacles of modern history. It explosively peopled the Pacific West, forever changed the face of America and the character of the American people, and altered the course of history in so many ways that scholars will never trace them all.

As drama and spectacle, the Gold Rush has been continuously exciting to the imagination, from 1849 to the present. The rich resulting literature has been agreeably surveyed by Carl I. Wheat in *Books of the California Gold Rush* (San Francisco, 1949), which discusses the first promotional books and guides, the narratives of travel by the several routes, accounts of life in the diggings, and serious scholarly studies of later eras, 239 books being individually described, and a good many more mentioned in passing.

That literature, to the extent that it is a record of personal experience, had its inception in the hometown newspapers of the Forty-niners. The fragments of autobiography recorded in the letters and diaries sent home by the Argonauts to this day make the reading of newspaper files of 1849-1850 an adventure. No one has ever written quite so well of the Forty-niners as they wrote of themselves, and scarcely a newspaper was published in any corner of the Union but had a stake in the Gold Rush as reflected in the fortunes of some townsman.

Soon separately printed accounts of the Gold Rush began to appear, narratives of personal experience which commenced to issue from the press as early as 1850. With emigration still swelling toward high tide, these narratives were often published for sale as overland guides, as in the case of G. S. Isham's diary, or John Stemmons' letters.[1] But other motives were at work; men

---

1. For Isham, see Bibliography. Stemmons is mentioned to direct attention

like John Hale, "aware that tens of thousands of American citizens have been sacrificed in consequence of being deceived [by false reports in regard to . . . California]," resolutely prepared accounts of their experiences on the Western trails and in the diggings as a means of exerting "all the influence in [their] power to prevent [their] fellow-citizens from emigrating to that country."

Yet other narratives, like the diary of Samuel Rutherford Dundass, presently were published as memorials to men who died after reaching California, or on the way West. And of course there were men of journalistic bent, like William Kelly, who from the outset saw the Gold Rush as a literary vein free for the mining; and others, like Alonzo Delano, whose correspondence to hometown newspapers opened up possibilities within themselves they may never have suspected, their experiences transmuted as time went on into mature books descriptive of the trails and the mines.[2]

As the years went by, the aging "California Pioneers" commenced to produce a richly anecdotal literature of reminiscence. And in our own day scholars bringing a lively new appreciation to the starkly contemporary records of the Gold Rush have actively sought them out; diaries and letters of Forty-niners have been gathered up for preservation in many great libraries, particularly in California, and have also been published in ever-increasing numbers, sometimes merely thrown into print, but more often edited with care and discrimination, and sometimes converted by scholars in love with their subject into absolute

---

to an overland narrative of which no copy has yet been discovered. Published by Fisher & Bennett of St. Louis, it was noticed in the St. Louis *Missouri Republican*, February 21, 1850, as "A Book for Californians," this "little book" being further described as "the journal of Maj. John Stemmons, of Rocheport, Mo., noted down in the shape of familiar letters to his friends, and embracing every incident connected with his trip to California, over the Plains, last year."

2. For Hale, Dundass, Kelly, and Delano, see Bibliography.

tours de force, as when Georgia Willis Read and Ruth P. Gaines wrought upon the diaries of J. Goldsborough Bruff.[3]

So sizeable has the literature become that each letter or diary now published has to make its way against a stultifying impression—perhaps more prevalent among scholars, who often know just enough to be immunized against further knowledge, than among general readers, who are inclined to accept any new work on its own terms—that everything worth knowing about the California Gold Rush is already known.

A major purpose of the present book, while endeavoring to organize our knowledge about one sector of a single aspect of the California Gold Rush, the overland emigration across South Pass in 1849, is to point out that on the contrary much painstaking investigation will have to be undertaken, and many fortunate finds made, before we can feel that at any point we are approaching the limits of the subject.

A more profound national experience than the Gold Rush, intimately invading as it did the life and society of every State and virtually every county of the Union, would be difficult to name. Even the wars of the Republic are of a different order of experience. Yet the impact of the Gold Rush upon the several States has been studied in only a few instances. Octavius Thorndyke Howe has written about Massachusetts; Fred W. Lorch has made a shorter study of Iowa; Kate L. Gregg began a series of studies about Missouri, interrupted by other preoccupations and her death; and Robert Thomas has made a beginning on Ohio.[4] Such local studies are productive of insights on the highest

---

3. Published as *Gold Rush* (New York, 1944, 2 vols.).

4. See O. T. Howe, *Argonauts of '49* (Cambridge, 1923); Fred W. Lorch, "Iowa and the California Gold Rush of 1849," *Iowa Journal of History and Politics,* vol. 30, July, 1932, pp. 307-376; Kate L. Gregg, "Missourians in the Gold Rush," and "Boonslickers in the Gold Rush to California," *Missouri Historical Review,* vol. 39, January, 1945, pp. 137-164; vol. 41, July, 1947, pp. 345-360; and Robert Thomas, "Buckeye Argonauts," *Ohio State Archaeological and Historical Quarterly,* vol. 59, July, 1950, pp. 256-269.

level, and we should welcome more of them. St. Louis newspaper correspondents, remarking in the spring of 1849 on the emigration gathering on the Missouri River frontier, noted that every State in the Union was represented by an organized company— an astonishing observation when it is considered that sea routes would appeal to inheritors of the maritime tradition of the Atlantic coast, and that routes through Mexico, Texas, and New Mexico would attract overland emigrants starting from southern States; the observation serves to indicate how much we might learn from a State-by-State study of the Gold Rush, drawing upon the diaries here reported to supplement information in county histories and the indispensable letters and news reports now largely buried in newspaper files difficult of access to general scholars.

When on this local level the Gold Rush shall have been comprehensively studied, we shall be on the road to comprehending its whole significance in American history, for the departure of Forty-niners gave towns and counties everywhere a personal stake in the West such as few had had before, as well as home-town eyes to take a look at this far-off country, and what can be learned of the shifting relationships between those who went and those who stayed home must have surpassing interest. A corollary study would scrutinize the organized companies of goldseekers, with their constitutions, bylaws, financial arrangements, and eventual fate. The St. Louis newspapers in particular, reporting between March and May, 1849, on the companies assembling at the frontier, listing companies by the hundred and members by the thousand, suggest the fruitful inquiries that might be made.

Ere long we shall also expect to have a study of the Gold Rush as an aggregate of human experience, distilled from the absolutely contemporary record. Why and under what conditions men journeyed to California in 1849, and with what outfits; how they reacted to one another and the characteristic experiences of the trail; what those experiences were; where the trails went, and why; why one trail was used instead of another, or why at one time and not at another; why some parties held together when others were torn asunder; what social values are observable; why some values stood up when others did not; the nature of home ties and how men were affected by them; and the whole range of experience after reaching the gold fields—these are just a few of the many questions posed by the emerging diaries of the Forty-niners. Most of what has thus far been published has been based upon too little directly contemporary documentation. Archer B. Hulbert's *Forty-niners* (Boston, 1931) was one effort to convey to the uninitiated a living sense of what it was like to journey overland to the mines in 1849, but Hulbert's medium was a fictitious diary, the materials for which he drew from diaries of travel to California written all through the Fifties, and without much regard for the subtle differences that set each year apart from every other. The job should be done all over again, and someone will do it, for the accumulating original documents of 1849 cannot but strike fire in the imagination of some passing scholar.

The primary contribution of the present book is that for the first time it brings the actual overland diaries of 1849 (excluding, however, those kept on southern routes) under scholarly discipline. With a chronologically arranged chart and an alphabetically arranged list of diaries, each complementing the other, every known diary kept on the northern route to California during the first year of the Gold Rush has been reported, showing the State and community from which the diarist came, the name of his company (if it had one, or if known), the date on which he passed more than fifty landmarks along the trail, the effective terminal date of his diary as a record of an overland journey, and, at least indicatively, how long this diary was kept afterwards. (If not otherwise stated, the diarist was still in California when his record closes; but it would swell this book to unmanageable proportions to attempt a description of how the diarist fared after reaching California: any interested scholar is invited to go on from where the present book must leave off.) The better to bring out the relationships of the various diarists to all others on the trail, each has been entered on the chart approximately in accordance with the date he arrived at Fort Laramie, where the various trails from the Missouri River came finally together. Although some Forty-niners, approaching tangentially from the south, entered the established California Trail for the first time west of Fort Laramie, no diarists on these routes have appeared.[5]

Altogether, 132 diaries or equivalent, including eight collections of letters, are entered in list and chart. If compared with the known diaries for any previous year in the history of overland travel, the number seems large. In fact, it is statistically small —less than one-half of one per cent of the estimated 30,000 people who in 1849 traveled to California across South Pass.[6]

---

5. Such routes were principally three. The "Cherokee Trail," which came north along the Front Range of the Rockies to the Cache la Poudre, then went via the Laramie Plains and Bitter Creek to strike the Salt Lake Road east of Fort Bridger, was traveled in 1849 by members of the Lewis Evans party from the Cherokee Nation; letters written by various members of this party are reprinted by Ralph B. Bieber in *Southern Trails to California in 1849* (Glendale, 1937), pp. 325-350. An actual diary on this route in 1850 is that of John Lowery Brown, edited by Muriel H. Wright in *Chronicles of Oklahoma*, vol. 12, June, 1934, pp. 177-213. As will be seen, *post*, Note 1, the Ithaca Company in 1849 followed this route as far as the Laramie Plains and the North Platte, but then took a more southerly course via Browns Hole, old Fort Uintah, and Utah Valley. Some members of this company may then have gone on to California by the northern or Humboldt route, but the company itself finished its journey from the Mormon settlements via the southern road to Los Angeles. Thus it never actually touched at any point the main northern trails with which this book is concerned. The third principal route was the old Spanish Trail from Santa Fe to Utah Valley. No party has yet been identified as having traveled this route, but I believe this information will be forthcoming in the course of time, and that some who entered Utah by the Spanish Trail will be found to have gone on to California by the Humboldt route. See, *post*, Note 104.

Yet the sampling is the first from which general conclusions may be drawn, having any statistical validity; and in one sense the smallness of the sampling is more apparent than real: Emigrants traveled in companies, not as individuals, and a single diary consequently may encompass the experiences of several dozen travelers. (On the other hand, against all the laws of probability, an astonishing number of diaries have emerged, kept by members of the same company—Gould and Staples of one party; Bruff and Austin of another; Bowman, Hackney, Kirkpatrick, Page, and Tappan of yet another; and consider the statistical unlikelihood that three different diaries should turn up, kept by men named Clark!)

A few of the statistical implications of this mass of diaries I shall remark later, but I wish to discuss the diaries as individual records of experience on the trail in 1849, point out some areas of persisting ignorance, and touch lightly upon the gap between the absolute limits of our knowledge and the record as represented in the diaries.

First, and by way of putting the overland emigration of 1849 in perspective, let us note that the earliest travelers to reach California across the Sierra Nevada this year started not from the Missouri River but from the Mormon settlements in the valley of the Great Salt Lake. As early as March 21, 1849, eight wagons and families left Great Salt Lake City "preparatory to going to the gold mines." How many in all departed the Mormon Zion for Babylon during the next month is not known; one of the Forty-niners, Joseph Hackney, noted in August that "sixty teams left salt Lake for California this spring," but evidently

---

6. The estimates have run between 25,000 and 35,000 for the emigration to California across South Pass in 1849. I am content to adopt Georgia Willis Read's "golden mean" of 30,000 for present purposes, especially because the question receives more extended consideration in a forthcoming work by J. S. Holliday. It should be added that the year's Oregon emigration is estimated at from 400 to 500, and the Mormon emigration to Utah at about 1,400 souls.

many packers went as well. Somewhere in this advance emigration traveled one of Brigham Young's apostles, Amasa Lyman, sent to California with an epistle to "the faithful Saints," and the only definite dates from any source about the movements of these home-grown Forty-niners come from Lyman's subsequent report to Young from Sacramento July 6 that he had reached Sutter's May 25, "45 days from Salt Lake City by the northern route."[7]

No diary detailing the experiences of these earliest goldseekers who crossed the Sierra in 1849 has yet appeared, but we may hope that such a record will be found. Abner Blackburn has left some remarkable reminiscences of a journey from Utah to California this spring, enlivened by recollections of his discovery of gold at what became known as Gold Canyon, in Nevada, but Blackburn gives the name of only one companion, William Lane, and says merely that he "joined a pack train for the gold mines," leaving us to infer that some went independent of the wagon company.[8]

These all but forgotten Forty-niners who began their journey from Salt Lake made an earlier start than those who set out from the Missouri River, where throngs had been gathering since the beginning of March. The spring was slow and wet in 1849, after a severe winter, and only a few risked a start before the beginning of May. (Some, it is true, felt afterward that this had been a mistake, and that they could just as well have got off two weeks earlier; Pritchard was of this mind.) The earliest company to get away from St. Joseph was that of Colonel Vital Jarrot, identified by the *Missouri Republican* on April 20, 1849, as the "St. Clair Mining Company" from St. Clair County, Illinois. By a happy

---

7. See Latter-day Saints' Journal History, MS. compilation in L. D. S. Church Historian's Office, Salt Lake City, Utah, entries for March 21 and July 6, 1849; for Hackney, see Bibliography.

8. Abner Blackburn, MS. Reminiscences, typed transcript in my possession through the courtesy of Robert A. Allen.

stroke of fortune, a small party from Belleville, Illinois, which included the diarist Daniel Gelwicks, joined Jarrot on April 14 and embarked out into the plains with him on April 19. Since Jarrot went ahead in leisurely fashion, he was overtaken east of the Big Blue on April 26 by a party of Kentuckians, "all old men, gentlemanly and affable, and full of enthusiasm," Gelwicks says, and soon after by other companies from Iowa, Kentucky, Michigan, and Indiana, so that from this time forward we no longer have a diary reflecting conditions at the apex of the emigration. Nevertheless, the diaries of Joshua D. Breyfogle, Franklin Starr, Charles A. Tinker, G. S. Isham, Peter Decker, and Charles E. Boyle, in the first wave out of St. Joseph, unite with that of Gelwicks to present a graphic picture of this portion of the year's emigration.

At Independence the first company to get away seems to have been that of G. W. Paul, and a diary reporting its experiences would be a happy discovery. The *Missouri Republican* of April 12, 1849, prints an Independence dispatch of April 7 which tells of visiting this company at its encampment on the Santa Fe road about 10 miles from town; at this time 10 emigrants composed the party; with a majority of Missourians, it included men from Massachusetts, New Jersey, New Hampshire, and Pennsylvania. William G. Johnston tells of Paul's departure for the prairies on April 14, the first to leave, and the *Missouri Republican* of April 23, 1849, in another Independence dispatch of April 17, mentions that no companies had yet made a final start "except those of Lieut. Paul and Capt. [William] Pye"—the latter actually leaving later with Johnston's party. If, as he asserts, William Kelly got away from the frontier two days later, on April 16, the fact has left no deposit in the records of the emigration.[9] In any event, after another week the emigration began to

9. Kelly has to be taken with a grain of salt throughout, as for literary effect he placed himself at the front of the emigration from the time he set out. He also appropriated unto himself at least one incident that belongs to Paul's party;

roll in force from Independence, the earliest diarists to record departure being Delos R. Ashley and his companion of the Monroe Company, David Cosad, William G. Johnston, Amos P. Josselyn, and Samuel Rutherford Dundass.

The first diarist on the Old Fort Kearny road is John Boggs, who passed that point May 3; we have no concrete information as to who may have preceded him. A *Missouri Republican* correspondent, "M. M.," writing on May 2 from the vicinity of Old Fort Kearny, said: "We have heard of but one company that has started yet, that of Colonel Jarrot. . . . Captain Miller, with a small company, will leave in two or three days from Fort Kearny, taking a central route between St. Joseph and the northern route from Council Bluffs." This would place the laconic Boggs as among the earliest on this route. By the northernmost road, via Council Bluffs and the north bank of the Platte, we have no diarists who left the Missouri ahead of George E. Jewett and Isaac Foster on May 16; Foster gives us to think that the first company north of the Platte traveled four days ahead of his own, eventually reaching Fort Laramie on June 12. It seems likely that any who set out from the Council Bluffs area prior to this time went down the Missouri to cross at Old Fort Kearny, going on by the south bank of the Platte.[10]

Paul's driver John Fuller who accidentally shot himself at the Big Blue on April 28, as recorded in Johnston's diary and several newspapers of 1849, becomes "John Coulter" and one of Kelly's party in the latter's narrative.

10. This route was taken by the first Mormon company of 1849, that captained by Howard Egan, which is not included among the five organized companies usually defined as the Mormon emigration of 1849. A combination of letter and diary by Egan, May 13-June 1, ending on arrival at (New) Fort Kearny is printed in *Frontier Guardian*, July 14, 1849. Egan found the trail south of the Platte so congested that he considered going up the north bank of the Platte after reaching the head of Grand Island, if it was possible to cross the river. It does not appear that he did so. Egan reached Salt Lake July 29 in advance of his company, which came in August 8. He later traveled the southern road to Los Angeles, and his diary, November 18, 1849-February 23, 1850, is

South of the Platte, the three main trails came together at the head of Grand Island, where "new" Fort Kearny, the post now thought of by that name, was established in 1848. Here we can first measure the effectiveness of the diaries as general reportage on the emigration—the first and the last, as well as the mass traveling in between. On May 18 a Fort Kearny correspondent wrote the *Missouri Republican* that "The first specimen [of gold digger], with a large pick axe over his shoulder, a long rifle in his hand, and two revolvers and a Bowie knife stuck in his belt, made his appearance here a week ago last Sunday [May 6]. . . . Since then wagons have been constantly passing."[11] The mountain man Miles M. Goodyear wrote the *Republican* from the same point the day before, "About three hundred wagons have passed; the foremost train about ten days ago. They are said to be go-ahead boys from St. Louis"[12]—which would indicate that Paul's company managed to keep out ahead of the trains from Independence thus far, at least, and that the diaries are nearly up with the vanguard of the emigration; it will be seen that Breyfogle reached Fort Kearny on May 8, Kelly apparently the same day, and Gelwicks on May 9. Our own diarist, James A. Pritchard, having delayed at Independence until May 3, did not reach this point until May 18.

The subsequent movement of the great mass of the emigration past Fort Kearny is well displayed by the chart. The *Republican's* correspondent, in a final letter written from the fort, says that as

---

printed in Howard R. Egan, ed., *Pioneering the West* (Richmond, Utah, 1917), pp. 169-81. (I have not been able to include it in the analysis, or to enter it in chart or bibliography, but belatedly I learn of a MS. diary with Egan's company, April 18-August 7, kept by Peter O. Hansen; original in L. D. S. Church Historian's Office.)

11. St. Louis *Missouri Republican*, June 4, 1849. In the Galena *Weekly North-Western Gazette*, July 4, 1849, is a letter by Edward W. Morrison, "Near Fort Child, May 6, 1849," saying, "There is but one company ahead of us, and that in sight this morning." He was one of the company, mostly from St. Louis, whose Captain Lafferty separated from Jarrot April 30.

12. *Ibid.*, July 6, 1849.

of June 23 a total of 5,516 wagons had passed on the south bank of the Platte, with perhaps another 600 on the north bank.[13] James M. Hutchings, who came along June 24, is the only California-bound diarist who reached Fort Kearny afterward, though some travelers bound for Salt Lake subsequently passed along the opposite bank of the Platte. Unreported in diaries or contemporary newspapers are parties that came along in the very late summer; one called Critcher's, undoubtedly the final company on the northern plains in 1849, left the Missouri River as late as September 24, and could scarcely have reached Fort Kearny before the first week of October; they were caught by snow in the Wasatch Mountains, and reached Salt Lake City, stripped of all property, on December 1.[14] We will have a much ampler view of the overland emigration of 1849 when a diary kept in such a party shall be found.

At the next major checkpoint on the trail, Fort Laramie, we find a gap opening up between the foremost travelers and the foremost diarists. According to a letter written on May 24 from Fort Laramie by Bruce Husband, then in charge, the advance guard of the emigration had arrived a little before, almost the whole force of the fort being employed in crossing their wagons

---

13. *Ibid.*, August 6, 1849. I think that this correspondent, who signed himself "Pawnee," may have been Captain Stewart Van Vliet, then quartermaster at Fort Kearny.

14. Critcher's party is so named by Gunnison, in an entry in his journal made in January, 1850. The Third General Epistle of the Presidency, April 12, 1850, printed in *Frontier Guardian*, June 12, 1850, said of it, "Nineteen emigrants arrived December 1st, in a very destitute situation, having left their wagons more than forty miles back, and their teams about twenty; themselves without provision. They reported having left the States on the 24th September, and having passed Elder [John] Taylor's [east-bound] company at Independence Rock, November 6th. . . ." See also the MS. diary of Hosea Stout for December 1, 1849 (photocopies in Utah State Historical Society and Henry E. Huntington Library); and Maybelle Harmon Anderson, ed., *Appleton Milo Harmon Goes West* (Berkeley, 1946), p. 61. Some 49ers, like P. L. Platt of the 1852 *Guide*, wintered at Fort Laramie (*Oquawka Spectator*, Oct. 2, 1850).

over the Laramie River.[15] It was not until May 27 that Breyfogle, the first diarist to arrive, reached the east bank of the Laramie.

Those who were now five days ahead of the diarists maintained their margin through the Black Hills and on to the upper crossing of the North Platte. Lorenzo D. Young, who had come east with a Mormon party intending to operate a ferry across the North Platte at present Casper, Wyoming, tells of accompanying his brethren to the ferry site, of crossing the river on May 28 after arriving the day before, and of then continuing on to Deer Creek; he adds, "This day commenced meeting emigrants for the mines."[16] Charles Shumway, in charge of the ferry, in a letter to Brigham Young soon after, similarly says that his company arrived "on the 27th, raised their boats, and found them in good order. . . . On the 29th the first company of emigrants for the California gold mines reached the ferry, who stated that the road thence to the Missouri river was lined with emigrant wagons for the same destination."[17] Thus the foremost Forty-niners were across the North Platte before any of the known diarists had advanced beyond Fort Laramie, 125 miles below.[18]

15. LeRoy R. Hafen and F. M. Young, *Fort Laramie and the Pageant of the West* (Glendale, 1938), pp. 132-133. Husband is ambiguous as to the actual date of arrival, but the *Frontier Guardian*, June 27, 1849, recording the arrival of Mormon mail carriers from Salt Lake, says they met the first emigrants at Fort Laramie May 23. It seems likely the advance party arrived May 22 and stayed on till the 23rd, for an emigrant, "Joaquin," writing from the fort July 21 in the *Missouri Republican*, August 29, 1849, said the first train, from St. Louis, came up on May 22. The earliest emigrant letter from Fort Laramie yet seen is by A. J. Harris, May 24, in the Galena *Gazette*, July 25, 1849; Harris said only one company, Paul's, was ahead, then about 25 miles in advance.

16. "Diary of Lorenzo Dow Young," *Utah Historical Quarterly*, vol. 14, 1946, p. 169.

17. Quoted in L. D. S. Journal History, May 27, 1849.

18. It might be noted that "Joaquin," as cited in Note 15, reported that the majority of the emigration passed Fort Laramie before July 1, that 5,500 wagons had gone by, and only 100 families. A correspondent of the Columbus *Ohio*

Beyond the North Platte, less information is available on the trail situation as it developed during June and July of 1849. We have no dates for the first arrivals at South Pass, or at the junction between the Greenwood Cutoff (this year renamed the Sublette Cutoff) and the Salt Lake Road west of the Pass. A little information has come forth about the first arrival of Forty-niners at Great Salt Lake City, one account giving the date as June 16, another naming Captain Paul's company as the first to get there.[19] The earliest reference to arriving Forty-niners thus far found in a Mormon diary is by Eliza R. Snow on June 19, "People with pack animals arrive from the States going to California. They expect wagons in 2 or 3 days." The next remark of the kind occurs in Alexander Neibaur's journal on June 20, "A company of men from Ohio bound for California arrived in Great Salt Lake City."[20] It can be shown that William Kelly did not reach the Mormon settlement till June 22, Breyfogle the same day, and Johnston next morning, so the first diarists on this southerly branch of the South Pass route had lost still more ground to the nameless Forty-niners out in front.

Statesman, as summarized in the Galena *Gazette* of September 19, 1849, contradictorily reported from the fort on July 22 that 7,000 wagons had passed, with 500 yet to come up, including the Mormon trains and excluding the government military trains.

19. See *L. D. S. Millennial Star*, vol. 11, November 15, 1849, pp. 337-338; December 1, 1849, pp. 366-367. A perplexing thing is that Johnston, who is our principal source of information about Paul's progress along the trail, on arrival at Fort Bridger June 17, "learned . . . that Captain Paul, who is in the lead of all emigrant parties, is but thirty-six hours in advance of us. He . . . followed from this point the Oregon trail, going northward via Fort Hall." Either Johnston is twice incorrect or the information from Mormon sources is erroneous; Paul could not have reached Salt Lake by the 16th if at Fort Bridger on the 15th or 16th. For later references to Paul's company, see Johnston's diary entries for July 2, 13, and 16; as of July 16 Paul had been at the Carson River "a few nights since," which would be well ahead of Cosad.

20. LeRoi C. Snow, ed., "Pioneer Diary of Eliza R. Snow," *Improvement Era*, vol. 47, April, 1944, p. 241; L. D. S. Journal History, June 20, 1849.

On the main branch of the trail west of South Pass, the more direct Sublette Cutoff, David Cosad is the leading diarist, first to reach Green River, first at Fort Hall, first to reach the junction with the Salt Lake Cutoff near City of Rocks, first to cross the Forty-mile Desert to the Carson River—and, indeed, first to reach the diggings. He gained in time and space relative to those who traveled via Salt Lake, but we have no sufficient information on how far he trailed those absolutely first among the emigration. A remark in Joseph Hackney's diary, on meeting an eastbound company of Mormons on the Humboldt August 20, is to the effect that the first overland arrivals reached Sutter's the same day they left, five weeks before; and more exactly, Kimball Webster on September 5 was told that these Mormons had left Sutter's 53 days before, *i.e.*, July 14. Both notations should be compared with Isaac Lord's, *post*, note 94, and Cosad's July 25 arrival at Placerville appraised accordingly.

The California newspapers displayed no particular excitement over what was, from the long view back to the Missouri River, a considerable event. The San Francisco *Alta California* of August 2, 1849, was moved only to remark: "The advance companies of the Rocky Mountain emigration are entering the country by the northern route. A few members of the first party are in this place. A letter from Sacramento city, dated July 24, contains the following intelligence:—'Emigrants from Missouri, over the mountains, are now arriving daily. The first party of *packers* has been here five or six days, and reports four wagons in Pleasant Valley, about 100 miles above, and five or six thousand wagons on the way and not far behind'."

A somewhat more enlightening report was written to the New York *Tribune* from Sacramento on Saturday, July 28: "I saw last week [*i.e.*, July 21 or earlier] the first company of adventurers who have arrived by the overland route—Capt. [Miles M.] Goodyear's party which started from San Jose [St. Joseph] on the Missouri River in May last. They report but 67 traveling days through, and all the party look hearty and rugged. Capt. Goodyear thinks that the first wagon train will enter the valley of the Sacramento on the 15th of July. Capt. G. expresses the belief that most of the wagon trains will suffer unaccountably from scarcity of grass for animals, although he represents the yield of grass as more than ordinary good, and this is his third trip across the mountains. There has another small party arrived, both of which took the Salt Lake Valley route. . . ."[21] If, in fact, Goodyear's was the first party to reach California across South Pass in 1849, he had made good time from Fort Laramie, where Lorenzo D. Young had encountered him on June 1; despite having gone the Salt Lake route, he had outpaced all others.[22]

How much remains to be found out about the overland emigration of 1849 is at least suggested by this running account of a single aspect of its history, emphasis placed upon swiftest passages, with attention to the gap between the vanguard and the earliest known diarists. But other stories await investigation and the providential coming forth of new documentation. In particular, the tail end of the 1849 emigration would reward study. The last diarists to cross the Sierra by the Carson route, nearly all in the first two weeks of October, were Timothy Judge, J. M. Hutchings, David Dewolf, O. J. Hall, and Sarah Royce; no diarists on the Truckee route in October have appeared, and it

21. The letter is reprinted from the *Tribune* in the Springfield *Illinois Journal*, September 21, 1849. In a second letter the correspondent passes on information obtained from James Stewart, the guide of Johnston's party, "one of the foremost parties through from St. Louis by the Salt Lake route, by the way of the Mormon cut-off."

22. Compare Dale L. Morgan, "Miles Goodyear and the Founding of Ogden," *Utah Historical Quarterly*, vol. 21, October, 1953, pp. 321-329, and Charles Kelly and Maurice L. Howe, *Miles Goodyear* (Salt Lake City, 1937), pp. 108-115. That William Kelly is at pains to intimate he preceded Goodyear into California may validate Goodyear's priority! Kelly did not reach Weaverville before July 30.

seems that there was no travel on this branch of the trail after September. One of several government relief trains sent out from Sacramento on September 14, having found no emigrants on the Truckee, crossed over to the Carson River and found stragglers still arriving there. A second relief train, coming across the Sierra on the Carson road, took over the responsibility of shepherding in the emigration, and brought in the last family, that of Charles Sacket from St. Louis, reaching Weaverville about October 29.[23]

Enough diaries have appeared that we can date exactly the opening of the Hudspeth Cutoff west of the Bear River, July 19-24; there are even diarists who entered upon the new cutoff the same day Benoni M. Hudspeth and John J. Myers took the pioneer train upon it. Nearly as much can be said of the opening of the Lassen Cutoff on August 11, when the first Forty-niners under Milton McGee headed west from the Humboldt into the Black Rock Desert to reach California the "quick and easy" way. Yet in neither case do we have diaries kept by members of the pioneer companies.

Still other gaps in the documentation of the northern trail to California open up when we examine even so many as 132 diaries. Oblique references to parties which had traveled via Santa Fe and Salt Lake to reach the Humboldt (thus by-passing South Pass) strongly suggest that the old Spanish Trail saw its share of travel, though neither diary nor letter describing such a journey has yet appeared. Even more definitely, several parties are known to have packed west from Great Salt Lake City at the beginning

---

23. The official reports of the relief, including those of John J. Chandler, Robert W. Hunt, Ferris Foreman, and Captain Charles L. Kilburn to Major D. H. Rucker are very enlightening, printed in 31st Congress, 1st Session, *Senate Executive Document 52* (Serial 561), along with much more voluminous reports by John H. Peoples concerning his labors on the Lassen Cutoff. W. A. George, in a letter of February 12, 1850, printed in the *Missouri Republican*, April 19, 1850, tells of accompanying Hunt's detachment.

of September, 1849, by way of the Hastings Cutoff, around the south shore of Great Salt Lake and on across the Salt Desert. Some were members of a New York company called the Colony Guards; others were from Milwaukee; yet others, called Dutchmen by their fellow travelers, may have been part of a well-known company of Germans from New York which originally included H. B. Scharmann and Louis Nusbaumer, but only passing mentions in the diaries of fellow emigrants report their experiences.[24]

In these remarks, emphasis has been placed upon the overland journey, especially because so many overland emigrants—Pritchard among them—ceased to keep a full diary after reaching the mines. But information on life in the mines and among the diggings is not the least valuable part of many of the diaries. Some, when kept at all, degenerate into records of the weather, about as dismal as the California rainy season itself, but many illuminate unexpected aspects of the life and society into which emigrants entered at the end of the trail. A good many Forty-niners discovered quickly that, notwithstanding all the hardships,

---

24. For a summary, see Charles Kelly, "Gold Seekers on the Hastings Cutoff," *Utah Historical Quarterly*, vol. 20, January, 1952, pp. 9-13. Since that article appeared, further information has come from the diaries of J. M. Hutchings and Timothy Judge, and some notes gathered by Benjamin I. Hayes from Jacob Grewell on January 30, 1850 (Bancroft Library MS., C-E 92; see Bibliography under Shearer). Grewell left his family to go the southern road from Utah Valley, while he himself "left his wagons on the last of August in Eutaw valley" to go via the Hastings Cutoff on horseback. He and his brother "Suffered much for water—crossing a desert of 90 miles, from Tuesday till Thursday, nothing to drink except the blood from a cow that had been dead for some time," and losing "his hearing & speech before they got through." He afterward took the Lassen Cutoff, "crossed the summit Oct. 7th entered the valley Nov. 7th, [and] got to Sutter's about 15th . . . ." A letter by J. W. Temple, Sacramento, October 2, 1849, in *Knoxville*, Illinois, *Journal*, January 9, 1850, tells of using the Hastings Cutoff but says merely that he and three companions, with six horses, crossed the 85-mile desert in 30 hours.

they had enjoyed going West, associating in a great and historic adventure while seeing the country and far places, experiencing both the freedom and the discipline of life on the trail. By contrast, rooting among gravels in search of a substance not nearly so glamorous at close range as from the distance of several thousand miles appealed scarcely at all. It was not economic necessity or opportunity alone that set men to working at all sorts of alternative occupations—running boarding houses, butchering, gardening, blacksmithing, freighting and contracting, doctoring and lawyering. Pritchard himself, though he is said at last to have made some money at mining, we find engaged in a herding enterprise when, in May, 1850, we take leave of him.

Something more must be said about the charted diaries as a whole, with their statistical implications. Five of 132 were kept by U. S. officers or attachés traveling to Oregon or Utah, and as a special class these may be ignored in an analysis. Of the remainder, 122 were kept by California-bound emigrants (including one who wintered at Salt Lake and went on the following spring), 3 were kept by Oregon-bound emigrants, and 2 by Mormons destined for Salt Lake. Thus, as a sampling, Oregon diaries are surprisingly over-represented, Mormon diaries as surprisingly under-represented, but non-California diaries more nearly proportional to California diaries, if not statistically quite in line.

A reasoned if questionable analysis of the sex distribution of the 1849 overland emigration, by Georgia Willis Read,[25] is that 85 per cent were men, 10 per cent women, and 5 per cent children. Hence 2 diaries out of 122 kept by women is slight over-representation for a presumptive 3,000 women on the trail in 1849—and the latter figure itself seems excessive.

---

25. See her "Women and Children on the Oregon-California Trail in the Gold-Rush Years," *Missouri Historical Review*, vol. 39, October, 1944, pp. 1-23.

To study the diarists in relation to the State from which they emigrated is too much of an undertaking for the present work; information afforded by the diaries should be assimilated with the mass of information still locked up in contemporary newspapers; and in any event would best be pursued on the largest scale, taking into account all avenues of approach to the gold fields—sea routes, routes through Mexico and Nicaragua, and southern land routes via the Gila Valley, as well as the northern routes across South Pass. It does, however, seem worth while to note that of 125 diarists for whom sufficient information is available, 54 started from St. Joseph and vicinity, 40 from Independence or its environs, 12 from Old Fort Kearny, and 14 from Council Bluffs by the trail north of the Platte, with 5 "military diarists" launching out from Fort Leavenworth. Most of those who crossed the Missouri at Old Fort Kearny had outfitted in or around St. Joseph; and thus far the diaries confirm the contemporary newspaper reports of an emigration out of St. Joseph considerably larger than that out of Independence, with 12 non-Mormon diarists on the Council Bluffs route slightly over-representing the 2,400 emigrants hitherto supposed to have traveled that route. (Perhaps that estimate should be revised upward.)

More interesting reporting comes beyond South Pass, where until now we have had little solid data to work with. It has been believed that emigrants who took the Sublette Cutoff outnumbered those who went via Salt Lake by perhaps 4 to 1. Our sampling, first limited to 129 diarists on whom we have sufficient information, then leaving out of consideration 10 bound for Oregon or Utah, finds 78 going via the Sublette Cutoff, 2 via the Old Oregon Trail, and 39 via Salt Lake. Figures with such revolutionary implications should be examined still more closely. During the first few weeks the 4 to 1 ratio holds; 42 took the Sublette Cutoff, 9 the Salt Lake Road. But of those who crossed South Pass after July 4, 36 traveled the Sublette Cutoff and 30 took the Salt Lake Road; that is, during the latter part of the season over 45 per cent of the emigration went via Salt Lake; and for the whole year, over 35 per cent. If the California emigration totaled 30,000, some 10,500 passed through Salt Lake. It will be interesting if a thorough study of the letters written by Forty-niners should hereafter support these conclusions from the diaries.

That no diary has been found for the Hastings Cutoff west of Salt Lake in 1849 is not unreasonable; so few traveled this route that even one diary would be statistically out of line for the whole emigration. There was heavier travel by the southern road from Salt Lake to Los Angeles, during and after October, 1849, and 6 diarists on this route seems by no means disproportionate. As for those who went on to California by the main Humboldt trail, whether or not by way of Salt Lake, it is surprising that 41 of 110 diarists chose the Lassen Cutoff, despite the fact that none had taken it prior to August 11. Of the 69 who continued down the Humboldt to its Sink, 37 took the Truckee route across the Sierra, and 32 chose the Carson route—a pattern of choice the more interesting in that we know from the reports of the U. S. relief expeditions that the Truckee route was not used at all after September, 1849, those who had not taken the Lassen Cutoff continuing by the Carson road.

Rather than attempt to exploit myself all the statistical possibilities inherent in the diaries, I invite the attention of students, who will find here points of departure for investigations which could be productive of many new insights.

By a happy circumstance the account of James Pritchard which prefaces his diary is written by his grandnephew, Hugh Pritchard Williamson. An assistant attorney-general for the State of Missouri, and himself the author of a book on the Middle Border, Mr. Williamson provides a sympathetic and intimately informed picture of Pritchard the man, and leaves to me the congenial responsibility of saying something about the diary itself.

Pritchard is one of the very few Forty-niners who describes a journey by land across Missouri, from St. Louis to Independence. This first part of his diary, continued until he passed the junction of the Independence and St. Joseph roads west of the Big Blue, was published some years ago in the *Missouri Historical Review,* and thus his name has echoed familiarly through all the books about the overland trails written in recent years. That part of his diary previously unpublished is no less interesting. To his superior descriptions of Independence and the approaches to the Kansas River, he adds detailed accounts of the ford at the South Fork of the Platte, Ash Hollow, the Black Hills, the North Platte and Green River ferries, the Snake Indians, Fort Hall, the City of Rocks, the Forty-mile Desert, Carson Valley and Canyon, the Sierra Nevada and its foothill country, Coloma, and the environs of Sacramento. He throws fresh light on many persons who stand up above their fellows in American history, from Dr. John Sappington to Lansford W. Hastings; and better than most diarists, he shows us the problems attendant on the breakup of companies en route.

Pritchard got off early, ahead of the cholera scourge, and he kept moving, usually among the first dozen diarists for any particular stretch of the trail. This is a comment upon his sensible management, but it also gives his diary a special value when contrasted with a record like that of J. Goldsborough Bruff or William Swain, who traveled near the tail-end of the emigration; the stresses, strains, and changing conditions of travel during 1849 become manifest. With all this, Pritchard was not a diarist exclusively, or even very largely, preoccupied with himself. His diary tells much about the kind of person he was, and sometimes gives oblique glimpses of his past, but on the whole it is an interestingly impersonal record.

The original diary, bound in brown leather, measures 19 x 12.5 cm., and is written in brown ink on 203 numbered pages. Pritchard has written his name in pencil on the flyleaf. After three blank pages there is a leaf bearing the memorandum, "Mr. N E Breinham San Hosay." Although the diary was written on the trail, Pritchard obviously wrote it up at intervals from brief daily memoranda, so that occasionally he writes retrospectively. In printing the diary, I have rendered the text quite literally, the better to convey its directness and informality. However, Pritchard was much given to the use of short dashes, not only between sentences, phrases and words, but even within words. These I have largely eliminated or converted into other punctuation; I have also closed up some words he spaced as two, and in a few instances have modified his capitalization and punctuation, also breaking up into shorter passages some of the longest of his paragraphs.

The frontispiece portrait of Pritchard is reproduced from an oil painting in the possession of Mr. Williamson, from whom also the diary was obtained for the collection of Mr. Fred A. Rosenstock. The unpublished Bruff maps, as set forth in the special note, are reproduced by courtesy of the National Archives and Mr. Herman R. Friis, head of its Cartographic Branch; and the section from the Goddard map has been made available by Mr. Francis P. Farquhar, who owns one of the extremely rare originals.

I was persuaded to edit the Pritchard diary by Mr. Rosenstock, who is not only one of America's most notable antiquarian booksellers and publishers of distinctive Western Americana, but a friend of long standing. To the book he has contributed much, including information on half a dozen Forty-niner diaries I should otherwise have known nothing about. I am also immensely indebted to Mr. J. S. Holliday, whose own book on the Gold Rush will appear on the heels of this one; with notable generosity he placed at my disposal the fruits of years of research, made new investigations responsive to my special needs, personally examined all the diaries in the Henry E. Huntington Library for my benefit, and enriched chart and bibliography by at least a dozen interesting diaries.

Mrs. Marjorie Borland capably transcribed the manuscript to start the whole work. While the book was in preparation, my colleagues on the Bancroft Library staff aided in solving many problems. In particular I thank the Director, Mr. George P. Hammond, Mrs. Julia H. Macleod, Mr. John Barr Tompkins, Mr. Robert Becker, Mrs. Helen H. Bretnor, Mr. Richard Bernard, Mrs. Elisabeth Gudde, Mrs. Ruth Rodriguez, Mrs. Vivian Fisher, and Miss Estelle Rebec. Other divisions of the University of California Library helped, the General Library, the Documents, Periodical, and Map divisions; and especially Mr. William R. Hawken and his staff of the Library's Photographic Service, whose skills have become indispensable for scholars who frequent the Berkeley campus.

Any writer on Western history must soon become indebted to the directors, archivists, librarians, and other staff members of the historical societies, and public and private libraries which have systematically gathered up the documents of our national history. Many have made special searches, provided information, and counseled me. In particular I thank Mr. Archibald Hanna and his secretary, Mrs. Ruthe Smith, of the Yale University Library; Mrs. Ruth Lapham Butler of the Newberry Library; Miss Carolyn E. Jakeman of the Harvard University Library; Mrs. Hazel W. Hopper of the Indiana State Library; Mr. Allen Ottley of the California State Library; Mr. W. D. Aeschbacker and Mr. Donald F. Denker of the Nebraska State Historical Society; Mr. James Abaijan of the California Historical Society; Mr. Reginald R. Stuart of the California Historical Foundation, College of the Pacific; Mrs. Frances H. Stadler of the Missouri Historical Society at St. Louis; Mr. Floyd C. Shoemaker of the State Historical Society of Missouri at Columbia; Mr. Nyle H. Miller and Mr. Edgar Langsdorff of the Kansas State Historical Society; Mrs. Aylis Freeze of the Denver Public Library; Mr. Maurice Frink of the State Historical Society of Colorado; Mrs. Frances L. Goudy of the Ohio Historical Society; Miss Helen

T. Kessler of the Peoria Public Library; Miss Margaret A. Flint of the Illinois State Historical Library; Miss Blanche Jantzen of the Chicago Historical Society; Mr. A. William Lund of the L. D. S. Church Historian's Office; Mr. A. R. Mortensen, Mr. John James, and Mr. Everett Cooley of the Utah State Historical Society; Mr. Paul G. Sotirin of the Milwaukee Public Library; Miss Josephine L. Harper and Miss Margaret Gleason of the State Historical Society of Wisconsin; Miss Doris M. Reed of the Indiana University Library; Mr. William Peterson of the State Historical Society of Iowa; Mr. Thomas Vaughan and Miss Priscilla Knuth of the Oregon Historical Society; Mr. David P. Mearns of the Library of Congress; Mrs. Helen S. Giffen of the Society of California Pioneers; Miss Lucile Kane of the Minnesota Historical Society; Miss Haydée Noya of the Henry E. Huntington Library; Mr. Donald F. Carmony of the *Indiana Magazine of History;* and Miss Mabel Weeks and Mrs. Dorothy T. Cullen of The Filson Club.

In addition to this institutional aid, I have had much valuable help from friends and students of Western history, notably including Mr. Carl I. Wheat, Mr. Francis Coleman Rosenberger; Mrs. Irene D. Paden; Mr. Everett D. Graff; Mr. Thomas D. Clark; Mrs. Madeline R. McQuown; Mr. Thomas E. McQuown; Mr. Francis Farquhar, Mr. Charles L. Camp; Mr. Merrill J. Mattes; Mr. John B. Goodman III; Mrs. Thomas Lorraine Campbell; Mrs. Eva Breyfogle Lovelace; Mr. James N. Adams; Col. Fred B. Rogers; and Mr. Devere Helfrich. A work printed by Lawton R. Kennedy speaks for itself, but it is fitting to conclude these acknowledgments with a word of personal appreciation and professional thanks to Lawton and Freda Kennedy.

Attention is directed to the Addenda at the close of the Bibliography.

DALE L. MORGAN
Berkeley, California

JAMES AVERY PRITCHARD

1816-1862

JAMES AVERY PRITCHARD was born in Bourbon County, Kentucky, on December 25, 1816. His father, William, was the son of James, a native of Virginia, a soldier in the Revolutionary War, and a farmer. William Pritchard was also a farmer, the owner of a considerable amount of land and a number of slaves. In 1815 he was married to America Grimes, the daughter of Avery Grimes, who was the son of Philip, of Loudoun County, Virginia. The Grimes family were extensive, solid, and somewhat distinguished, reputedly close kin to the immortal Thomas Jonathan "Stonewall" Jackson.

William Pritchard and America Grimes had two children, Sarah, who married James N. Hall, and James Avery. In 1828 his wife died, and soon thereafter William remarried. By his second wife, Lydia, he had nine children, five of them boys, of whom we know almost nothing. William Pritchard died in 1837. His widow lived until 1859.

At about the age of fifteen, which would have been in 1831, James left home. Why he left, where he went, and what he did during the next thirteen years, we do not know. Somewhere along the way, however, he acquired, or supplemented, an education which must have been above the average of his time, evidenced by his vocabulary, and by his knowledge of history, science, and mathematics, all revealed in his diary. Revelatory, too, are his books, many of which are now in my possession. These include: *Elements of Natural History, Embracing Zoology, Botany, and Geology*, by Ruschenberger; *The Prince of the House of David*, and *Pillar of Fire*, by Ingraham; *Bible Defense of Slavery*, by Josiah Priest; Buffon's *Natural History*; *Arctic Explorations*, by Elisha Kent Kane; *Antiquities of the Jews*, by Flavius Josephus; *Ancient History* (5 Volumes) by Charles Rollins; Hume's *History of England* (3 Volumes); *Pictorial*

37

History of the United States (3 Volumes), by John Frost; *Poems by Amelia; History of the Reformation,* by D'Aubigne; *Life of John Randolph of Roanoke; Proverbial Philosophy,* by Martin Tupper; *Abridgments of the Law,* by Matthew Bacon; *The Works of Washington Irving* (10 Volumes); *Poems of Robert Burns;* and *Moore's Poetical Works.* This is the library of a scholar and a thinker, as well as a man of culture. Moreover, in many of these volumes are numerous underscored passages and marginal notes in Pritchard's handwriting. How much of his education was formal, and how much self-acquired, is not known.

It seems likely that Pritchard had been a farmer, stockman, and trader, for in his diary he displays a continued interest in, and a considerable knowledge of, soils, crops, timber, and domestic animals. It is known too that after his removal to Missouri he engaged in farming and stock-raising for a period of some nine years. As will appear later, he seems to have been very successful financially during this period.

Apparently he was active and interested in politics, at least on the town and county level. He must also have been a conscientious church-goer, for his diary reveals him to have been a man of deep and sincere piety.

The record of Pritchard's life becomes more concrete in the spring of 1844. That year, at the April Term of the County Court of Boone County, Kentucky (located in the northernmost part of the State, and about sixty miles from Bourbon County), Pritchard was appointed constable of the village of Petersburg, which is situated at the western edge of Boone County, on the Ohio River. At the February, 1845, Term, he was appointed deputy sheriff of the county, and by 1847, whether through election or appointment, he was sheriff.

Pritchard was then thirty-one years of age, and unmarried. We infer that his economic condition was sound; he was well-educated and intelligent; he occupied one of the highest official positions in his county, which would indicate that he was popular and respected; he was obviously somewhat of a dreamer and poet, but practical and realistic, and probably somewhat of a Puritan in his personal life. Pleasant, affable, just, and generous, he was also decisive, adventurous, and patriotic. He stood just over six feet tall, slender but very strong and active. His portrait, now in my possession, shows that he had perfectly black hair, which he wore rather long in the style of the times, and that he also had dark eyes of a greenish cast, and features extraordinarily handsome, refined, and sensitive. There is more than a suggestion of an Indian strain in him, although his complexion was fair.

The pull and pressure of events in this year 1847 was too great for Pritchard to remain longer at home, war with Mexico having been in progress for a year. If then, as later, his political loyalties were given to the Whigs, he may until now have opposed the war, an opposition that gave way at last before love of country. In any event, resigning his office, he raised a company of 98 men, was elected Captain, received from the ladies of Boone County a beautiful silk United States flag (now in the museum at Arrow Rock Tavern, Saline County, Missouri), and rode off to Louisville. There, on October 5, 1847, he and his men became Company "D," Third Regiment, Kentucky Foot Volunteers, United States Army. Manlius V. Thomson was Colonel, Thomas L. Crittenden Lieutenant-Colonel, and John C. Breckinridge Major, a distinguished outfit, truly! And so away to glory and conquest!

Company "D" and the Third Regiment, however, scarcely tasted either, being much too late in reaching the field. Mexico City surrendered to the obdurate General Winfield Scott on September 13, nearly a month before the boys from Boone County joined up. It was occupied by American troops until after the signing of the Treaty of Guadalupe Hidalgo, in February, 1848. Company "D" proceeded, by what route or in what manner I do not know, to the Mexican capital city, where it was quartered in the majestic Hall of the Montezumas—over which its flag (it is alleged) was raised, and flaunted its beauty, and doubtless received the baleful glare of countless Mexicans!

These investing troops probably did patrol duty; they may have hunted down and mopped up some Mexican die-hards. They no doubt sharply depleted the supply of alcoholic beverages, and begot numerous progeny. Certainly some of them died of disease, intemperance, and general commotions. And that was their war. By July 21, 1848, they were back in Louisville to be mustered out. Medals and renown had eluded them, but they were heroes to the homefolks (as indeed they should have been, simply for having withstood the rigors of such a trip)—and little old Boone County would never seem the same to them again.

What Captain Pritchard did in the Mexican expedition I do not know. Neither do I know how he occupied himself after his return, but part of his time was spent in courtship, for on the following October 5 he was united in the holy bonds of matrimony to Mathilda Frances Williamson, daughter of Colonel John Williamson, formerly of Stamping Ground, Scott County, Kentucky, but more lately of Petersburg.

Judging from a still clear daguerreotype that has been handed down to me, Mathilda would have been almost beautiful had it not been for her fixed expression of resigned melancholy and general gloom. This was an unfortunate characteristic of her family, and she probably could not help it. Deeply in love with death, tragedy, and sorrow, her chief activity was the writing of funeral poems and obituaries, both of which she did well. She believed that she was a hopeless invalid, and comported herself accordingly, though she lived to a rather advanced age, and showed herself capable of enduring almost incredible hardships and exposures without ill effect or the slightest discomposure. Doubtless she was a hypochondriac with numerous complicated neuroses. She could hardly have been a very cheerful companion, but in a spiritual way she did deeply love her Captain, and certainly her Captain loved her.

The fall and early winter of 1848 passed away; the moment-
ous year of 1849 came in with snow and cold—and Mathilda
wrote a poem:

> Oh death! Come take me in thy horrid
>   arms, and make me thine!
> Take thou my feeble heart with fingers
>   cold, and make it thine!
> I long for thee, oh death! Deny me not!
> Oh death! Oh love! Forget me not tonight!

Sleet rattled on the windowpane; wind moaned in the chimney; Captain Pritchard manfully said: "That is a very beautiful
poem, dear. Quite, ah, lovely." And let his thoughts drift to
gold, lately discovered in California, to plains, mountains, and
far adventures. Maybe Mathilda's poem was the final motivat-
ing cause, and maybe not, but he began to make preparations to
depart for California. He talked several of his friends into going
along; bought mules, wagons, camp equipment, and gold-mining
paraphernalia; studied maps and routes; and engaged passage
on a steamer from Petersburg to St. Louis, Missouri, from which
point he would start overland.

The Captain's diary describes his life during the next year, as
he crossed the Plains by the northern route and labored in the
mines. Family legend is that Pritchard was moderately successful there; that, in company with another man, he started back
to the States and encamped one night in a dry canyon; that during the night a heavy rain fell, and that when the flood water
roared down the canyon, Pritchard and his companion barely
escaped with their lives, losing everything they possessed except
one small bag of gold dust which the Captain picked up in his
flight. A buckskin bag, containing a few ounces of black, glitter-
ing dust, has been in the possession of my family since my earliest
recollection. I was always told that Pritchard had brought it back
from California—and that he brought nothing else. So perhaps
this particular legend is true.

How he made his way back home I cannot say, but he landed in Petersburg March 2, 1851. He had had a long, hard, financially disastrous trip, and he had acquired many disillusions about his fellow men. His mood could not have been too good.

His first evening at home was taken up by a reading of the whole of a packet of some forty poems upon which Mathilda had been weakly but perseveringly engaged during his long absence. One will suffice us, entitled "Death in the Wilderness":

> What voice is this I hear from out the blackness
>   of yon winter's night?
> What cry of pain, what sobbing of despair?
> Tis he! Tis he! My love, my heart of hearts!
> Pale, bleeding, dying in the wilderness.

Comparatively, this poem is frivolous and gay. All of the others were really graveyard stuff. Nevertheless, he had come back to a serenity and grace he had not found in California, and the Captain did not leave Mathilda again until wrenched from her by war.

Still, Pritchard responded to the pull of the West, for in the spring of 1852 he left Kentucky, moving with his wife and possessions to Carroll County, Missouri, where lived his brother-in-law, John Williamson. He purchased 640 acres of land, some five miles north of Carrollton, but after a short time disposed of this and bought a large farm near the eastern edge of the county, near the village of Windsor City, the name of which he subsequently had changed to DeWitt. There he built a home of considerable pretensions, and called it "Rose Wild." (I shall always believe that Mathilda chose the name.) He had negro slaves—how many I do not know. Obviously Rose Wild was quite an establishment, which indicates that between 1831 and 1844 Pritchard must have made a good deal of money, for he had not made much since.

There now began for him the most settled and perhaps the most enjoyable period of his life, lasting nine years. From all I can learn, he lived the life of a country squire. He directed the work of his plantation, engaged in small business ventures, visited his neighbors and kinfolk, spent many hours in his library, and doubtless reflected much upon his experiences in Mexico and California. It would also appear that he was active in religion, for he was appointed Elder of the First Christian Church in Carrollton in 1853, and continued so until his death.

Mathilda was related to nearly all of the prominent families in Carrollton and in the county. Among them were many people of learning and intellect, whose company Pritchard enjoyed. The extensive social life they carried on was gracious, easy, and refined. We can picture the Captain and Mathilda setting out from Rose Wild in a handsome carriage, drawn by a mettlesome team, a colored driver in the box, bound for Carrollton and a weekend in one of the stately houses, where there would be good food, good talk, and good company. About these homes there was an air of security, orderliness, and elegance. In them were heard the crackle of wood fires, the subdued murmur of conversation, the tinkle of pianofortes, the sound of violins, the laughter of youth: There was gaiety, comfort, joviality, and good cheer, all in vast contrast to the violence, misery, and debauchery of Old Mexico, the savage sun and blinding dust of the California trail, the reckless violence, intemperance, and struggle for gold in Hangtown, Coloma, and Sacramento.

In 1858 Pritchard reëntered politics, announcing as a Whig for the Missouri legislature. In his campaign he steadfastly advocated maintenance of the Union. Although Carroll County was overwhelmingly Democratic and there was increasing hostility toward the Federal Government, Pritchard was elected, defeating his close friend, Colonel Stephen Stafford, the Democratic nominee. This success must be attributed to Pritchard's personal popularity. Thereafter, on December 27, 1858, he answered the roll call at the opening of the 20th General Assembly, in Jefferson City.

Pritchard's career as a legislator was more active than that of the ordinary first-term member. On January 11, 1859, he introduced an act to establish a Probate Court in Carroll County, which was done in the fall session. On the same day he introduced another act to change the name of Windsor City to DeWitt, which was also done. Two days later he offered an amendment to an act to set up a State Police to protect the western boundary of Missouri. The amendment was stronger than the original act, and more clear and definite. It was, too, more nearly in accord with the expressed desires of Governor R. M. Stewart. On February 2 Pritchard introduced an act to "establish a state road from Carrollton to J. H. Snowden's, in Ray County." Throughout the term he worked actively for the establishment of State and private road laws and for the extension of railroads. On March 9 he introduced an act "for the benefit of William A. Darr," of Carroll County. The House adjourned March 12. Sessions were resumed November 28, and continued until January 16, 1860. Pritchard further occupied himself in promoting the establishment of roads and railroads. During both sessions his attendance record was excellent.

In 1860 he failed of reëlection to the Legislature. Concerning this campaign the *History of Carroll County, Missouri,* published in 1911, comments:

James A. Pritchard, an old Whig, had been elected to the Legislature although the county was largely Democratic. His personal popularity and his acknowledged ability made him the dread of the Democratic aspirants for seats in the lower House. In this year he was the nominee of the Bell-Everett Party. The Democrats nominated William M. Eads, a young lawyer, recently from Kentucky. The two candidates spoke 37 times in various places in the county. Both branches of the Democratic Party supported Mr. Eads and he was elected. The vote was: Eads— 852; Pritchard—687.

During the Civil War it so chanced that Pritchard who, in 1860, was a pronounced and decided Union man, became a Colonel in the Confederate Army (and a gallant officer) and Mr. Eads, the choice of the Democratic Party, became a Captain in the Union Army. And yet there was nothing inconsistent in the conduct of either of the gentlemen.

Although so late as 1860 Pritchard was a strong Union man, about this time he underwent a change in attitude, apparently because he was a strong believer in states' rights, and had come to believe these rights threatened by the United States Government. At a public meeting held at the courthouse in Carrollton on May 6, 1861, he and his former rival, Colonel Stafford, were the speakers. The resolutions adopted were: "Resolved, to tender a loan of $10,000 by Carroll County to the State for arming forces. Resolved, that we view with scorn and disdain the marshalling and arming of Northern troops, and the act of sending them to our borders will be regarded as insulting to a free people. Resolved, that under no circumstances will we permit or allow the armed bands of Abraham Lincoln to enter, quarter in, or pass through our State under pretense of enforcing the laws; and that we will not look on with indifference while Northern troops are being congregated on Southern soil."

War had come. Soon after, Pritchard wrote his brother-in-law, John Williamson, "You well know there has been a dark, gloomy cloud of foreboding hanging over my mind for several years in regard to my country. I have resisted dis-union in every shape that it has presented itself. But the crisis has been forced upon us, and we must make the best of it we can." In a second letter, written after he had joined the Confederate army, he said: "I feel that this is a just and holy cause we are engaged in and that it is my indispensable duty to be here. In fact, I would hate myself if I were anywhere else. Could I be base enough to desert my country, in this, her hour of danger, I feel that the curse of Heaven would beset my path with thorns at every turn in life. This may be a mistaken view of the subject, but it is my religious and conscientious view of it; if I am mistaken I hope God will forgive me."

So the lines between North and South were drawn, and Pritchard responded to what he deemed the clear call of duty. Of his departure Mathilda wrote after his death:

He left home for the Army on the 18th of June, 1861. As I sit here this mournful autumn eve, gathering up these fragments of the past, as that date drops from my pen, a curtain has slowly lifted from a sacred picture in memory's halls. I see a mansion looming up amid waving forest trees. Flowers are blooming around it, for it is the month of roses. The air is musical with the songs of wild birds. Canaries are trilling in their cages. Squirrels run up and down the trees or bask contentedly in the sunshine, for in that house everything is protected—no wanton gun is ever drawn on bird or squirrel, so everything grows tame and happy. It is a breezy summer morn, and in the wide halls of that mansion a weeping group are gathered to bid husband, friend and kind, indulgent master a last farewell. His face works convulsively, for he has a tender, loving heart, yet a firm resolve is on his brow as he takes the hands, one after another, of his faithful servants, over whose dusky cheeks the tears are streaming, bids adieu to another dear as his life, and turns his back upon his home—his beautiful Rose Wild, little as he thought so then—to return no more. For never again were the quiet shadows of Rose Wild brightened by his presence.

I shall not describe in detail Pritchard's experiences in the war. He was attached to the command of General Sterling Price, with the rank of Captain, and within a short time was made a Colonel. He fought in many battles and established a reputation for courage and leadership. On October 4, 1862, at the Battle of Corinth in Mississippi, while leading a charge against a Federal breastworks, he was mortally wounded. He died October 20 and was buried at the nearby village of Coffeyville.

I infer that Pritchard must have been a soldier of unusual qualities, and that he was recognized as such. This impression comes largely from reading the marked passages (marked by Mathilda years afterward, and bedewed by her tears) of a book entitled, *History of the First and Second Missouri Confederate Brigades,* by R. S. Bevier, published in 1879. This book contains a five-page narrative by Pritchard of the Battle of Wilsons Creek, fought near Springfield, Missouri, on August 10, 1861. Pritchard was in the thickest of this hard-fought battle, and his report was written not more than one or two days afterward; it is clear, concise, and full. To Pritchard's death Bevier devotes two and one-half pages, recounting how he received his fatal wound, what he said—"Boys, do your duty!"—and the "Resolutions of Regret" drawn up at "Camp Near Lumpkin's Mill, Mississippi, November 2, 1862." The whole concludes with a poem (Pritchard simply could not, even in death, get away from these poems) by James Bradley, a member of his command:

Colonel Pritchard

The Autumn leaves have fallen
The Summer rose has gone;
  So fell our noble Colonel,
  The brave, the gallant one,
  Upon the field of Corinth;
He fell—ever brave and true,
  Sternly charging on the foe,
Obedient to his high devoir.

He stood with us at Springfield,
Where patriots fought and died;
  And again at Lexington,
  With honor by his side;
  And on Elkhorn's bloody field,
Where Freedom's sons fell full fast,
  He firmly stood, or led on,
The foremost to face the blast.

Iuka, too, we remember well,
How there he most nobly stood
  Against the cow'ring foe,
  On field of flowing blood;
  And alas! at Corinth fell—
A bright flower of noble fame
  Who long shall bear—
Tho' gone from us a hero's name.

Now bring the fairest, loveliest flowers,
And strew them 'round his tomb;
 Embalm his name with truth
 Of bright and brilliant bloom;
 Let his wife weep no more,
But wipe those sorrowing tears away,
 For him she loved shall wear
The crown of an immortal day.

Today, in Oak Hill Cemetery, near Carrollton, there stands a plain, weather-worn monument erected to his memory. A man and a child (who are no blood relation to him) bear his name. Some old land records in Kentucky and Missouri, filed away and forgotten, bear his signature. Some of the books he read and marked are still preserved. His deeds and death in the Southern War are recorded in a book which few, now, ever read. Near the hamlet of Coffeyville, Mississippi, he lies in a grave probably unmarked and lost. There are no men now alive who ever looked upon his face, or felt the pressure of his hand, or heard his voice. But through the medium of his diary he comes to us from out of the long past, and lives again.

HUGH PRITCHARD WILLIAMSON
Fulton, Missouri

I

THE BLUE WALL OF THE SKY
Petersburg to Fort Kearny

On the night of the 10th of April 1849 I left my residence in the town of Petersburgh, Ky, on the Steamer *Cambria* with my travelling companions & mules & wagons Samuel Hardesty, William Wilkie, T. [P.?] P. Youell, M. Stephens, Perry McNeely, John Wilkie, & N. P. Norris, for an overland rout across the Rocky Mountains to California, and arrived at St Louis on the night of the 13th without any accident occuring or anything of moment transpireing. On board the *Cambria* we found several Companies from different parts of the States, and among the rest was the Ethica company of New York, a joint Stock association composed of 50 members with a capital invested of $25,000.00 &c. &c.[1]

The forenoon of the 14th was spent in getting our Mules ashore & finishing our outfit for the journey. This all done, at 4 P. M. I with Hardesty J. Wilkie & M. Stephens started from St Louis to Indipendance through the country with the Mules while W. Wilkie McNeely Norris & Youell continued on board the Steamer with our Baggage to Indipendance landing [Wayne City].[2] There were two young men with their Mules & Horses travelled across the country with us—Mitchell of New York & Burr Runnells of Ohio. After a very amuseing romp through the Streets with our Mules jurking the riders off occasionally we pushed out of the City at a pretty rapid rate, & sunset found us 16 miles on our road, at an Inn kept by a widow Lady by the name of Martin formily of Madison Co. Ky. We had good accommodations for our selves & Mules. The land through here is handsome & furtile. Distance 16 miles.

SUNDAY APRIL 15TH   After an early breakfast we found ourselves on the road, merrily pushing along towards the place of
our destination. As our Mules were fresh it was impossible to
keep them back. We Struck the Missori River in 4 miles from
w[h]ere we started this morning, opposite the Town of St
Charles. The bottom on the South Side of the river at this point
is rather wide, low, & furtile than otherwise & looks as if it was
Subject to overflow in time of high freshits. There is a good
steem-ferry Boad [boat] Kept at this place. Here, after a laps of
27 years my Eyes rested once more on the turbid waters of this
most Singular River, my mind was irresistable carried back to
the seens of my Childhood—and assosiations which were not of
the most agreeable character forced themselves upon it—tho it
is generally pleasant to reflect upon our youthful seens.

St Charles is rather a neat looking little Town built between
the river & the hill that rises to som considerable hight in its
reare, & Stratches along up and down the river for a miles or
more. St Charles is situated on the North or upper Side of the
Missouri River and 20 miles above its confluence with the Mississippi. At a distance of 14 miles we haulted to take some refresh-
ments for ourselves & Animals at an Inn Kept by an elderly
Gentleman by the name of Campbell (New Stone House) a
Virginian. Here we saw quite a number of Emegrants encamped
& resting over Lord's day, good accommodations & low prices.
At 2 P. M. we resumed our journey and reached the farm house
of a Gent by the name of Coleman to the right of the road who
entertained travellers when called upon. Coleman was from
Gallatine Co, Ky. Distance this afternoone 15 ms. Whole distance today 33 ms.

MONDAY 16TH   This morning when we awoke, for the first
time, we were Salluted by a multitude of Prairie Chickens with
their dolorous sounds. The land through here is high rolling
Prairie. The land is furtile & the farms finely improved. The
weather has been clear with a strong East wind, which renders it

extreamly disagreeable travelling over this Prairie country. At 7 A. M. we left Coleman's & Passed through several large Prairies this forenoon interspeared with low shruby timber & underbrush. On one of those Prairies at 9 this morning we had a heavy fall of Snow for about 15 or 20 minutes which rendered it exeedingly unpleasant travelling on *Muleback*. We got to Jones's tavern by noon a distance of 20 ms. & here we overtook 8 or 10 Ox teams bound for California. At 1½ past we continued our journey & found the road fine runing across a fine leavel (or undulated) Prairie country rich furtile & enviting good farmes & well improved. About 5 P.M. we passed through a little Town called Danville, and 5 ms. farther on we crossed a large Creek high hills rough roads. 1½ ms. farther at the top of the hill we reached Cranes Tavern Stand, where we put up for the night. Distance 42 ms.

TUESDAY 17TH   We resumed our journey at 7 this morning passed through some woodland & in 7 ms. we came to Williamsburgh & took the middle road which led through Columbia to Roachport where we desine crossing the River again. And at noon we were at A. Allens tavern Stand, 19 ms. from Crane's. At 2 P. M. we left Allens & immediately struck a large Prairie 15 miles across. We then had timbered land for 6 or 8 ms. The wind blew a cold Chilling blast from the N West all day. At about 6 P M we reached the residence of Mr. Thos. Grant formily of Scott co. Ky & related to the Grants of that State. We applyed to stay all night & he told us he never turned off travellers. And we found him to possess all the hospitality Characteristic of the well bread Kentuckyan. He has a fine farm & Brick house, with everything in abundance around him. 23 ms this afternoon. Distance today 42 ms.

WEDNESDAY 18TH   This was a cold frosty morning. We were now in the district of country that suffered so much from the hale & Sleet during the last winter. The timber in many places was literally crushed to the earth. The branches were all or nearly so broken off and nothing but the snags & stubs left standing as the liveing mon[u]ment of the great distress that had once been there. The timber is plenty through this part of the State & the soil decidedly the best that we have seen since we left St. Louis. Six miles from Grant's we reached Columbia, one of the neatest and handsomes little Towns that I have seen in my life. In this place there is a fine College or institution of learning.[3] It is 14 miles from Columbia to River at Roachport, at which place we arrived by noon. We passed between these two points the large train from St. Louis.

When we got to the river there were so many ahead of us, the ferryman told us that we could not cross for 3 days. So I took dinner at the tavern and hurryed off to Booneville a handsome Town situated 12 miles above Roachport & on the Southwest side of the Missouri River. At this place we found a first rate Steam ferry Boat that could cross all the teams at the lower ferry in one day.[4] At this point we met the Steam Boat *Cambria* that had on board our Baggage & the ballance of our Company. I rode down to the landing & went on Board & Changed my Cloths &c. Here Stephens and Youell changed places. We travelled 3 ms. out to Thomas's Stand and put up for the night. Distance 35 ms. THURSDAY 19TH   At 7 this morning we were on the road, and in 5 ms. we Struck, and crossed the Lamoine River passing on through fine country & well improved farmes & clever People. By noon we reached the fine and extensive residence of the renowned Dr Sapington the Daddy of all the Pills—and with him we took dinner. I found him to be a very adroit & singularly eccentric Character, jocular & lively & rather quisical possessing a high degree of hospitality and Gentlemanly demeanor. He is a large fine looking man about 6 feet high and looks to be about 70 years of age with heavy Suit of hair & it as white as Snow. His Beard was as white as his head and hung to his breast. His wife was a pleasant agreeable Lady and appeared to be much his junior.[5]

Just through this region of country, its mostly Prairie, but the land is very furtile. The Farmers raise hemp extensively through here. This afternoon we saw 2 deer & a great number of Prairie Chickens. At sunset we reached Capt Kise's, but he was so crouded with Emegrants the [that] he could not accomodate us. We turned and road back about one mile and Stayed at a farme house owned by a Mr Webb, who was a virginian. Distance 37 miles.

FRIDAY 20TH   The farmes along here are mostly in Prairies & the farmers many of them have to haul their railes to fence their farmes from 10 to 15 ms. Notwithstanding this to us a great disadvantage they say that they can fence their farmes sooner than they could clear of the timbered land. The soil is admirably addapted to the culture of hemp which formes one of their principal articles of agriculture & trade. And corn grass and everything in proportion. We reached Crissman's to dinner a distance of 16 ms. Soone after dinner we resumed our journey and during the afternoon we crossed the river Tarban 8 miles this side of Lexington. We reached Catrens this evening and put up for the night. Distance 37 ms.

SATURDAY 21ST   In four miles we reached Lexington a handsome Town, part of it is situated immediately on the Mo River & part on the hill about 1 mile back. The lands around this place cannot be surpassed either in beauty or fertility. The timber is very heavy and of a fine quality. We travelled 18 ms. and haulted for dinner at the farm house of Mr. Arnold. He was a very clever Gentleman & read to us a letter that had just been re'd in the Neighbourhood from a gentleman in California who had emegrated the year before from that neighborhood Who gave flattering accounts of the gold discoverys. While we were eating dinner a Mr. St[e]wart & 2 other Gentlemen came & called for dinner. Stwart recognized Hardesty & made himself known to him. Stewart had once lived in Petersburgh. During our afternoons travell we crossed a fine large Creek (late in the evening) upon which was a fine looking Mill owned by Rice. We stoped on the hill 1½ ms. from the creek and put up for the night withe the widow Adams—plain old fassion sort of folks. Distance 40 [miles].

SUNDAY 22D   We reached Indipendence this morning at 8 Oclk A. M & continued to the river where we found the ballance of our company & Baggage. It was 6 ms from where we stayed last night to Indipendance & 3 from there to the landing. We commenced hearnessed up our mules & loaded in our goods & chattles and moved out one mile to a good camping place on the road towards Town where we encamped for several days. Distance to Indipendance 6 miles.

The whole distance from St Louis Mo. to Indipendance according to the sta[te]ment of distances as given to me by the inhabitance along the road—from place to place & from time to time which I presume to be correct as I got it from the most relyable sources—is two hundred & Eighty Eight miles. We were all ready to start on our trip across the plaines by the 24 of April but we were perswaded by the old setlers that, that was too early as we would find no grass upon the plains for our Stock. In fiew of these statements we postponed starting till the 3 of May. And remained during the time encamped in and around Indipendance. But this advice we found to be extreamly detrimental to us. It served only to place us in the reare of a great number of large traines which we were compelled eventually to pass. We were prepaired to take with us grane enough to feed our mules twice pr day for a distance of 400 miles. Therefore we Should have started at least 10 or 12 days sooner, which would have given us great advantages in the way of selecting good camping places

Indipendance is a handsome flourishing town with a high healthy situation, three miles from the Missouri River on the South side And Surrounded by one of the most beautiful & fertile countries of any Town in the Nation. The land is well

timbered with the most luxuriant groth of black Walnut Blue &
Black Ash, Hackbury large Bur White & black Oak Buckey[e]
Boxelder Coffee mut [nut?] etc. Soil with that groth of timeber
cannot help being abundantly productive besides it has a lime
Stone foundation. Its geographical position is such that the
climate is unsurpassed in the Union. The Emegrants were
encamped in every direction for miles around the place awaiting
the time to come for their departure. Such were the crouded condition of the Streets of Ind by long traines of Ox teams mule
teams men there with stock for Sale and men there to purchase
stock that it was all most impossible to pass along. And the
California fever rageing to such a fearful extent that it was
carrying off its thousands pr day.[6] Being all ready now to bid
adieu to homes, friends, and happy Country, as it ware—for we
were about Separating ourselves from the abodes of Civilization,
its peace, comeforts, and its saf[e]ty, for a period we knew not
how long, and to some for ever, to launch away upon the broad
and extensive plaines, which Straches away and away, untill it
fades from the sight in the dim distance, and bounded only by
the blue wall of the Sky.

While thus laying round in suspence the reflections of home
were forcibly crouding upon our minds the happy influences
that we had torne ourselves from to enter upon a wild and in all
probability a chimerical enterprize. In this state of suspence we
had wandered along in search of grass for our Mules, and for
the purpose of accustoming them to the use of the Larriet & the
Stake—untill on the 2nd of May we found ourselves some
13 ms from Indipendance.

THURSDAY MAY 3RD 1849 W. W. Abbott of Burbane [Bour-
bon] Co. Ky haveing attached himself to our company on the
evening previous, We were all ready this morning to take up the
line of march—which did at an early hour. We crossed the state
line at about 9 A. M. where we found a great number of Emegrants—among the rest was the large train commanded by Mr

Headspeath the great Mountaineerer.[7] We were now on the large Prairie, and in the Indian Territory. These lands through here are very Rich indeed the road was fine all day. It Showered a little on us during the day. At 3 P. M. we reached the noted lone Elm, where we encamped for the night. This lone tree stands on the bank of a small stream, with no other tree or shrub in sight, all the branches have been cut from it by traders & Emegrans for the purpos of fuel. At this place we found some 40 or 50 Emegrant Wagons. Haulted for the night. Distance from Indipendance 34 miles.[8]

FRIDAY MAY 4   It was raining this morning and we did not start to [till?] 9 and in 8 miles came to where the Sante Fe road leaves the old Orregon trail. It still continued to rain and the roads became somewhat heavy. Still passing over high rolling Prairie we continued till 3 P. M. which brought us to a large creek, called Bool [Bull] Creek.[9] There is an abundance of timber along its banks and bottoms. Just before we reached the creek we found one unfortunate fellow with the tongue broken square off at th[e] hou[n]ds of his wagon. We crossed the creek and encamped for the night. It had been raining all day & were wet & chilled by the exposure. We discovered a dead Oak close by and in a few minutes it was converted into a splendid log fire, by which we cooked our supper & got comefortably warm before bed time. We pased some 70 wagons today. Distance 18.

SATURDAY 5TH   We left our camp this morning and travelled over rolling Prairie land crossing severall creeks withe steep banks and made a heard days march passing during the day some 80 teams, and late in the evening s[t]oped to camp at what is called coons point, on a small ravine with some timber along its banks   Distance 28 ms.[10]

SUNDAY 6TH   We left camp this morning early & travelled over country pretty much such as we did yesterday, in fact the general face of the country through here is pretty much alike. At 2 P. M. we reached a fine large creek called Shunganung. We found a

large number of wagons crossing. They had to take it by turnes
and let their wagons dow[n] the steep banks.[11] Thay all crossed
and encamped for the night. We did the same. There was something near 100 wagons, some Ox & some mule teams. The grass
was good along the creek bottoms. We are now in the Potiwatimy
destrict and in sight of one of their villages. A number of them
came into our camp this afternoon. One of them spoke good
English. The boys spent some time in Shooting at marks with
them. They had plenty of horses & asked a good price for them.[12]
Distance 16 ms.

MONDAY 7TH   We had to travel 16 miles to upper ferry or 3
to the lower ferry. What we lost on this side by travelling to the
upper ferry we gained on the other and as nearly all the Emegrants were going to the lower ferry, we took the upper one.[13]
And one mile before strikeing the Kansas river is a mission and
trading post called Potiwatimi. There are several white familys
liveing there & some 4 or 5 stores blacksmith shop &c. A number
of the Indians are liveing in the village. We called a hault of an
hour or such a matter in the town and let the boys trade a little.
We reached the River about 12 M, and crossed at 3 P. M. There
was 2 ferry boats, one Kept by a half breed Indian (Michegan)
& the other by a white man. This river is about 120 yards wide,
with a strong bold current; the water is rather turbed. After
crossing we came out to creek about 2 miles & encamped for the
night, grass good. Distance 18 ms.[14]

TUESDAY 8TH   About one mile above our camp we crossed the
creek. Here we were compelled to double teams in order to get
through the bank very steep & muddy. Our rout today was along
the Kansas bottom principally, the bottom being soft made it
very heard pulling. We crossed a number of creeks & mud holes,
with steep banks. We passed an Indian village about 9 A. M.
where their was a saw mill, and a temporary brdge thrown across
a bad muddy creek by an Old Indian who charged us 25 cts apiece
for our wagons. In about 10 ms from where we started this

morning we came to a Catholic mission, surrounded with a number of Indian Wigwams.[15] At three P. M. we reached the big Vermillion. About one mile before reaching the river, the bottom Road and hill road as it is called came togeather. The hill road is said to be the best early or of a wet time. The Vermillion is the largest that we have crossed since we left the Kansas—it watters are clear bold & beautiful with stomy bead [stony bed]. Its banks are steep. The bottoms are about one mile in width & finely timbered in places for some distance out. We crossed and encamped for the night, good grass. The weather being warm we took a baith in its clear blue water. Distance 23 ms.

WEDNESDAY 9TH   We are now out in the Indian country and [as] there are various rumers afloat, with regard to their commiting depradations on Emegrant parties, we deemed it necessary to keep a strict guard over our Mules during the night.[16] Last evening after we encamped there came to our camp a gentleman who had been left at the Kansas crossing by his party. We took him in and kept with us till this evening when we overtook his train. His name was Jacob Hoover, from Eeagle Village, Ind. Five miles after leaveing camp this morning M. Stephens drove his wagon into [a] deep mudhole & broke the Tongue. We howevur were not detained long with that. We laid it smothly togeather and roped it with Twine and drove on till noon, where we stopped on a fine stream of water rested & grazed our Animals one hour & a half. After which we resumed our march and at dark overtook the Indiana train Commanded by Capt. Fash, compossed of 17 wagons and 60 men. We temporarily attached ourselves to his train untill we could make further arrangments.[17] Distance 27 ms.

THURSDAY 10TH   We made an early start this morning in order to pass a large Ox train which had encamped just ahead of us. The road was rather hilly today. We nooned 2 hours after crossing a small stream, and continued our march till 4 P. M. when we came to the big Blue. This is a fine large Stream with a bold

rapid current & gravelly bottom. We had here to lower our
wagons down with ropes, which consumed the ballance of the
evening in crossing all the train.[18] The Soil is very fine on this
river, and the bottoms are well timbered. This will doubtless
become a fine farming country—and that before many years.
Here we encamped for the night. Distance 22 ms.

FRIDAY 11   By noone today we came to where the St. Joseph
road & Indipendance road came togeather [8 miles beyond the
Big Blue]. It was allarming to see the long strings of wagons
that were on the road. I counted just passing before us as we
came into the St. Jo. road 90 Ox teams in one string. And as far
as the Eye could reach forward and back the road was just lined
with them. It would appear from the sight befor us that the
Nation was disgorgeing its self and sending off its whole inhabitance. We were not able to pass this train till they stoped for the
night. Came by them 3 ms & stoped where there was neithe[r]
wood water nor but little grass. We however found a hole of
water after so long a time and a little brush some mile or so down
the branch. Seven of our 8 were put on guard tonight. I told the
boys that, that way of doing business was rather too exciting to
be pleasant. And that did not suit me. So we determined to leave
the train at the earlyest opportunity. Distance 22 ms.

SATURDAY 12TH MAY   Nothing of any moment occurred today. We made an early start this morning. Our rout today lay
across rather a broken country, or high table lands. The face of
the country all day has appeared like climbing an encline plain—
the top of which we never could gane. We crossed several
branches today one of which we had to bridge with willow brush.
Occasionally we see a tree or a clump of bushes at a distance
which indicates a Spring of [or] Pool of water. We noond of
[on] a small branch that had the appearance of being dry except
in wet weather. This afternoon we crossed several dry branches
with gravelly beds—and encamped on one of the tributarys of
the little Blue. Distance 20 ms

SUNDAY 13TH   We left our camp this morning with the view of moveing to a good camping place, and in 9 ms we found it and encamped on a broad creek with deep sandy gravelly bottom. The water was not running in it, but Stood in large pools. Here the men Spent the remainder of the day sunning their clothing lightning up their loading, and readjusting things in general. The evening was very warm and pleasant. The little Blue was to [*sic*] in full view—about 4 ms distant to our left. Its bottoms are broad and heavily timbered the groth of which is principally Cotton wood & Oak. The Seenary was so enviting that it induced Stephens Wilkie and myself to take a stroll down that way. We spent several hours in wandering along the bank of the Blue. We found beautiful Spots an[d] romantic Situations. The current was very Swift and rapid, yet the water rippled over its gravelly bed as clear as a chrystle. We came finally to a cheerful pleasant looking Spot—and regardless of any danger from Indians who doubtless were then learking in the brush watching our movements, but were held at bay by the appearance of our Ky. Rifles, we deliberately undressed and pitched into the transparent Stream to take a bathe. But to our surprize it was not so pleasant to be in as to look at. The water was so cold that we could not bear its touch—it chilled us through instantly. This was a consideration that had not presented its self to us, tho we had slaked our thirst in its pure sweet & refreshing waters time & again while sporting upon its banks. It was here that we got sight of the first Antelope—it was mearly a sight for we could not approach within a half mile of them. A few wild Turkeys were also seen on the river by some of the party. Distance today 9 ms

MONDAY 14TH   We had during the past night a tremendos heard rain & acompanied by heavy wind and loud peels of thunder and fearce lighting. Ma[n]y of the tents were upset and the men were exposed to the storme—stakeing down their tents—till their clothing were perfectly saturated with water. Ours however was not of that number. We made but slow progress this morning on account of the heavy fall of rain last night which left the roads muddy and slippery. The country over which we passed this forenoon was somewhat broken, the road runs across the heads of the small branches that put into the Blue. At noon we had only made six miles.

Wilkie & myself took our guns this morning and starte to hunt we killed several ducks Prairie chickens Curleus, &c, and headed into the road some 4 or 5 ms ahead of the train & had to walk back to get our dinners. After resting 2 hours we resumed our march and at about 6 in the afternoon we struck the Bottom of the little Blue River. The bottom here is about one mile wide. We travelled 1½ ms up it and encamped for the night. We found the grass very fine along the bottoms of the River. In a very few minutes after we haulted nearly the whole train was found angleing in the river, nor was this effort in vain for they all caught a fine mess of fish principally Cat Fish. Distance 16 ms.

TUESDAY MAY 15TH Our course today lies along the bottom of the little Blue. The river here is about 50 feet wide with a rapid current. The soil of the bottom is furtile and yields grass most luxuriantly. Timber abundant. At noon today I went to Capt Fash and told him that I wished to leave his train—not that I, or any of our Company, had any objections to him as Capt. but that the train was too large to get along with convenience and speed. To which he agreed and said that there were no objections upon his part to our withdrawal. I caught up our Mules harnessed them and drove out and was followed by 3 teams from Ill.[19] I drove till pretty late and encamped for the night on the banks of the river. About dark a wagon with 5 men from Pendleton Co. Ky came up to us, and requested to join us which was agreed too. Distance 20 ms.

WEDNESDAY 16TH This morning shortly after starting We passed the large train of 50 wagons commanded by Capt. Sublett the Old Mountaineerer and the discoverer of the Sublett or Greenwood cut off.[20] They however as was the common lot of large Companies had had a split that morning—27 of wagons remained with Sublett & 23 with some Dr of Mo, I did not learn his name. By noon we had assended the little Blue, to the point at which we left it Strike across to the Platte River. While nooning 2 other wagons came up to us of Fashe's train and requested admission, which was granted. These were A. W. Harrison & co of Indianopolis & Jacobe Hoover & co of Eagle Village.[21] After supplying ourselves with wood and water to last us across to the Platte, we moved on till night. About Dark P. S. Hamline & co of 6 men from the lower part of Ky came up & requested admission which was granted. It has been showering upon us for several days. The road good. Distance 23 ms.

THURSDAY 17TH   Last evening we formed our Camp regardless of shape or convenience, there being no one whos duty it was to attend to the forming the compny in proper shape. Therefore we were unable to picket our Mules so as to guard them conven[ien]tly. About 10 at night just as the Camp had become quiet, a large Mountain Woolf made his Debut and brought one of those hideous howls that will startle one from the profoundest sleep—and make him think that one of the Fiends of the infurnal regions was standing befor him. And away went Picket ropes & pins, at a single dash about 40 [of] the mules were loosed. The camp was aroused, and in a sho[r]t time all but 5 Mules & one horse was recovered, all qu[i]eted. Guards were detached to go in various directions. After scowering the country round for a mile or two they returned without success. This morning several parties were sent out on horseback & about 11 A M they returned with all of the Mules & horse[s].

It was now apparrant to all, that it was indispensible to have a Capt—or commander to the train—and that it must be organized with proper rules & restrictions. Thereupon a motion was made to elect a Capt who should take charge of the company till further regulations could be made. Thereupon James A. Pritchard was put in nomination by P. S. Hamline. Perry McNeely then put P. S. Hamline and James Croslin in nomination.[22] The respe[c]tive candidates were then requested to take their stand so as to allow the men to form on their choice. The word was then given to form on their candidate. Thirty eight of the forty formed on Pritchard and McNeely on Croslin, Croslin himself voting for Pritchard. Hamline got none he vowed his intention to vot for Pritchard in the start. A few appropriate remarks were then made by the Capt. with regard to the heardships and difficulties that men had to encounter upon an expedition like the one in which we are now engagued. Also the relative & respective duties due each other &c &c. At the close one universal shout rose from the croud. And orders were immediately given to catch up and move forward to the Plat that night, which were as promptly obeyed. The Capt then made a motion to have one man selected by the members of each wagon to meet at the earliest hour to draft a constitution & bylaws for the farther organization & government of the company, which motion was carried. The train was then put in motion & reached the Platte by 6 P M opposite or nearly at the head of Grand Island where we encamped for the night. Distance 17 ms.

FRIDAY MAY 18TH   Our rout today has been along the bank of the Platte, the general course of which is nearly from the West to East. We passed the head of Grand Island about 2 ms above our encampment, here the river expands in breadth, presenting a Surface of water from 1½ to 2 miles wide; it has a strong resemblance of the Missouri river. Although the channel is so broad, and presenting to the Eye such a volum of water, the Stream is, nevertheless so Shallow that it can be forded without difficulty in many places. The bed of the river is compossed of sand, and this is all the time shifting its possition and fresh deposits are constantly being made. The fall is great the current strong and waters turbid. The banks of the Platte are low and at this time (the river being high) do not rise more than 18 inches or two feet above the surface of the water. I judge that the bottom at this point is rarely if ever inundated. Such is the breadth of the channel that an immence quantity of water would be required to raise it above its banks. The stream is beyond the possibility of ever being made navigable. The Soil of the Platte bottom generaly appears to be thin and sandy and not very productive of grass or other vegitation. Occasionally there are marshy places which produce grass tolerably luxuriently, but these are easily av[o]ided in travelling. Besides these the road is generally firm and solled. There is little or no timber along the banks or bottoms of the Platte, and in many places for long distances none at all.

At noon we reached Fort Kerney, passed through the place 1 mile and stoped to greaze & rest a couplet of hours. Here we found a Military post established and some 80 or 90 Dregoons posted here—also a kind of Post office establishment, which gave us an opportunity of sending back letters. The Fort is about 12 ms above the head of Grand Island, and the houses are built of adob[e]s or sun dried brick.[23] At 2 P. M. we continued our march till 5 P. M. and haulted for the night. Distance 25.

II

ARCH, PILLAR, DOME & MINARET
Fort Kearny to Fort Laramie

SATURDAY MAY 19TH   We travelled till noon and haulted to-day at noon in order to give the men an opportunity to wash their clothing Shoe mules cut off wagon bed & readjust their loading Etc. Last night we had a tremendous storme—"The Storme it raged, the thunders rolled, fearce Lightning split the skye, & all the heavens seemed fringed with gold, while on my couch I lye." Our camp was located upon a slough, this evening—which furnished us with good clear water, in which we saw swarmes of small fish. At this point we found first-rate grass. The evening was busily spent in making preparations for an Early start next morning. Distance 14 ms.

SUNDAY MAY 20TH   Our rout today is still along the banks of the Platte & frequently near the river. We crossed during the day several small streams with low banks and marshy bed that gave our teams some trouble in pulling through. The waters of these streams are rather brackish and disagreeable to the tast[e], and considered not to be condusive to health. The river here still presents the same general outline, except that its surface is dotted with a number of small Islands which present every veriety of shape. They are from 30 feet in diameter to one half mile. The green urbage & vegitation and shrubry upon them, from their singular configuration, appear rather fantastick to Eye than other wise—when viewed from the distance.

At noon we grazed our Mules one hour & a half &c & resumed the march again at 2 P M. This afternoon a large number of antelope wer[e] to be seen. A number of our party gave chase to them but to no effect. I never saw an animal that can run with the same speed, grace, ease, and elegance of these Antelope. When hotly pursued on our best horses they fled almost with the fleetness of the wind. The Antelope were very soon t[w]o or three miles distant, nothwithstanding fresh horses were put in at almost every stage of the game, as they ran pa[s]t the different trains along the road. And as if in derission of the slow progress, of their pursueres, would stop occasionally and look round untill we came near to them, when again they would bound off, with their former fleetness—and in a few minutes be again out of sight. In Shape they resemble the goat in many particulars, being between in hight the size of the Goat and the common deer. They are very finely formed, with heavy quarters and deep chest. Their limbs are very small and sinewy. Their hair is course, and of a light chestnut or roneish color mingled with white. On their thighs behind there is a small ovalshaped spot of white hair. All efforts to approach them within gunshot are entirely fruitless unless you can steal a march on them behind an object or hill. The chase might have been considered good sport to the men, but not so agreeable to the horses.

We crossed several small streams this afternoon. We passed a broken down wagon just before we stoped to camp, which the boys geathered up for cooking purposes. They gave chase to a woolf and made him take the river. Just here we struck the river and encamped for the night. We are passing vast numbers of Emegrant wagons now every day.[24] Distance 24 ms.

MONDAY MAY 21ST   One of our party Mr Rollins came in this last evening with a fine Antelope which he had shot, during the afternoon. That gave us all this morning a keen relish for hunting. I appointed a man to manage the train, and in campany with several others struck for the Bluffs. We spent the forenoon in travelling over hills and broken ground, in chase of Antelope (which are abundant along here), but without success. The forward movements of the train is so rapid that it gives a man but little chance to walk, hunt, and keep up.

The Bluffs are becom[ing] as we assend the river, of greater elevation more broken, and cragy. They sometimes appear of gentle elevation, then they assume the appearance of overhanging rocks when viewed at a distance. We crossed several dry branches today. At 5 P M we encamped for the night. The grass was becoming short and indifferent. We had to depend tonight for fuel upon some willow brush which was procured from an Island that lay just opposite to us. Here we met several Mountain trappers with their wagons heavily ladened with bailes of furs and Buffalo skins. This presented a good opportunity of sending back letters to the States which we all gladly embraced. Their price for carrying letters was only 25 cts—which to us was a small consideration. Distance 25 ms.

TUESDAY MAY 22ND   Just at this point, the road leaves the river—runs midway between the River & the bluffs for a distance of eight miles where it comes to the river again. The road along here is firm and solled, but the grass low, thin, and indifferent. We selected the best spot we could find & grazed our Mules two hours at noon.

While here McNeely found on an Island where they had been turned to graze the night before two Oxen that had been left in the hurry to start this morning. They belong to different men. They were loos cattle—and the 2 trains e[n]deavering to get the start overlooked them, and did not miss them till noon. About 4 P M we met the Owners of the cattle returning for them. We had tied them to the hind part of our wagons. I Supposed that the catching and bringing the cattle along was entirely a matter of accommodation in McNeely to the Owners, and when the Gentleman road up and claimed the cattle I told them, to loos them, and take them. They said that they would see the man who caught the steers first & Satify him for his trouble. They road on and met McNeely who charged them $5 apiec for his trouble. They said that was too much. They gave McNeely $5,50 cts and he claimed the $10. The gentlemen came to me as Commandant of the train, to Know whether they could get their cattle. I told them that they could—and that they should have them. Some sharp words ensued when I proposed to leave it to 5 disinterested men which was agreed to. And they decided instantly that the Gentlemen had paid McNeely enough, whereupon the cattle were given up and the Owners took them off. It is a well Known fact that every Emegrants stock is liable to go a Stray, as they have no other pastureage than the wide, and unbounded domain, which is equally free and accessable to all—And the common practice amongst the Emegrants is to catch for and assist each other to protect their stock without the hope of fee or reward.

I took a horse and went ahead of the train, as was my practice all the time, to select a camping sight—and about two miles to the right of the road, on a Slough and at the mouth of a ravine I found tolerable good grass & timber. I rode back and conducted the train to the spot. The correl was formed as usual. Being apprehensive of a stampeed that night from woolfs or Indians a Strong guard was put out that night. It was dark and raining. The gard fired the alarm gun several times through the night. Our mules were Kept in a constant state of allarme by the Woolfs that were prowleing around our camp that night. Here I will just remark that a woolf will frighten Mules equally as bad as an Indian who appears in their midst and discovers to them a Buffalo rug with the rong side out—And the only way to Keep them from being stampeeded is to be in their midst and talking to them all the time. Ones preasants with Mules, and the voice of consiliation will all ways quiet their fears. Distance 25 ms.

WEDNESDAY 23RD   We were detained this morning some what latar than usual in consequence of an unfortunate difficulty which took place between Charles Hodges & P. S. Hamline, last evening whilst they were engagued in their culinary operations. Some unpleasant woords passed whereupon Hodges Struck Hamline & Knocked him down—and was beating him sevearly.

When the cry of fight was given, I was the first who got there and pulled Hodges off of Hamline—when Knives & Pistols were drawn. I caught Hamline just in the act of stabing Hodges with a large Bouy-Knife, and in the effort to arest the stroke I recived a slight cut myself about one and a half inches long across my right arm. Other men interfeard by this time, and the combattants were finely seperated. Hamline re'c a very bad cut on his upper lip done when Hodges frist [*sic*] struck him. Hodges withdrew from the mess next morning—& we left him on the road side with his Mules & good & chattles—and what became of him I Know not.

One of our party Killed an Antelope today. The road today runs near the base of the Bluffs, leaveing the [river?] at [?] some distance to our right. The Soil was of a sandy nature, and vegetation short grass indifferent. In passing today I saw ledges of stone in the Bluffs of a calcareous formation. I saw a most beautiful grove of seder today in a cove in the side of the Bluff. The sight of which was most agreeable haveing seen nothing of the kind since I started. We nooned on a stream of water running paralell with the river. Our fuel consisted of Buffalo chips. We are now about opposite the junction of the North & South Platte. The road is still near the Bluffs, & continued so till towards evening, when the bottom began to narrow in towards the river. We encamped this evening between the Bluffs (which have become more sloping and gradual) and a marshy place where we found in spots very good grass. Distance 25 ms.

THURSDAY 24TH   The morning was dark and lowering and at about 6 A M the rain commenced falling, and as the day advanced the rain increased. The wind was from the North East which rendered it very disagreeable. Soon after leaveing Camp we passed an Ox train of 30 wagons which had encamped just above us. Just here we left the bottom and raised the Bluffs by a gradual ascent, and in about 5 ms. struck the south fork of the Platte. Meantime we passed the Cincinnati Train a joint Stock

association of 50 members. They had 8 mules to the wagon.[25]
Our course is now up the South fork of the Platte and along its
bottom. We continued some 3 or 4 miles up the river. And the
rain continued to fall in such profusion that we were compelled
to stop for the day—which we did oposite to an Island from
which the men procured wood by fording across to it on horseback and bringing the wood back, before them. We found vegitation greener and grass better on the South fork than it was on
the main river.

At 3 P. M. we had a meeting of the whole company at the
tent of the Capt for the purpose of receiveing and addopting
the Constitution that was to be reported this evening by the Committee of 9 who had been selected for that purpose. The Constitution was then read by the Chairman of the Committee and
addopted by sections, togeather with some accompanying bylaws.
After which a few remarks was made by several members of the
meeting and it adjourned.[26] Distance 12 ms.

FRIDAY 25TH   It ceased raining some time during the night,
and the wind continued strong from the N East which rendered
it cold and chilly all day. About 9 A. M. a heard of about 25 or
30 head of Buffalo were discried on the oposite side of the river
quietly feeding along the bottom. I procured a horse and in company withe several others we made several attempts to cross the
river, but our efforts were all vain. The water was too deep to
be forded and to[o] wide to attempt to swim our horses all the
way across. So we were necessarily tho sadly compelled to give
up the chase and leave the quadrupeds to their quiet enjoyment.

The South fork of the Platte is not very dissimilar in its general
appearance from the main stream, except the Surface is not quite
so distended. The banks, bed bottom & waters are pretty much
the same—except the bottoms are much narrower. The river
here is from three forths to one mile and a forth wide. The Bluffs
are much more gentle and slopeing than they are on the main
river, and out back in many places the soil is entirely destitute
of vegitation.

P. F. Harrison and myself took a hunting excursion this fore noon on horse back, in surch of Buffalo. We went out back from the river some 8 or 10 miles but found none—we crippelled several Antelope but got none. We road through a number of those dog-towns. Their Towns cover an Eria of several acres & some times they are one forth of a mile in diameter. They burrow in the ground, dig out large holes and throw up oval shaped moun[d]s of from 4 to 6 feet in diameter and from 1 to 2 feet high. It is extreamly dangerous to ride through those towns on horse-back at full seep [speed]. If your horse steps on one of those mowns he goes through to his breast. I Shot one of them today and examined him manutely. They are about the size of the largest Kind of ground hogs in our country—perhap their boddies are heavyer and more lengthy—with small heads and sharp keen noses and faces. Their legs are short and their feet are rather in the shap[e] of a Molds [mole's], with long sharp nails. Their couler is rather sand—between the Fox & ground hog. They are rather shy and cunning in their appearance. Mr. E. Bryant in his work on California mistook the Gofer [gopher] for the Prairie dog.[27] The Gofer lives in the ground also* and they throw up little oval shaped mouns about the size of a bushel. They are about the size of our Norway rats & of the coller, with short Ears & round chuby heads, but they do not all ways live in towns—but promiscusly all over the face of the earth in many places. Then there is the Prairie—Ground Squirl—that is about the size of the Goffer or something larger than the common ground squirl in our country. They resemble our ground Squirl somewhat. I have eaten of these and they are quite a dellicacy on the plaines. About sunset we struck the bottom 2 ms below where the train had haulted for the night.

---

*It is the Badger that I have been describing. Bryant is right & I am rong— J. A. Pritchard. This is the Prairie dog & not Gofer as I afterwards learned. The Prairie Ground Squirl is a diffrant animal—as I also afterwards learned.

J. A. P.

I saw today a village of Woolfs. These Prairie or Mountain Woolfs [coyotes] are very large, larger than our largest dogs in the States. They are of a grayish yellow, with sharp peked Ears big heads and long drooping tails. I found one of their dens today and came very near catching some of the Puppys that lay on the outside sunning themselves. I saw some 40 or 50 old one setting round, and I rode down that way in order to get a shot at them, but at my approach the[y] disapeared. I thought it singular as but 8 or 10 of them ran off and when I got there I found that their houses were under ground. They had large subterneraneous passages running in every direction. There appeared to be holes enough for one hundred to go in at once. The passages were large enough for a man to have crolled round in with ease. My curiosity led me to mak a close examination. I dismounted and looked into the holes. But I was not so curious as was Genl. [Israel] Putnam who entered with Rifle in hand and brought one out by the Ears. It was while looking round that I found the 3 young *whelps*. I made a dart at them but they being near their dens sliped in and I missed them. It was a thoughtless thing in me to be down on the ground alone amongst a den of perhaps 500 of the largest size of these feroceous animals of the Plaines. And if I had caught one of their young and it had raised the cry for help, I would perhap have been devoured instantly. All wild animals, however cowardly they may be on ordinary occasions, will fight most furiously for their young. Distance today 24 ms.

SATURDAY 26TH   We made an early start this morning and by noon reached the ford, 15 ms distant.[28] And by 3 P M we were all safely landed across the river notwithstanding the great number of teams ahead of us. The river here is about one mile wide, with a bottom composed of quick sand. The sand breaks under the wagon wheels and it jares worse than if it was passing over the roughest kind of frozen ground. We were compelled to put two teams to each wagon in order to pul through. If the wagon is permitted to stand for one minute they bury down in the sand.

It was somewhat difficult finding the road across on account of the holes in the bed of the river caused by the action of the current which was constantly shifting the sand. There was a Frenchman there who acted as pilott—his charge was a tin full of sugar & coffee to the wagon, which was generally given. I watch the crossing of one train whilst the boys were doubling on the teams. And when the next started I put in after them with 4 of our wagons, and made the crossing in perfect safty. We then took our Mules back and doubled on to the five wagons & through ceourtesy to Old man we got him to pilot us. Mules frequently mire in the qu[i]ck sand and fall when crossing. It was a matter of general congratulation when we found ourselves safely landed on the oposite side of the river. There is no timber of any kind at the crossing of the South Platte and but very little any where from the mouth up here—and that little manly brush.

There is a village of the Sioux Indians two miles above the crossing. And some 2 or 300 of them of all sex ages & size wer loitering round our wagons pretending to trade Mockisons & Skins &c for something to eat. The men are large well proportioned & fine looking the woman are rather fine looking. The Sioux Indians have never been hostile to the whites. We encamped about one mile above the ford, where we found good grass. There are some ten or a dozen Frenchmen liveing here in lodges or wigwams, withe Squaws for their wives. After we had encamped a large number of the men came round our camp. I was not all togeather pleassed with their appearance. So I told the boys about sunset to bring out their Guns & Stacke them in the center of the *Corral*. And in a very short time they all drew off by twos 3 & a half dozen at a time. Meantime I told a Frenchman who spoke their language to tell them that, if any of them came round our camp that night, that the Guard would fire upon them. After seeing the guns they took very good care to stay away. Distance 18 ms.[29]

SUNDAY 27TH   At 5 A M we bid adieu to the South Platte and all its inhabitance. Mounted the Bluffs & struck for Ash hollow on the North fork. There being neither water nor grass we we [*sic*] have to make it across in one drive, a distance of 22 miles. At 11 A M we struck the head of Ash hollow 2 ms from the river—so called from the fact that there are a few clumps of Ash trees standing along a hollow that puts into the North Platte with high bold cragy Bluffs on either side with a few seedar bushes sticking along the side. The decent into the hollow [Windlass Hill] is very steep and difficult to get down. The bed of the branch is sandy and heavy pulling with several good springs of clear cold water breaking out of the ground.[30] When we reached the river we rested two hours. After which we resumed our march drove 8 ms & encamped for the night; most of this distance the road is sandy and heavy pulling. The bottom is narrow here and the road runs near the Bluff. The Bluffs are much higher along here than any that we have seen [on] our rout. And of a rough cragy appearance—and sparcely covered with seeder [juniper]. The North fork of the Platte here beares some resemblance to the main stream, yet the channel is not so wide—the banks are higher and the current much more rapid.

We passed several trains today, that had haulted to rest their Mules wash their clothing sun their goods & etc, etc. Among the rest was the Chicago train that passed us soone after we struck the main Platte. They went by us in a trot and said that they were going to beat everyboddy to California. I told the boys that I could beat any train to California that troted their Mules to loded wagons. Distance 30 ms.

MONDAY MAY 28TH   Just along here the bluffs are a greater distance from the river & the bottom more expa[n]sive. The bottom is covered with sand hills and pools of stagnant water, strongly impregnated with Alkali and Saltpeter—so much so that it is rendered entirely unfit for use, and danger[ous] to our Stock. The Grass in spots here is good. The weather is warm and plasant, with a fine brisk breze from the South—which keeps the light sand drifting across the road, in light and floting clouds, giveing to vegitation a greyish hue. The road has [been] heavy all day with the exception of small spot. At noon we found good grass. In places we find marshe spots, that are very heavy getting through. We were overtaken this afternoon by Capt Basye of Ill. with 6 mule teams. Basye was formily of Bourbon Co, Ky and in the same neighbourhood of my Fathers family.[31] At our camp tonight the bluffs ran down to the rivers edge—the Grass was indifferent. Distance 23 ms.

TUESDAY 29TH   In consequence of the shortness of grass we left our camp this morning at 4 A M & travelled 4 ms where we found good grass. We haulted 2 hours to graze & breakfast. One of our party killed an Antelope this morning. After which we resumed our march. At 11 A M I road forward to select a nooning spot. I found the place near the edge of the bluffs good grass & a fine cold spring of water to the right of the road. The bluffs ran so near the river that we have to cross them occasionally—this was at one of those points.

As I was returning I met 2 of wagon from Ill. comeing on. I haulted them till the ballanc of the train cam up which had been haulted on a small creek, untill the spot for nooning could be found. This movement upon their part was a violation of the orders of the Capt. The rest of the train took umbrage at it. Charges were prefured against them, and an Executive Committee called for, to consist of nine, one from each wagon to be selected by the Capt. to enquire into the causes of their violation of Constitution and disobediance of Orders.

The road is much better this evening. About 3 P M we came in sight of the Court house rock. It presents to the Eye the appearance of an artificial Superstructure. It has a round top with doams and Spires. This Court house rock is about 4 ms to the left of the road. At about the same time we came in sight of the Chimney rock. It has the appearance from here of a house with a tall chimney on the south side. We are now some 15 or 16 ms this side of it.[32] We are now in one of the Platts broadest bottoms, with exelant grass.

At 4 P M I discovered in the southwest a very angry looking cloud arising. I haulted the train, and gave orders to Stake the Mules & Pitch tents a[s] quick as possible which was done. The cloud changed round west North West and then bore Square down upon us—and at 5 P M it commenced raining accompanied withe hail and heavy wind, with fearce and vived flashes of lightning, and loud crashing peels of thunder. It raged with increased fury for the space of an hour and a half. Tent pins gave way, and tents went by the board—nearly all the tents round the camp were blown down and the men exposed to the fury of the storm which raged with such violence that it was impossible for a man to stand erect in it, trying to save their tents; and their beding from being wet. Ours being round top tents were not disturbed by the storm. The storm abated somewhat in the course of an hour and a half, but the rain continued during during [*sic*] the night without intermission. Distance 24 ms.

WEDNESDAY 30TH   It is still raining this morning with a cold chiling wind from the North. There is scarcely fuel enough in camp this morning to boile a coffee pot, and none that we know of to be had in this vecinity. The men's clothing and beding are perfectly saturated with water—And they stand shivering round with cold no fire nor anything else to warm them, not so much as a cup of hot coffee. It is stormeing to[o] much to leave here— besides we do not know that we would find wood by leaving here. Towards noon all hands mounted on horses or Mules went [in] serch of wood, and on the plaines back from the river they found an abundance of pine [k]nots and pitch pine timber drifted about in spots—or rather it was scattered promiscusly all over the face of the earth. There was no mountains—no growing timber in view—yet this timber was lying all over the high barren plaines from 40 to 70 feet above the level of the river. This wood was evidently carried there by Wind or Water, who can determine which. The sight of wood to us, hungary wet, and shivering creatures at such a time was most greatful to the feelings.

Men are passing our camp continually in surch of stock. There are a number of trains encamped in sight, and their Mules & cattle have been drifted away by the Storme—And some have been recovered this forenoon 15 miles from camp way out on the plains. The Executive committee met this evening to examine the case of violating order refured to. The party Dr Eckley was summoned before the committee and sent some insulting language back to them & for the two offences his wagon was expelled from the train. A written report to that effect was handed to me by the Chairman of the Committee & I gave him notice of the fact. The rain continues.

THURSDAY MAY 31ST   The Camp was called at 3 A M (the rain haveing stoped at 2) and at 5 we were in motion. The dark and lowering Clouds that hung over us so long with such fearful and threatening forebodings have been chased away by a dismal night. A pure azure Sky displayed its self this morning at the dawn of day, arrayed in all of its magnificence and splendor. The God of day rose clear, unobscured, and beautifully bright— When the fury of the storm was hushed, and nothing but a low gentle breeze was heard whispering across the plaines—peace— peace—be still—how greatful must be the feelings of man to that God who gave him his existance.

A large number of trains had encamped during the storm just along in this bottom. We found this morning where they had been ligh[t]ing up their loading & throwing away their provisions. They had left Bacon, flour, dried beef, Beens, coffee, d[r]ied apples peaches &c &c. Our boys picked up some of the articles.[33] The road was heavy, being saturated with water. Our boys concluded this morning to cary a surveyers chain, in order to ascertain how fast we were travelling & how far we travelled pr day. They walked by my side all day and carryed it against

time. Our common gate on firm roads averaged 3 ms pr hour &
when the roads wer heavy (marshy or sandy) from 2½ to 2¾
ms per hour. We nooned today 3 hours. Our expelled wagon fell
back this morning and 2 others from the same county by permis-
sion went with it.

We passed this afternoon the chimney rock. It stands about 3
miles to the left of the road. Its elevation is said to be between
250 & 300 feet. Its composition is sand stone or rather sand &
Clay. Its shape is simply a round nole [knoll] or mound thrown
up to a great hight with benches or Storys—and from the center
this chimney runs up from 75 to an hundred feet above the main
boddy. When you are clost to it, its shap is a Squair or rather so
with chimney appearance.[34]

There has been a great croud on the road in sight all day and
as great a rush. We have taken it leasurely & the croud is still
with us. The stronger teames are gaining the frount and the
weeker are falling back. At 6 P M we encamped on the banks
of the river, and 5 ms above chimney rock and in full view of it.
The grass is good tonight. Our excommunacated wagon & companions are encamped near by. The high rough craggy bluffs
display themselves in bold relief to our left, from 1 to 3 ms from
the river. Distance 24 ms.

FRIDAY JUNE 1ST 1849   At 5 A M we resumed our march, and
at 10 A M we were at the point from which the road leaves the
river to pass to the left of Scotts bluffs. We gained the top of the
bluffs by gradual ascent and kept in the direction of the bluffs
till noon. The road runs here along a vally that lies between
Scotts bluffs on the right and a range of bluffs on the left, till the
vally gradually narrows down to a p[o]int—at which place the
road ascends the summit of the bluffs which are connected by a
ridge over which we pass, which might properly be called the
connecting Ridge of the 2 bluffs.

Scotts bluffs took its name from a man of that name, who was
a trapper, and in decending the river he was taken sick—and

left, by his ungreatful companions to perish. They returned and reported that he had died and that they burryed him. The next year his remains were found by some Trappers who were passing that way, and with him a journal that gave a full account of the whole transaction. And from that circumstance the bluffs took their name.[35] This bluff is a very large and isolated pile of soft sandstone or rather a Calcareous formation of sand and clay. As you are passing it bye and the differ[ent] faces are exhibited, it presents almost every variety of architectural shape that you can immagion. There is arch, pillar, dome, spire, minaret, temple, gothic castle, modern fortification—round, top and tower. These of course hav not that nice pollish and finish about it, that the construction of human art, would have given it, but upon a scale of magnifficence and grandure fair surpassing the constructive efforts of human Strength and energy. While passing along I surveyed this Scenery, which is continuous for 15 or 20 miles. I involuntearily immagioned myself in the midst of the dessolate, and deserted ruins of vast cities of the Old world, to which Petral Thebes, Babylon and Nineveh, were but pigmas in point of grandure and magnificence. At the base of the bluffs we encamped for the night. About half way up the hill we found a spring of cold water which served by diging it out to furnishe water for all the men & stock that were encamped round there that night and there were a number of trains.[36] Distance 24 ms.

SATURDAY JUNE 2ND   We left camp this morning at 4 A M to get ahead of the tra[i]ns that were crouding us. The road was heavy and sandy all day. Nothing of moment occured today. Basye & myself road ahead this evening & found fine grass, and a fine well of water that had been sunk by some one several days before. We formed a correl togeather this evening. Distance 20 ms. (P S   I lost a leaf out of my memorandam book)*

SUNDAY JUNE 3RD   As the grass was short and indifferent I

---

*This day's entry is written at the bottom of two pages of the diary, but no pages are missing from the diary itself.—D. L. M.

gave orders to the Guard to call the camp at 2 A. M. so that the Mules might be staked out, in order to graze before leaveing camp. That done, we were ready to take up the line of march at 4. We ascended the dividing Ridge—and from the top of which, we had a view of several peaks of the Rocky Mountains. The morning being clear we could see the snow on Laramie's peak with perfect distinctness, and several other elevations about 100 or 150 miles off. The boys immagioned, that they could see the summit of the Wind River Mountains distant about 400 ms— but in that I think [and rightly!] they were mistaken.

Descending from the ridge, we passed over barren plaines, cut up and hollowed out by the action of winds and the torrents of water that came rushing from the hills during the wet seasons. In 12 miles we reached Horse Creek, crossed and in a mile or so furthe found good grass and stoped at 10 A M to noon. Capt Basye's train was still with us and had been for several days. After resting 2 hours we commenced the line of march and crossed over a ridge of sand & struck the river—continued up it till we came to Laramie's fork about one and a half miles this side of the Fort. After a few minutes examination we commenced crossing and succeded without difficulty. The water just struck the fore part of the beds of the wagons. At 4 P M we were at the Fort. We haulted a few minutes, and drove one mile above and encamped for the night. Distance 20 ms.

III

STERILITY, SNOWBANKS & FLOWERS
Fort Laramie to Fort Hall

Monday June 4th   Fort Laramie is built of adob[e]s or sun-dried brick. It is a one story house with several out houses, dwellings &c. It is surrounded by high wall, of the same material, and stands immediatly on the North banks of Laramie's [fork] of the Platte. And it looks more like a place of dessolation than like a place for protection.[37]

I[n] consequence of the disagreement among several of the members of our company, we were here driven to the necessity of dividing it. The Company in the division stood thus—Wm Wilkie, Saml Hardesty Perry McNeely, N. P. Norris, and John Wilkie on one side, and P. P. Youell, Marian Stephens, W. W. Abbott and James A Pritchard on the other side. Abbott was not one of the Company proper, he was attached mearly to travel across the country. Hardesty was selected by his friends to meet Pritchard who was selected by the other boys to divide out the Mules wagons supplys &c &c. In the division of the wagons & provisions there was no disagreement. As there was 5 to 3 we gave them the large wagon, and ⅝th of the provisions were conceded to them and all private property to revert back to its proper owner. The Mules then became the principal objects in the division. Heardesty and myself met and I proposed several plans of dividing which I thought fair. There was 8 men & 10 mules—8 of the mules were old work mules & 2 young unbroke ones.

My first proposition was, to put the name of each of the 8 old mule on a blank piece of paper and let the men draw and take the mule he drew, and then fix the division of the 2 young one afterwards. That proposition was rejected. I then proposed to give them first choice and choice [*sic*] and I the next till we had drawn 2 each—and then give him 2 next time, and I one—and he the next which would have given, us 3 and he 5. He would then [have] had first choice of the first four, I the 2nd, he the 3rd, I the 4th, then of the next four he would have had the first choice of 2, I the 3 choice & he the 4 choice, the young mules afterwards to be divided. And that proposition was also rejected. There was 2 large mules that were considered to be worth a good deal more than any other 2, and he said that he would not divide unless he could get both of those. I then told him that I would give him the 2 big mules John & Nance if he would give me choice of the next 2, and he the 5 I the 6 & he the 7 & 8—and he refused to do that. I then told him I did not see how we could fix it. So he went & consulted his friends & came back, to me, with this proposition—That we were to let them have of the mules choice of the first six, towit 1 John 2 Nancy 3 Jack 4th Dan 5 Fanny 6th Rock, all old well broke mules and further the big wagon ⅝ of all the provisions, The Gold washer, The Gold Scales & $75.00 dollars in money. And we were left the little black mule, the wild untamable yellow mare mule & the 2 little unbrok 3 year olds that we purchased in Indipendance—caught them wild out of the street—& the little wagon & ⅜ of the provision. The provisions & big wagon were conceeded to them all the time.

I at once indignantly rejected the proposition. And told Hardesty that under the circumstances I considered the proposition, not only ungentlemanly but dishonorable. I had been at all the trouble of makeing the outfit. I had spent my time, and part [of] my own personal funds without one cents charge to the company. And not one member of the company had been to one cents expence or one hours trouble, except to put into the Treasury the amount due the company to make the outfit. And not only that—that I was doing this thing of seperating because Wilkie

& Hardesty could not agree with Youell & Stephens. And that Youell, Stephens, Abbott, McNeely, and Norris, could not agree. I rema[r]ked to Hardesty, Thus you see Squire, I am driven to the exceedingly unpleasant necessity of seperating with you and Wilkie entirely for your sakes and on account of others not for myself. These things being true, I have been induced to use the strong language I have towards you. The Squire rema[r]ked that, he did not wish me to consider that the proposition had been made by him that it was mad by others &c &c. Hardesty then withdrew from the task of dividing, and Mr. Wilkie was put in his place.

I met Wilkie, and after a few words of friendly conversation explanatory of my & Hardesty's attempt, I made a proposition to him which he agreed to. It was this that I would or he might as he plased value all the Mules & wagons &c &c and the other take them at the valueation—& he told me to value & he would or would not tak. I there upon fixed the valuations and he took and divided so as to make the number of mules &c and valuation thereof beare as nearly as could be, the relative proportion of 3 to 5. In that way we very soon effected a division of everything. If I wanted anything I paid to him the worth [of] it. If he wanted anything (that could not be divided) he paid the worth of it to me. Untill we got through with all the goods & effects of the company proper. But they still claimed $75.00 off of us, because Abbott joined our mess to travel with us across the plaines and therefor his mules would be put to our wagon. But this I refused to give because I considered it unjust.

I told Mr. Wilkie that, as he would not agree to a final settlement without the money, I was willing to leeve it to 3 disinterested men one to be chose by him, one by me, and they 2 to select the 3 person. This he agreed too. I then told Mr. Wilkie to write out a statement of our contract with Abbott & that we would submit the matter in writing without comment to the Refferrees. Which Mr. Wilkie did. Wilkie selected P. S. Hamline and I selected P. F. Harrison & they selected as thirdsman M. M. Basye Capt of a company of Illinoians. The statement is in these words—

Statement

About the 3rd of May 8 men with 2 waggons & 10 mules overtaken by W. W. Abbott & his 2 mules & his white horse with about 200 lbs of baggage, and provisions & proposed to those 8 men to give them his provisions and the use of his 2 mules to work in the waggons, and the use of his poney when we wanted to chase buffalo upon only—and to carry his baggage to California and he to be as one of us in the mess. Now we want to divide the company into 2 parts, and each of us origional 8 men mutually agree to a dessolution 5 men in one mess, and 3 in the other—Abbott joining with the 3 members of the former company. Now these 5 men claim money from the 3 men for the use of the 2 mules of Abbott's from this to California. The amount we submit to your honourable decision.

Here follows the descision of the referees—

Agreeable to the above statement, we can see no just cause why the mess of 3 men Should pay anything to the mess of 5 men. It being as Stated above a mutual and simultaneous agreement to desolve the origional contract. The fact that Abbott joines in with the 3 men does not alter in our opinion the matter of the case—for the dessolution being mutually agreed upon, all the parties Stand in the Same relation to each other which they did, before any contract was entered into. And Abbott might or not just as he chose unite with either party. If he chose to unite with neither party, then clearly neither could claim of the other. If he United with a foreign party then who could think of claiming any thing of such a party.

> M M Basye
> P. S. Hamline
> F. P. [P. F.] Harrison

In the descision we all acquiessed. Meantime we went on & completed the work of dividing. And by night each party had their waggon loaded and fitted up ready for an early start next morning.

TUESDAY JUNE 5 1849   At an early hour this morning we resumed the line of march. At this point we leeve the river and commence crossing what is called the black hills.[38] Our rout today was over a rough broken country of sandy soil, barron & destitute of vegitation. At noon we reached a small stream of water about 20 ms from the fort. We ascended it about 2 or 3 miles and stoped to noon at 2 P. M. At about 3 Oclock a dark cloud rose and it commenced a heavy fall of rain which lasted till night. We remained in camp this afternoon. Here Wilkie & co. travelled in the rain to get ahead of us. They left our train finally and joined with the 3 Illinois wagons that had withdrawn from our train. We picketed our mules on the oposite side of the creek & hearded them. We found plenty of good timber on this creek. Distance 25 ms.

WEDNESDAY JUNE 6TH   We left our camp this morning at half past four and continued to ascend the creek crossing it several times for a distance 5 or 6 miles when the road turned squar to the right. And ascended a creek with a dry, sandy broad bed for a considerable distance, when we came to several fine large springs of clear pure cold water, the largest of these however is a warm spring from which the place takes its name. We continued to ascend the branch to its head and untill we had gained the hights of the bluff wher we nooned, timber & grass plenty. The face of the country was broken and carpeted with a beautiful coat of grass, besides the hills were covered with beautiful groves of Seeder and pine. We were at this point just oposite Laramie's peak and near to it. Its Snow caped summit seemed to pier to the Skys. Thus winter Stood aloft, in bold relief upon the left, beautifully reflecting the rays of the sun through the light fleeces of cloud that floated across the blue vault of heavens, while upon the right Nature was clad in all the soft, sweet, and gentle beauty of vernal bloom. While the one presented the bold, fearce, and lofty figure of the Fridged Zone, the other presented one (as it were) eternal spring embellished and beautified with perenneal Flowers. Upon the whole it was a most pictureque and liveing landscape, most beautiful to the Eye, most greatful to the feelings.

While nooning a mule Kicked C. K. Snyder with both feet in the brest, and he fell to the ground lifeless to all appearance. I with several others ran to him and raised him upon my lap. There was not the slightest appearance of life in him. I rubed his pulse, bathed his head in water rubed him with camphor for a considerable length of time before the slightest appearance of life was percieveable. And when we had partially resussitated him he fainted away, and it was several minutes before he began to recover from that. But he finally recovered & and [from] the effects, from which he received no serious injury, and in a few days able to do duty. While nooning the Chicago train passed us again but this time on pack mules. It was the same train that had troted past us, on the main Platte. They had broken down their teams, & threw away their wagons at fort Laramie, and now were bound to pack to California.

We continued our rout at 2 P M and crossing a number of branches ravines & hollows, we came to a large creek [Horseshoe Creek]. We crossed the creek. Capt Basye who was with us camped on the creek. We raised the hill, it was decidedly the Steepest and longest that we have encountered. On the hill we encamped for the night. In the head of a ravine we found good grass & wood. Distance 22 ms.

THURSDAY JUNE 7TH   Our rout today has been across what may properly be termed the Black hills. The road runs across high rolling broken country. The principal production is the wild Sage, except along the streams. There you find timber. We crossed several small streams this forenoon. In 15 ms. we came to La. Bonte River (called by some [*i.e.*, Edwin Bryant] Beaver creek) where we nooned. After crossing the river and desending some 2 ms, turned Our mules across to the oposite side of the stream. While nooning we had a heavy rain with considerable hail. After the rain was over we hitched up and came 8 ms to small creek [La Prele Creek] where we encamped for the night. On the oposite side of the creek we found good grass where we put our mules to graze. We are now in the neighbourhood of the Red hills. The rain rendered the roads slippery travelling this afternoon. Distance 23 ms.

FRIDAY JUNE 8TH   During the night a very heavy rain fell, which made the roads muddy and heavy travelling. Soon after leaveing camp this morning we passed the red hills. Our camp last night was surrounded by cragy hills thrown up to a great hight by the up heaveing of volcanoe eruptions. The face of the country today has been barron and sterile. We nooned in a vally formed by two erregular cliffs of Sandstone thrown up to a great elevation evidently by some volcanoe eruption. By night we had completed our journey across the black hills. And encamped on a fine bold running stream 4 miles this side of the North fork of the Platte. The Stream is called Foaurche Bois [Fourche Boise] River. We are getting into a region of country where the water is all cold. Distance 25 ms.

SATURDAY JUNE 9TH   In 4 miles this morning we struck the river. Here we found good grass & plenty of timber. In 5 miles we struck Deer Creek—a fine camping spot. The Stream is large & handsom & said to contain an abundance of Fish. The road has been fine today, by noon we had travelled 15 ms. Here we found in the bend of the river a splendid bottom of blue grass. It was from 12 to 15 inches high and heavily seeded. It resembles very much the blue grass of Ky—it is somewhat courser with very heavy heads, and of a more nutritious [character] than any grass I ever saw in any country.

Just as we were in the act of leaveing camp a Buffalo Bull was chased into camp. A great excitement was instantly created [and] every man Sprang to his gun. Each man took a shot at the old

Gentleman as he went bounding along. Not one shot seemed to tak effect or turn his course. I caught my Gun after I saw that he was still on his feet (for I [s]tood till all the party fired expecting every shot to see him fall) and mounted a horse & was about overtakeing him when he pitched into the River, I however dismounted and took a deliberate fire at him as he swam off, placeing the ball back of the wethers, rather on the right side. The ball took effect and sank him down, but rose & made shore and finally made his escape as we had no means of crossing after him.[39] The general appearance of the North Platte has muterily changed here. The channel is not over 150 or 200 yards wide, the water deeper & the current swifter. At 5 P M we encamped for the night in a bend of the river on a splendid spot of blue grass. Basye formed a correl with me this evening. Distance 25 ms.

SUNDAY JUNE 10TH   At 9 A M we reached the Ferry. I[t] was Kept by some Mormans from Salt Lake who had came clere there to Keep ferry for the season. We found about 175 wagon ahead of us & we had to tak our turn. We however joined another company or 2 & constructed a raft to cross our wagone on. After several efforts we succeded in crossing 2 wagons, but we found the current so strong and the Raft so heavy and unwiealdy that we abandoned the project and awaited our turn which came in on Wednesday morning. We are now getting into the region of mountains. The peak within 8 ms of us to our left [Casper Mountain] is covered with snow. I wrote several letters and left with Ferryman to send back to the states for me. Monday & Tuesday 11 & 12 were sepent in washing our cloths shoeing mules fixing wagons Etc. Etc. Distance Sunday 10th 10 miles. A young man by the name of [James] Brown from Howard county Mo. was drown[ed] in attempting to swim his stock across the river.[40]

WEDNESDAY JUNE 13TH   We commenced crossing our wagons this morning at the dawn of day, and by 8½ A. M. Basye's and my train were both over. We joined to assist each other in crossing. Our mules were brought in the morning by daylight from

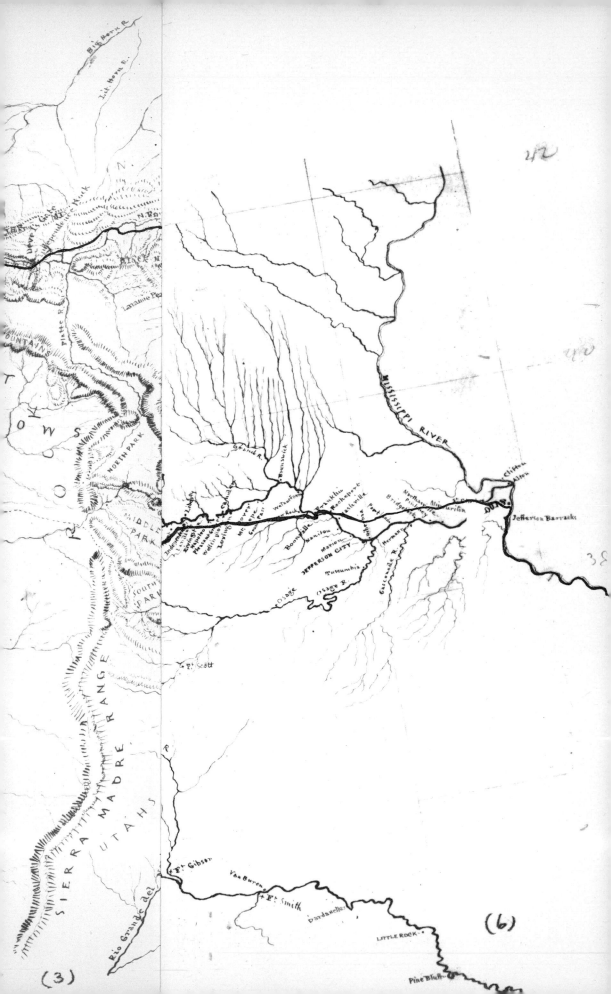

where we had been grazeing them some 6 or 8 ms out towards the bluff [Casper Mountain]. We put them all togeather, and swam them over the river before the sun rose, it being the best time to swim animals at this point. We crossed all safe. Our course was up the river on the North side for about 9 miles. The road there bore to the right across the bluff in the direction of Sweetwater. The road has been heavy & sandy today. The country over which we passed today has been arid & sterile, no vegitation except the wild sage brush.

In 5 miles after leaveing the river we came to a mineral lake and mineral spring. At 3 P. M. we struck a dry branch, and passing down it some distance we came to a spring & Pool of water, strongly impregnated with Sulpher & Alkali. We there watered ourselves & Animals and continued till 7 when we struck a small branch that afforded a scanty supply of water that was impregnated with the Carbonet of Soda & Alkeli. We could bearly use it for coffee. The grass was tolerable but we had to keep a guard with the mules all the time to keep them from swamping in the spouty places. A man would sind [sink] to his neck instantly. Several of the men fell in during the night. I saw 5 head of Oxen sunk down to their hornes, and their owners had extracate them by attaching ropes to their heads & puling them out. Distance 30 ms.[41]

THURSDAY JUNE 14TH   At 4 A M this morning we were on the road, endeavouring to get away from the unpleasant and dangerous place at which we were compeled to spend the night. During the night 3 of the mules belonging to Basye's train fell into the Quagmire and were unable to get out without help. The men belonging to an Ox train spent the morning in diging & hauling out their cattle. Some 7 or 8 of them had sunk down head hornes and all. We enjoyed several hearty laughs at the boys to see *them* walk right into the Soda fountains up to their Eyes without the formality of Knocking at the door.

Quite a number of Antelope were discovered feeding on the

plaines, and as the surface of the ground was somewhat broken
it afforded a good opportunity for shooting them. Several of the
boys took their guns & started on the chase, I & P F Harrison
among the rest. We pretty soon got one & sent it up by a couple
of the boys, & continued around a Mountain expecting to mak
a cut off. And when we traveled 8 or 10 miles we found no end
to the mountain as we expected. We clome the mountain an when
we gained the top we found the road bore to the left, and the
train was just in sight some 10 miles off. We bore down the
Mountain for the road, and struck it at the Willow Spring. Here
we took a cool refreshing drink, rested a while & then pushed on
& 15 ms from that place we came up to the train nooning on a
fine creek [Fish Creek] to the left of road. The other boys that
had gone to the left of the road had succeeded in killing some
5 or 6 Antelope. They being in sight of the train theirs were
brought in on horse back. Harrison & myself walked before we
caught up to the train in all about 26 or 8 miles.[42]

At 2 P M we resumed our march and at about 4 we came to
several large lakes of pure salaratus. It was as genuine an article
as I ever saw. I geathered several pounds & used it in bread—
one of these lakes looked at a distance of 300 yards like a river
disgorgeing its self of Ice & with its broken flakes upheaved in
all manner of shapes. The water had dried away & the pure
genuine double refined Salaratus as white as chalk was left on
the ground from one to ten inches thick. At seven this evening
we struck Sweetwater river and about one mile from where we
struck we came to the well known place called Indipendance
Rock. Here we encamped for the night. Distance 34 ms.

FRIDAY JUNE 15TH   This morning all the curious were clamb-
ering to the top of "Indipendance Rock I among the rest. I saw
name[s] to the number of several thousand—some graven some
painted. I did not follow their example. It is an isolated elevation composed of masses of granite rock piled one upon another,
about one hundred feet high, and about one mile in circumfer-

ence, located on the northern bank of the Sweetwater river.[43] This river is from 60 to 80 feet wide deep channel, gravelly bed & swift current. At this point we cross the river and in 5 miles come to what is calld the deavels [Devils] gate. It [is] a singular fissure or cannon [canyon] in the Mountains through which sweetwater forces its way. The fissure is about 30 feet wide and about one half mile through, with vertical walls from 350 to 400 feet high. The range of Mountans run parillel with the river for some distance and near to it.

In ten miles from the Deavils Gate the road leaves the river to cutt off a bend. The road is here heavy and sandy. We crossed during the forenoon several smal streams that flow into the Sweetwater, the waters of which were as cold as Ice. They were fresh from the melted snows. We nooned before leaveing the river. This afternoon was the first time that we had a view of the Wind river Mountains. When we struck the river after crossing the bend we encamped for the night. I purchased during the day from a gentleman with an Ox train a wagon Tongue, to suply the one that was broken by Stephens between the Vermillion & Big Blue river. He had brought it along as an extra tongue. I spent the evening in putting it in which was done in splendid style. Distance 25 miles.

SATURDAY JUNE 16TH   We left the river this morning soon after we left our camp and in six miles we struck it again. We watered our mules & in a mile or so we left it again, and struck it in 8 mil[e]s where we nooned. When we leave the river we have deep heavy sand to pull through. The grass is good on Sweetwater but no timber, we find willow brush occasionly. The ballance of the time we have to depend on sage bushes for fuel. After nooning we struck across the country to avoid a bend in the river. In ten miles from where we left the river we came to an Ice Spring one of the strangest & mos[t] singular phenomena in the whole trip, and one of the most singular in Nature. This Spring as it is called is, rather a bason surounded by sand plains, about one mile in length & from 150 to 300 yards wide. But does not all contain Ice. The Ice is found about 8 to 10 inches beneath the surface. There is from 4 to 6 inches water above the Ice, and as turf or sod of grass appearantly floating on the water, upon which you can walk all over it. You can stand and Shake for 2 or 3 rods Squar. The water above the Ice is pretty strongly impregnated with Alk[a]li. The upper end of the marsh is entirely of that kind of water mixture. Tho there is good fresh water in spots. To get to the Ice you take a spade or Ax & cut away the sod & then strike down & cut it out in Squar blocks. The Ice is clear & pure entirely free from any Alkali or other unpleasant tast. It is from 4 to 10 inches thick, and as good as any I ever cut from the streams in Kentucky. I cut and filled my water bucket & took it to camp with me and so did all the ballance of the men.[44] This marsh is not nearer any stream of water than 8 miles, and 15 or 20 miles from the Mountains. We encamped here for the night, and as the grass was sparce we turned our mules loos on the plains & placed a guard to heard them. No fuel but sage brush. Distance 24 miles.

SUNDAY JUNE 17   We left our camp at the Ice Springs at 4 A. M. and travelled to the river a distance of 12 miles on account of the scarcity of grass & bad water for our stock. We reached there at 9 A M and rested 2 hours grazed our mules & tooke breakfast our selves. P F Harrison one of our party Killed an Antelope this morning & we had a feast. I consider the flesh of the Antelope to be far superior in every point of view to venison or Mutton. At 11 A M we commenced our journey again & crossed a large hill, struck the river in 3 ms. We then crossed the river several times to avoid bad roads. We travelled up the river several miles & left it[45] cross what is called Stony [Rocky] Ridge—A very high elevation. On top of the hill in the head of a ravine we found a good camping spot and stoped for the night. We had good grass & found several fine springs breaking out of the top of the mountain—water as cold as melted Ice. Distance 24 miles.

MONDAY JUNE 18TH   The line of march was resumed this morning by our train at 5 A M. And we bid adieu to the hights of Stony Ridge. We are now in the region of Snow. This morning the grass was stifened and white with frost. In three miles we came up to 3 or 4 trains of Ox wagons, we passed 14 of them as they were leaveing their camp. And 53 kept ahead of us till noon, when we passed them and some 20 or 30 others.

This forenoon we crossed several tributarys of the Sweetwater river, in crossing some of which we found Bank of snow from 2 to 20 feet deep. On one of those wintery looking spots, in a clear warm summers day the Boys took quite an exciting game of snow bawling in which a dozen or more took part. We crossed the Sweetwater river at noon, the last time.

About one half mile after crossing the river we noon[ed] on the hill or leavel.[46] About 4 P M we stood upon the Summit leavel of the Rocky Mountains. Nor could we have told from observation that we had gained such a great elevation had it not been for the knowledge of our geographical position & the imposeing land marks to our right, the Wind River Mountains, whos cold, Spiral, Snow caped summits were raised to such a great elevation. And the very perceptible change in the temprature of the climate. We are now upon the dividing Ridge or to use a more forcible figure "the Backbone of the North American Continent"—And from which the waters flow into the Atlantic & Pacific Ocean. The South Pass is about 300 miles distant from Fort Laramie. And about 980 miles from Indipendance. The Plat[e]au of the South Pass is from 15 to 20 miles wide—And as you approach the Summit level or the point of culmination it is gradually narrowed down. And the summit level lies immediately between 2 low hills from ¾ to one mile apart, which rise about 150 feet above the plain. The Altitude of the South Pass according to some observations is 7490 feet above the level of the sea. The Latitude North is 42 degrees 27 minuts, 15 seconds. Longitude west 109 Degr. 27 [21] minuts 32 seconds.[47]

Two miles west of the Pass is the Pacific Springs. It rises in a hollow and oozes in from both sides for a mile or more. It is nothing more nor less than a perfect Quagmire or marsh, covered with a thick mat or turf of grass, Suffitiently strong to bear an Ox with ease. So soft is the mud and water that I could shake 25 or 30 feet in diametor. At this place we found severel trains encamped. And grass being short we drove 3 ms down the creek [Pacific Creek] where we found good grass one mile to the left of the road and encamped for the night. We have to use sage brush for fuel which is a very good substitute when we get it plenty. Distance 30 ms.

TUESDAY JUNE 19TH   The camp was called at 3 A. M. And by half past 4 we were on the road. I placed a guard out with the mules and had them hearded during the night, where they fared well. This morning the grass was perfectly whitened and stiffined with what we would call in Ky a Black Frost. We nooned today at the forks of the road. The left hand of which led to Fort Bridger and to Salt Lake, and the right hand road led to the *Sublett* or Greenwood cutoff a distance of 19 ms from the South Pass. We here took the right hand road.[48] We crossed little Sandy filled our casks with water, and three miles this side at 4 P. M. we encamped for the night on fine grass. While we were nooning Mr. E. M. Hays one of our party Killed a fine fat Antelope. This evening Basye & Alexander from Ill with a mule train encamped with us. We had this evening a very heavy hail shower which lasted but for a few minutes and entirely partial in its character. Distance 24 ms.

WEDNESDAY JUNE 20TH   At the distance of 7 miles this morning we reached & crossed Big Sandy at 7 A M—The starting point to cross the Green wood or Sublett's cutoff. It was our intention in the first place to stop here and rest our mules till evening. Then start and make a night travel across this dessert of 45 ms. without water as the practice has heretofore been. But we came to the conclusion (and properly too) as the day was cool to take with us water for our mules & selves and travel till night which would bring us nearly to Green River. And then depend upon the dew to water our animals that night, and make the trip early next morning. At a distance of 7 ms we found a pool of water to the left of the road that had been left there by the re[c]ent raines. Here we watered our mules, and continued our rout till 11 A. M. when we stoped to noon on very good grass. After we had grazed and rested ourselves & animals one hour and a half or 2 hours, we caught up & continued the march till 4 P. M. at which time we haulted in the road and gave our mules what water we had left, Saveing about one quart to the man to make our coffee for supper & breakfast. At half past 6 P M we crossed a deep hollow and on the oposite side we found exelant grass. We here encamped for the night.

The general appearance of the face of the country lying between Big Sandy and Green River is leavel, Slightly undulated, no timber, but plenty of wild Sage, and in places the grass is very good. The road is firm and untill you get within 15 miles of Green River, is very fine and easy travelling. From there on to the river the country is cut up very much by deep ravines. We are now 30 miles from Big Sandy according to Our Roadometer. Capt Basye concluded to go through tonight & drove on.[49] I thought that Our mules were too much fatigued to go farther. While we were at supper two Gentlemen came from the ferry on their way back to meet their trains. They told us that it was still 18 miles to the river. I envited them to dismount and remain with us during the night, as their trains were not near, which they did. We divided our scanty meal with them (scanty on account of water). Distance 37 miles.

THURSDAY JUNE 21ST   At 4 O'clock we left our camp for the river, and in about 3 miles we came up to where Basye had encamped. The road was hilly & heavy and the day warm. At about 10 we began to see the course of the river as marked out by the timber that skirted its margin. At the joyful sight the boys began to lead off, to get there as soon as possible. We found our way into the river bottom by a precipitous and difficult decent from the top of a very high bluff. We reached the river at 11 A M, four miles above the ferry. We here watered our mules & from a cold spring drank some refreshing draughts ourselves. After resting a few minutes we drove down to the ferry. We found there 24 wagons before us, 14 of which were crossed by night. I succeded in effecting a hire of the boat for the night, which was not objected to by those who were ahead of me. We were to furnish the hands to man the boat and pay him $1.50 pr wagon or he would furnish the hands & charge $3.00 pr wagon. I prefered the former as we had men with us that could beat his best hands with ease. We commenced crossing our wagons at 9 O'clock and by 12 we had the whole train over, with all the Baggage. The ferry Boat was constructed of 4 small Canoes which were roughly rafted togeather. The ferry is kept by some Frenchmen who live in lodges made of skinns and proped up with poles. They have Indian Squaws for wifves. In this way they live and trade with the Indians for their Furrs & Skins etc etc.[50] Green River is a bold rapid stream about 350 to 400 feet wide with a good deal of water for a stream of its size. Distance 22 ms. The boys here caught a good many fine Fish.

FRIDAY JUNE 22ND   As early as the boys could get in with our mules this morning we swam them across the river without accident or loss. The road bour off down and to the right of the river for 4 ms and then turnes squar to the right up a deep hollow for some 2 ms untill it gaines the top of the hill. And then descends to a creek called Willow run [Fontenelle Creek]. We passed up the creek some 3 ms & haulted for the day. As we had good grass we concluded to rest our mules the ballance of the day. The Channel of the creek was about 40 feet wide with a dep rapid current.

W. W. Abbott purchased a horse this morning at the ferry of one of the Frenchman at $50. We here found quite a number of

Indians loitering round the ferry. They had a great number of fine horses. And for which they asked a big price. These are the Soshonees or Snake Indians. They are decidedly the best looking and most intelligent Indians that I ever saw. They possess an affability and Suavity of manners not common at all to the Red Men of the forest. Their Women are handsome delicate & genteel looking. All the circumstances taken into consideration the Soshonees are, and, have always been Kind and friendly to the Whites.

Shortly after stoping Dr Wm L Thomas of Augusta Ky. came up and asked me if I hand any objection to his stoping, and, travelling with us from that on. I told him no, to turn in, which he did.[51] Dr. Roach from New York with 2 wagons asked the same privalege to which I assented.[52] They had been travelling in Capt Basye's train from the states, and were not altogeather satisfied with his way of doing business and prefured mine.

Late this evening the Old Chief of the Soshonee tribe came on from the ferry where he had been stoping for a time and encamped near to us with his family and a party of 25 or 30 men women & children. The Old Chief came down & enquired for the Capt. I was pointed out [to] him. He came up & shook hands with me and said in broken English that he wished to tell me that his people would not disturbe anything that belong to us. Nor would they interfear with our horses and mules. He said that his people were honest and would not steal. He continued to say that the White people were a big people—had big country—heap of cattle and horses—and lived in great big fine houses. And Indian little people—No big house—no many horses—no cattle—no big country. Laying his hand on his breast, he said—Indian Soshonee Indian—love white people —White people good people—White people love Indian— etc. etc. And I found the Old fellows words to be true.[53] And indeed such appears to be true with regard to these Snake Indians for such is their general character. There [?] men and Women go fantastically and Genteely dressed tho it be in skins principally. The boys caught several fine messes of Fish this afternoon. Distance 11 miles.

SATURDAY JUNE 23RD   We ascended the creek this morning some 3 miles before we came to the crossing place. And when we got there we found it so deep that (from the melting of the Snows in the mountains) [we] were compelled to raise our wagon beds to prevent the waters comeing into them. We left the creek to our right pretty shortly after crossing it, and struck the high table lands of the mountains. When we had gained the Summits we found large snow banks. It was a singular phenomina to see the snow banks that had drifted in the heads of the hollows and all the north hill sides literally covered with it, melting in the day and freezeing of a night, Surround[ed] by the most beautiful and luxuriant grasses and vegitation that ever grew out of the earth. Moreover the heavy frosts that was found on the grass every morning seemed not to injure its groth or other wise injure it, in the slighest degree. We encamped this evening on a small branch [Crow Creek]. The waters here are as cold as melted Ice. The grass on these mountains are very fine. Distance 22 ms.

SUNDAY JUNE 24TH   We travelled in the vally some 5 miles and then crossed a very high ridege of the mountains [Absaroka Ridge]. The descent on the west side was so abrupt that we were compelled to let our wagons down in part by attaching ropes and letting the men hold on behind. At the foot of the hill we came to What is called Hams fork of the Bear [*i.e.*, Green] River, it is about 50 feet wide at this place with a strong current as all these mountain streams have. We had to raise our wagon beds 8 or 10 inches to keep the water out. A Mr. Sidney Smith Joseph Fiffin & 3 others from Chiviot Ohio in attempting to cross had upset their wagon in the stream & had wet all of their things, and spoilt a great deal of their provisions. They however had succeded in getting their things out before we got there. I gave them a sack of Corn meal, which was very acceptably and cheer-fully received.

Our train was all safly crossed by moon [noon] when grazed our mules & rested 3 hours. The march was then resumed and in 2 ms we came to a hill [Hams Fork Plateau] that took us just two hours & 30 minutes to gain the top of strait forward travel-ling. From the Summit it looked as if we could trow a stone back to where we nooned. On top of this mountain was a beautiful level plain of as rich soil as I ever saw. It was [s]everal miles in extent. And peautifully Carpeted with a most luxuriant groth of elegant grass, that stood, in massive mats waveing in the breeze. In the reare of the plain there is an elevation in the mountains of about 70 feet which is covered with a fine groth of pine & in spots cotton wood timeber. Cold & never failing springs are gush-ing out of the rocks every few rods. Here we encamped for the night. Distance 15 ms.

MONDAY JUNE 25TH   The Musquetoes were so abundant here, that our men and animals saw no peace till about 9 when it was so cold that it chilled them. This morning after the sun rose and warmed the earth they were equally as anoying. I stood this morning on banks of snow and fought them off. It is most aston-ishing to find the Grasses on these mountains so abundant and of such an exelant quality. It looks nearly exactly like our Blue Grass, and in the absence of the proper (if that is not) name we call it Blue Grass. It groes from 10 to 18 inches high, and very heavily seeded. I regard it as being entirely equal to corn Oats & hay for stock. We descended after crossing the dividing ridge between Green River & Bear River a mountain one mile in length—there was about 200 feet of it over a precipice of stone that we had to take our mules from the wagons & let them down by hand & with ropes. After we gained the foot of the hill we crossed a small creek [Rock Creek] and ascended another high hill—descended it & struck Bear river vally at 3 P. M. In 6 or 8 ms came to Thomas's [*i.e.,* Smiths] fork of Bear River. We found it to deep to be forded with safty without raiseing our wagon beds some 15 or 18 inches. So the remainder of the afternoon was spent in cutting down cotton wood trees and cribing up our wagon beds. We lashed the timbers & beds fast to the Axels of the wagons. We here overtook the mule train of Col [William H.] Russell of Mo who left Indipendance 15 or 18 days befor we did.[54] The Col had just completed the job of ferrying his train over, by converting one of his wagon beds into a boat & pulling it backwards & forwards by a rope that was streatched across the stream. We found several Ox trains crossing this evening. One was the Howard Co. *Mo* train. Distance 20 ms.

TUESDAY JUNE 26TH Our wagons were driven early this morning to the ford. We commenced by swimming the mules over and then spliced our fifth cha[i]ns and made one end fast to the end of the tongue & laid the other across the river & hitched to it 2 spand [spans] of mules, leaveing a pr of the largest mules to the tongue—which could do no good after they struck the current, untill they began to strik shallow water again. The mules however that were suspended to the end of the chain drew the wagon through. This was done in order that the current should not carry the wagon and wheel mules off. As soone as the wagon was drawn near enough to shove we put on the other mules and took it out. In this way we suceeded in crossing all our wagons by 10 A M. The largest (15 hands ½) mules we had could just tuch bottom in the channel. We nooned shortly after crossing & travelled 14 ms down and encamped for the night on the banks of the main sream. This is the most beautiful vally that I ever beheld. I am sure that the Grass cannot be surpassed by any other spot of earth. And if I were to settle any where beyond the pales of civilization this should be the spot. What can be more enviting than a bold flowing river, a beautiful vally—and lofty Mountain scenary. Distance 14 ms. Bear river is about 200 feet wide at this point.

WEDNESDAY JUNE 27TH   From where we started this morning

the road runs across a large vally & in 5 miles crosses one of the tributaries of Bear river [Thomas Fork]. Here to we had to block up our wagons. After crossing the creek the road turns up a high long hill. The river beares immediately to the left and passes through an open cannon with high vertical wall that run to the waters edge. It is 6 miles from the last mentioned creek to where the road strikes the river again.[55] And when we reached the river we encamped for the day, as some of our boys, had become tired of the wagons & wished to pack through—and others were compelled to pack because their teams had failed so much that they were unabled longer to draw their wagons. So Hamline & mess sold their wagon & purchased at Smiths trading post (near to which we were then encamped) poneys for the purpose. M Stephens & P. P. Youell of Capt Pritchards mess came to the conclusion that they would prefur packing to going farther with the wagon consequently it was mutually agreed by all concerned they should exorcise their choice in the matter. So a division of mules & property was satisfactorily effected.

The wife of the Old Chief of whome I have been speaking was thrown from her horse today and killed. And a boy who was rideing behind her was also thrown and his arm broken. She was buried according to their custome. She was put into the ground & all of her things were put with her, and an equal share of all their provisions. They then shot the horse and put him into the grave for the woman to ride. They then fired a few guns into the grave & put up a most piteous howling, weeping, and waleing—and in that state of agony departed from the place.[56] This Old Smith who lives here has a cork leg—a rough looking man he is to. The place is better known as Smith's trading post. A Salt Lake Morman & wife wer here for the purpose of trading with the Emmegrants, & several Frenchmen.[57] Distance 14 ms.

THURSDAY 28TH   This morning Abbott & myself caught up our little team of 3 mules & one unbroke Indian horse. Tho Our team appeared small haveing reduced it one half, yet Our chances for getting along are still as good as they were when we had the whole team of 6, the load also being reduced in like proportion. After we had gone about one mile our new horse thought that he had gone far enough peacibly. So he set in to kicking and did not stop untill every peace of hearness had been removed by his heels that he could reach. And in fact he kicked after I had removed from his neck the cholar. I took him back and traded him to a packer for a first rate little mule, which just fited out our team of 4 mules.

We came on down Bear River vally crossing during the day quite a number of small streams. Towards evening the road turned up a branch and bour across the hills in order to avoid a bend in the river. After strikeing the bottom again which was within 3 miles from where we left it, We continued down the river for 5 ms, then turned to the left to strik the river in order to encamp for the night, there being no good stoping places exept on the river just along here. Distance 25 ms.

FRIDAY JUNE 29TH   At a distance of 4 ms this morning we came to a fine spring where we all haulted and took a good refreshing drink. We pushed on till 10 A. M. when we reached what is called the Soda or Beer Springs. These are so called on account of the acid tast and effervessing gasses contained in these waters. It is a place of very great interest. The water is clear and sparking, and in many places t[h]rown several feet in the air. The water is constantly boiling up with a kind [of] hissing nois. There are a great number of the springs bursting out of the ground but the principal one is near the river and comes out at the edge of the water near the lower part of the grove. The Springs are situated in a fine seeder Grove with a stony founddation. The Steam Boat Springs are about ½ mile below, the water of it are a little warmer than the others and escapes out of the ground through a crevis or apiture [aperture] in the stone about the size of a mans head. The effervescing gasses, being somewhat confined beneath the ledges of stone, presents this pufing appearance in its efforts to escape. The springs are in latitude North 42 degrees 39 minuts & 57 sects, and of west Longitude 111 degre, 46 minutes 00 sects. Altitude about 6000 feet above the level of the sea.[58] The road continues down the river 6 miles farther and at this point the river turnes to the left around the point of a mountain [Soda Point] which is beautifully clad with furr timber. The vally continues handsome & fertile—just here the road turnes to the right up a broad vally [Gem Valley].[59] In 5 or 6 miles we came to a small creek, and in one mile thereafter we found a splendid spring of water, that gushes from the base of the mountain. The Grass continues fine, the mountain sides are covered with stinted seeder. Distance 24 ms.

SATURDAY JUNE 30TH The road has been heavy today. We passed through a number of sloughs & branches, the waters of which were slightly impregnated with sulpher, with marshy beds. At 12 M to [we] struck a fine large creek [upper Portneuf River], on which we nooned. One of our mess caught a salm[o]n Trout, which afforded us a mess of Fish for dinner. Two young men belonging to the Howard Co. Mo. train came up to us today & stated that they crossed the line on the 20th of May, and that the grass was eaten down to the ground & that the croud was not yet past Fort Laramie, etc etc. I killed two Ducks this afternoon. We saw on our rout today a vast amount of volcanod eruptions evidently showing that the elements had been melted with a heat that was more exciting than pleasant. We arrived at the point where the road commences ascending the ridge that divides the waters of the Great basan from the waters of the Pacific, a[t] 6 P. M. where we encamped for the night.[60] Wood, grass & water plenty. Here the boys that we had left at Smith's trading post to fix up their packs came up with us. Distance 25 ms.

SUNDAY JULY 1ST We commenced the ascent this morning at 5 A M and by 9 we had gained the summit. In many places the hills were very steep. The descent on the west side is rather more gradual. After we reached the vally, on a small branch we nooned. At 6 P M we came to a large creek one of the forks [Ross's Fork] of the Port Neuf River, and encamped for the night. The grass was rather indifferent being principally wild barley. Today I found several bunches of roses, and they brought to mind recolections of the past which were exeedingly pleasant to reflect upon. Notwithstanding I was away in the midst of an uninhabited (except by wild beasts) wild mountain scenary, weary of a long and fatigueing journey, covered with dust, and immerced in care & anxiety, Still I found that my sensibilities were not so stu[lt]ified as to have lost all tast for the beautiful in nature. I geathered some dozen different kinds of Flowers and made a Boquet that would beare an honerble compairison to any made by the most fastidious exquisit of the States. They were wild Flowers, the liveing Poetry of those wild mountein seenaries. We had at noon a heavy Shower of rain, also one at sunset. Distance 20 ms. P S we have had frequent showers of rain latly. Monday July 2nd   Just as we were leaveing camp this morning it commenced raining, and continued till 10 A. M. We are today in the vally of several rivers. To wit—Port Neuf, Panack [Bannock], & Snake or Lewis's fork of the Columbia River. Fort Hall stands on the left bank of Lewis's fork or the Snake. It is surrounded by a vast plain, cut through and through with Rivers, creeks, branches & Sloughs running in every direction. And to all appearances one stream running paralell with anoth[er] in oposit directions, and but a short distance from each other. There is plenty of timber in this vally.

From where we nooned I rode back seven or 8 miles to trade with some Indians, the Panack's.[61] I effected a trade with one of them. I gave him a good Rifle a good blanket & some amunition for a very good young horse. Mean time the train moved on to the Fort, we crossed the Port Neuf river 4 or 5 miles before we reached the Fort. The train moved on by one mile & haulted for the night. I did not get back till after dark. The Indians are rather below in size the other Indians that we have seen on our rout, but the most perfectly formed men I ever saw and with all very keen and active, pleasant and rather agreeable in their manners. The women are small sprightly looking & handsom. They own a great number of horses in which they take great delight, and some of their horses are very fine. At the lodges were encamped some of the Soshonees & Senika's (I do not know whether the last name is spelt right or not).

Fort Hall is occupied by English traders. They pack their goods from Astoria and other trading points on the Pacific cost of Oregon. The buildings are composed of Sun dried brick. They have vast herds of Cattle & horses & Mules. They milk a great number of Cows and make a great deal of butter & Cheese. Their stock runs at large on the plaines which is covered with fine Grass, and every evening & morning you'll see several boys on horseback driveing up the stock. There are several families liveing here—some French, some English, and some Americans. It was quite a pleasant sight to see White women & children.[62] Distance 20 ms.

IV

SAND, SALT, FIRE & BRIMSTONE
Fort Hall to the Carson River

TUESDAY JULY 3RD   This morning was spent in tr[a]ding off wagons for pack horses. 3 of Our messes concluded to pack from this point. They became frightened at the alarming tails that were told them of the roads from Fort Hall to California. Dr. Roach & Co. of 9 men from N York sold their 2 good wagons & harness for one horse. Mullins's mess of Pendleton Co. Ky. Sold one wagon and all their spair provisions for one unbroke horse. A. W. Harrison sold his wagon & 2 sets of hearness for $6.00. The traders knew that the men were bound to sell at those prices or leave their wagons. And therefore they would give them no more.

At this place we joined messes with Harrison. That is A. W. Harrison & Saml Dunlop joined with Pritchard & Abbott. The Other 2 of their mess packed from this point. All the loading was put into Pritchard's wagon & 6 good mules hitched on. We were now fited Out with 4 men & 6 good mules to one wagon & an extra horse to ride, with provisions enough to take us through with safety. Those who packed from Smith's trading Post on Bear River were also here, and wateing for the others to get ready and all go on togeather. We left all hands at the Fort as busy as nailors fixing up pack saddles blankets &c &c. And at 3 P M we resumed the line of march with our train reduced more than one half. We had however enough left. There is no advantage in a large train. It is true that I felt rather unwilling to separate in this remote wilderness from Good hearted clever men with whom I had been so intimately connected for such a

107

length of time and surrounded by the trying circumstances through which we had passed in a journey of nealy 15 hundred miles, across dessert mountain & plain. At the same time I felt relieved from a heavy task, the charge of so many men & animals. In four miles we struck & crossed Port Neuf River. And passed on 3 miles farther to Panack River and encamped for the night. We here have to block up our wagons to keep them (beds) above water. Our train now consisted of Dr. Thomas's team & 3 men, Jacob Hoovers & 4 men, Sidney Smith's & 4 men, J A. Pritchard's & 4 men—A very respectible train.[63] Distance 7 ms.

WEDNESDAY JULY 4TH   By 6 A M this morning we were all safely landed on the oposite bank of Panack River, which is about one hundred and twenty yards wide, with gravely bottom. The bluffs of this river are high and steep; we had very heard puling to gain the top of them. We did it however without much difficulty. On the bluffs is a vast level plain, covered with wild sage bushes so thick that it is difficult to pass through them on foot. There is no grass on this plain. Our Fourth of July was spent in travelling in the dust and fighting off Musketoes. Their attacks were more fearce and determined, and more numerous, along this river, than any of the kind that I ever witnessed. I wrote a letter to my Wife today while nooning and forwarded it to California ba [by] a packer, who I thought would beat me in some 15 days. This forenoon we crossed a small stream not over 20 feet wide, but the channel was so deep & mirey that it was with the greatest difficulty that we could cross. The bank was so steep & the pitch into the water so abrupt that the men would have to hold on to the hind part of the wagon to keep the bed from pitching over the fore wheels. The water and mud was so deep that the mules would freequently go out of sight. I saw of the 6 mules in Dr. Thomas's wagon 4 of them entirely out of sight at once. We had encountered similar things for 1500 miles but we never found it quite so deep. Nothing of moment occured today.

We encamped this evening on Lewis's fork, and One mile

above the great American falls. The Musketoes were so bad this evening that they nearly ran Our mules crazy. They would break & run & lay down & roll, jirk up picket pines or break Lorrietts. We cut sage brush & grees wood & built large fires all round the camp—raised such a smok that it would suffocate the men & it did no good. And they would pursue & perforate your skin with their probossuses over the hotest fire that you could endure.[64] The grass was very fine & after the frost c[h]illed the Musketoes so that they could not disturb our mules they fared well. Distance 24 ms.

THURSDAY JULY 5TH In one mile from our encampment we passed the great American falls. The fall must be 40 or 50 feet in about 70 or 80 yards. There is not more than from 6 to 10 feet perpendicular fall at any place. The roaring of the waters can be heard for many miles. They rush with great velosity over and through the vast lumps that lay in massive piles in the channel. There is a Sollid mass of Black volcanick rock forming a complete [a]butment on either side of the river. This Stone is a composition of Volcanic Stone, sinder, & Smelted Oar of some sort. A thick heavy Spray is constantly emitted by the rushing of the waters; to tak it all in all, it is a most wonderful & beautiful sight. The river here is about 250 yards wide.[65] We crossed several small streams with steep banks today.

Just as we were encamping this afternoon an Indian of doubtful appearance came into camp. We gave him something to eat, and when I placed the Guard round the camp I told him he must make his bed by the fire and not move till he saw the sun rise next morning else the Guard would shoot him. I took his gun from him and Kept it till morning in order the more sur[e]ly to keep him in camp. When morning came I found the Indian still by the fire. I gave him his gun & something to eat and he departed. Distance 22 ms.

FRIDAY JULY 6TH Within one half mile of our encampment this morning we bid a final adieu to Lewis's fork of the Columbia

River and Struck across the hills for some distance, and descended into the bottom of Raft River. It is a small stream with a smooth strong current and gravely bed. We nooned on this stream some 5 or 6 miles above where we first struck it. It is at the crossing of this stream that the Oregon & California roads seperate.[66] Our course was still up raft river, and we crossed it the last time at 4 P M. We continued some 4 ms & found a splendid spring that burst out from the base of the Mts, where we found fine grass skirting the margin of the spring branch which sunk in about 400 yards. The Grass was to my wast and of an exelant quality. It was one mile to the right of the road and had not been discovered by any previous Emegrants. This was truly an Oasis in the dessert. Distance 25 ms.

SATURDAY JULY 7   The road was filled with round black stone for 4 or 5 ms, which made it bad travelling. Our course was towards the base of the mountains. In 4 ms we struck the north branch of Raft river up which we continued till noon, crossing it and its tributarys several times. We nooned 2 miles up the slope of the ridge that divides the waters that flow into Raft river and Cash Vally.[67] While nooning today the boys or some of them caught up with us. Cash Vally is most beautifully surrounded by high mountains the taller peaks of which are covered with perpetual snows. There are 3 creeks putting into this vally from the mountains, One from the South West, One from the West and one from the N. West, with irregular spurrs of mountains running down for some distance between each. The waters of all met near the center of the vally and found its outlet on the South Eastern side of the vally. We encamped tonight on the center stream where we found plenty of good grass wood and water. Here some more of Our boys came up & encamped with us. About sunset I found my way to the top of one of the nearest peaks, from the top of which I had a most spacious view of the surrounding country. The south side of this peak was covered with seeder & grass, and the top with shivered stone & the North with snow—and the whole with Musketoes. Distance 28 ms.

SUNDAY JULY 8TH   In 2 miles from our camp this morning we approached the mountain pass that leads out from Cash vally. This gorge in the mountains is dangerous to pass on account of the piles of large round stone that lay in the road, Over which we are compelled to pass. We had to use extream caution to prevent brakeing down our wagons. We found one wagon mashed down in the pass. This branch leads out into a small vally entirely surrounded by mts, with a narrow outlet about 30 feet wide with verticle walls from 3 to 500 feet high. The road strikes another vally. And at this point the Salt Lake and fort Hall roads come togeather again. We here overtook a wagon that came by Salt Lake. We had gained from 8 to 10 days on them according to their statement. They stated that provisions were scearce at Salt Lake, but that grass was good all the way across. They farther stated that not more than 30 wagons had passed on that road ahead of them. And that none had passed them since they left the Old Oregon road [Sublette Cutoff] 19 miles this side of the South Pass.[68] Our corse since noon has been over broken ridges & steep precipices. We had to ease our wagons down some of these hills by hand. At 7 P M we reached the vally of Goose Creek. We found severel trains & some packers encamped here. We passed them some ½ mile and encamped for the night. It is on this creek, that a Morman was said to have found Gold last year. Distance 24 ms.[69]

MONDAY JULY 9TH   Our corse his [has] been up Goose Creek or as it is called by some [*i.e.*, by Ware's *Guide*] Rattle Snake River. It is about 30 feet wide with a tolerable abundance of water. The road runs up this creek 22 miles. At 5 P. M. we reached the point from which the road leaves the headwater of the aforesaid creek and struck across the hills to what is called hot Spring Vally, a distance of 15 miles. We were compelled to make the whole distance this evening on account of finding no water, a thing unusual in this country. We reached the first watering place at 10 P. M. But to our surprise & mortification we found but little or no grass. We here found several trains encamped. We turned our mules loose a[nd] posted out a guard far enough to keep them from straying. Distance 37 ms.[70]

TUESDAY JULY 10TH   We rested & grazed our mules this morning till 9 A M on some patches of short grass that we found down the creek, when we continued our course down the branch some 9 ms—where the road turned to the right across some low sand hills for a short distance, when we entered the main vally. Up which we continued till 2 P. M. hunting grass and water—the finding of which seemed to be dubious. At length we found a patch of tolerable grass and a pool of miserably stagnant water which we were compeled to use for drinking and cooking. We rested 2 hours and traveled 6 miles farther up the vally where we found good grass and water, and encamped for the night. The surface of the ground was covered with an incrustation of Alkline [alkali] and the waters strongly impregnated with the same. We found however a spring of good water. Distance 24 ms.

WEDNESDAY JULY 11TH   In the vally which was a broad marsh, with deep pools of water standing about in places and covered with high swamp grass, we found plenty of Ducks. I shot 4, of which we served up a fine dinner. In about 6 ms we came to the hot springs. These Springs boile up in bold streams covering an area of several acres of marshy earth. The water that rises here formes quite a bold runing branch for several miles, which sink in the flats & rises along in places for some 25 or 30 miles. These waters are all boiling hot, and the water runs warm for a mile or so. I put my hand in several places, and it would have taken the skin off in less than no time. The water was strongly impregnated with the efflorescence of Alkali and mixed a little with sulpher.

At the head of this vally we nooned. We found a good Spring & good grass. While nooning, the New York boys caught up with us. This morning was cold, and the day hot dry and dusty. Six of Bryants men have been with us since yesterday morning. One of them is very sick. Dr. Thomas has agreed to take the sick man in his wagon, and use his mules. His friends have gone back to bring him up—who is some 4 or 5 ms behind.[71] We commenced the ascent of the ridge that divides the waters that flow into the Pacific from those that flow into the great bason of the Rocky Mountains. This is what might properly be called the Western Rim of the Great Bason.[72] The road leads out through a Cannon and by 4 P M we had gained the summit. We then commenced desending the slop of the ridge & by 8 we struck a small branch one of the tributaries of Mary's River, and encamped for the night. The roads have been very good today. The slopes of the ridges are of gentle acclivity, and generally smooth, grass & water good. Wild sage for fuel. Distance 27 ms.

THURSDAY JULY 12TH   We had a small stampeed last night among some packers, who were encamped just below us. It was supposed to be an Indian who had crept into camp for the purpose of stealing mules or horses. The men being up and among the mules they were stoped without any's escapeing. This morning as a pack train was leaveing camp they had a loos mule, which droped back a short distance behind—and it was instantly siezed by a party of Indians who were secreted in the Sage brush near the camp and hurryed off. They were discovered however by the men, 4 or 5 of whome instantly pursued them & in a short distance recovered the mule, but the Indians made their escape. We had a very White frost & Ice on my water bucket to the thickness of the 8th of an inch. The stream upon which we encamped last night looses its self in the sand after running some 4 or 5 ms and afterwards rises in the shape of first rate springs [Wells, Nevada]. At 6 P M we reached a point where the creek assumes a bold appearance; the water was about 18 inches deep. The evening being warm & pleasant, the boys all took a refreshing bathe. The water was clear pleasant & refreshing, grass good. Distance 23 ms.

FRIDAY JULY 13TH   In five miles after leaveing camp this

morning, we struck & crossed the main North fork of Marys River.[73] We found the ground on the oposite side to be very marshy & a train had nearly all their wagons & mules mired down. After prospecting a few minutes I found a way out that was tolerably good, and we passed out without any trouble. At noon we tried our luck at fishing but without success. The day has been oppressively warm, and whilest we were suffocating with dust and heat in the vally the Mountains on either side were covered with Snow.

As I was traveling leasurely along today I found a letter in the road written by a young lady who was on a visit to her Aunts in the State of New York To her Father at Indipendance Mo— Requesting the Old Gentleman to send her money to purchase a Black Silk dress. She made a great many excuses & many fine speeches. "The last one said she that you gave me I want to keep for parties, and if I ware it out on the street it will be so soiled, that it wont do for that purpose"—"I have not been idle, since I've been here, I have been makeing Pillow Cases for Aunt— besides this is not all the work that I have done" Etc, Etc, Etc —"Pa you write very good Poetry and no one here knows it. And Aunt wants me to put a piece in her Album & she does not want any but origional pieces—and I want you to write me a piece of Poetry & send it to me, and I will put it in her Album and no one will ever know but what it is mine." And a good deal more in like manner. I tore off both names & let the boys read it, and there was some tall laughing done over it.

We encamped this evening on the river after crossing a small stream puting in from the West—also a ridge to avoid a cannon through which the river passes.[74] Distance 25 ms.

SATURDAY JULY 14TH   We crossed a ridge this morning soone after starting, and in 3 miles crossed another. We have to cross hills along here to avoid bends in the river & also cannons. Our rout today has been down Marys river. We were compelled to travel till one P M before we could find a nooning spot. We reached a narrow place in the river with low stone bluffs, where we found tolerable grass. The day was oppressively warm and our mules very much jaded before we had a chance to rest & graze them. Mr Stuart the Gentleman that Dr Thomas took in his wagon is better. He is from Louisville Ky. The soil here is more porus & light than any that I ever before saw. It is not unfrequently the case that Our mules go Outside of the road sink to their knees in dry dirt—and almost swamp in dry earth. The one that I was rideing this forenoon came so near swamping that he fell to his brest and pitched me over his head with my rifle in my hand while strugling to get out. After resting some 2 hours we hitched up and travelled some 8 or 10 miles and encamped for the night. Distance 28 ms.

SUNDAY JULY 15TH   In 5 miles from our encampment this morning we struck the mountains and commenced its ascent. The road crosses the hills here in consequence of the river's running so near the point of the bluff that we cannot pass round the river road at this (present) stage of water [Moleen Canyon]. After passing through winding ways runing to all points of the Cumpas, we gained the summit at 10 A M. We commenced the descent immediately upon arriveing at the top of the hill, and by noon we had completed the trip across the mountains, a distance of 10 ms.[75]

Whilst nooning at the foot of the hill on a small branch E Bryant's pack train came up with us. They left the State line of Mo. 4 days after we did & this is the first sight that we have had of them. Capt Wm. Brown and Brother Samuel of Lexington Ky took dinner with us today. Several trains that had been pushing hard have came up with us and our boys began to feel alarmed. They thought we were travelling to slow and that all the trains would pass us and that there would be no grass left &c. I had some difficulty in disabuseing their minds of the falls impressions that had been made upon them by the appearances of things just at that particular time. By convinceing them of the fact that, while these men had already broken down their teams by excessively heard driveing in order to get ahead, that we had taken our time for it and taken good care of our teams & still done good travelling (for these are the first teams that have overtaken us—and they have only gained one day on us in 300 miles) and they are in as good plite to all appearances as when we left the States—And that this would be the last time in all probability that we would ever see any of those teams again. One of the messes (Smith's of Ohio) could not be convinced of these facts and they drove off and left us. We travelled to the river & 3 ms down and on a pretty little creek [Maggie Creek] we encamped for the night. A cloud came up this evening and a few drops of rain fell. Bryant's pack train passed on 10 miles farther and encamped at a spring half way over the hill. Distance 22 ms.

Monday July 16th   We hearded our mules last night on the oposite side of the creek in a bend where we found good grass, and they were ready to start this morning at a very early hour. We took the mountains shortly after leaveing camp, and by gradual approaches we gained the summit by 10 A M—a distance of 10 ms. Just over the turn of the hill we came to a splendid spring of pure cold water, where we slaked our thirst with the refreshing draughts that [were] drawn from it—besides it afforded an abundance for mules. Two miles below we came up to Bryant's train again. We descended this hill by and along a ravine. The hill was extreamly stony on this side, and no way to avoid them. We reached the river [at Gravelly Ford] by 2 P M—swam our mules across to grass. We found a luxury here such as we had not befor seen, in the shape of wild Currens. There was the Black Yellow & Red. The flavor of them was very fine indeed. We had as a rarity today, a fine pleasant shower of rain. After nooneing we crossed anoth[er] hill, and 8 miles struck the river & encamped for the night. We here came up with the boys who left us yesterday. Bryant camped in the bottom just above us. Grass short tonight. Distance 30 ms.[76]

TUESDAY JULY 17TH   We crossed a [hill?] and in 5 miles struck the river again. We continued through dust & Sunshine till noon both of which we found very oppressive. Here we found good grass & turned our mules loose on the plaines & let them run at large & rested ourselves & animal 3 hours. Whilst nooning Bryant passed us again. The road was good today. We are now leaveing the teams that are behind us, both Mules & Oxens, as none have made their appearance today. At 5 P M we encamped just below Bryant's train. We found a bend in the river that came so near forming a complet circle, that a small slough that ran across finished it. In that we found fine grass. It had but one narrow place of 6 feet that was at all accessible. We put our mules in there (the natural correl) and composed our selves tonight without a guard. The boys sunk a well—and in 3 feet found good water. We found some large willows tonight which answered our purposes for cooking. There is no timber the whole length so far as we have come but willow brush & occasionally cotten wood brush—in many places neither. The wild Sage is the principal dependance for fuel. Distance 25 ms.

WEDNESDAY JULY 18TH   We found our mules all safe in the lodgement where we left them through the night. The sun rose this morning from behind the mountains, bright, briliant, and beautifully clear, and scattered her blushing red along the verge of the far East and neighbouring mountains just as we were takeing Breakfast. And in a short time thereafter, as was usual with us, we were enjoying the benefits of the clouds of dust that were continually riseing by the motion of our teams on the road.

At about 10 O'clock last night I heard the report of a gun & some one, cry a stampeed. I raised myself up and listened to here the footsteps of mules & horses, but heard none—but still heard a bustle among some men who were encamped just below us. I examined and found that Our mules were all safe and quiet. I laid myself down to rest and heard nothing more of it. But upon enquiry this morning I found that the guard of a small pack train, had shot one of their Own company, who had thought-lessly gone out during the night to repicket his mules. The Guard hailed him when in the act of moveing his mule to a fresh place of grass & he answered not. He was hailed by the Guard several times but still made no answer. The Guard supposing it to be either and Indian or some one stealing a mules fired upon him & the ball took effect and passed through his breast, giveing him a mortal wound. The fact was the Old Gentleman was consider-ably deaf and did not here the guard when he was hailed. He was from Baltimore and by the name of Riddell, about 50 years of age. He was still alive this morning but no hope of his recovery. He appeared perfectly composed, whilst the certainty of death was before him. He had shipped round a saw mill & a good many other things to operate with when he arrived in California. He had left as I learned from his company a large family behind.[77]

Shortly after Bryant's train left camp this morning a Mr Bry-son of Louisville Ky, one of Bryant's company, was taken sud-ently sick. He was removed from his mule to an Ox wagon that was near at hand. And in 5 minutes thereafter was a dead man. He had not complained any till just at the time. He died with the disease of the heart. They were in sight & close behind us when it took place.[78] It is only in the sudent bends of the river, and places that have been hitherto unapproachible by those who have gone before us on account of sloughs that we find good grass. The water in Mary's river is getting to be very muddy and un-pleasant. We are encamped tonight with an Ox train of 3 wagons that has been clost along with us ever since we left Thomas's fork of Bear river, a distance of 550 miles. Seeman is the Capt. Distance 25 ms.

THURSDAY JULY 19TH   The bottoms of Mary's river has been today wide sterile & desolate except just along the margin of the stream, where in places we find spots of good grass. The road has been generally good today. The earth pretty generally this forenoon has been covered with a saline incrustation. The water in the river has become so warm muddy & disagreable that we can scearcely use it. We have resorted to an artifice that has thus far proven to be beneficial & well as comfortable. And that is to sink a well every noon & evening. We usually dig from 3 to 4 feet, and find water after setting that is cool and pleasant tasted. We find no game along this river exept an occasional sage hen or Hare—& we can rarely get a shot at them. Distance 25 ms.[79]

FRIDAY JULY 20TH   An attempt was made last night about 12 O'clock to stampeed Our mules & run them off. We were in the habit of picketing some 4 or 5 of Our leading mules & hearding the Others round them. At the time Stated Some one came dashing through Our camp on horseback at full speed. As he passed through the loose mules all took fright and sprang off after him. The Guard hapened to be in the diretion that the mules started and was very prompt & energetick in arresting their flight. I with 3 or 4 others sprang to Our feet instanter and assisted [in] quieting them. The individual passed through with such Spead that the Guard was unable to determin whether it was a White man or an Indian. It was very evident to me that it was an attempt made to frighten off and steal our mules. But their designs were fortunately thwarted by the promptness and vigilance of our Guard. I learned next day that a train just above us had a number of their horses and mules stollen that same night. The men took their trail next morning an puresued them some distance & were only fortunate enough to recover a part of their stolen property. It is a common occurrence along here to here of parties being robed of their animals.

Shortly after leaveing camp this morning we crossed a low sand hill, and in 5 ms struck the river again. Here a slough made out from the river & ran paralell with it for 15 ms. The grass all lay across the Slough except where the ground was so marshy that our stock could not feed on it.[80] The bottom was covered with Alkali and the water was so strongly impregnated with it that it was past being used either by man or beast. We thought of trying

to obviate its pernicious effects by sinking a well—which it did
to some extent. We nooned with Bryant's train today. A 6 P M
we haulted for the night on a broad flat. The Slough was still
between us and the river. The whole face of the country was
covered with a saline or Alkaline incrustation. Distance 24 ms.

SATURDAY JULY 21ST   The road today lay across sand hills,
strikeing the river occasionly. The wheels of the wagons will sink
from 6 to 10 inches in the sand, which makes it very heavy
drawing. I had the good fortune to kill a mountain Rabbit both
yesterday at noon & this forenoon. They furnished us a feast
worth[y] of note. To men completely tired out on Hard crackers,
Old Bacon & coffee nothing could be finer. Grass for Our mules
is getting to be quite an object. We find none except in obscure
places that are out of the way, which have been overlooked by
others. We had some trouble to find a spot of grass this evening
—we succeeded at last in finding a place in a bend of the river
amongst the willows where our mules faired tolerably well.
Distance 22 ms.

SUNDAY JULY 22ND   In 4 ms this morning we came to a hill
across which the road passes and does not strike the river again
for 16 miles. Here we found grass scearce. On the oposte side of
the river it was tolerable good so we swam our mules across &
let them graze till 6 P. M. when we started to make a night
travel—came 6 ms and haulted for the night.[81] The grass here
was very indifferent. The Ox teams are all failing on account of
the scearcity of grass & hot weather. Some of them travel of a
night and lay by in the day. But this is a bad plan as stock will
feed better of a night than they will in the day time of hot
weather. Cattle has never been known to make such time as they
have on this expedition. They have travelled from 20 to 30 ms
pr day for a distance of 1800 miles. Distance 23 ms.

MONDAY JULY 23RD   The grass was very indifferent last night
and this morning. In 4 miles we struck the bluffs again, and
travelled across them about 10 ms and haulted for the day. We

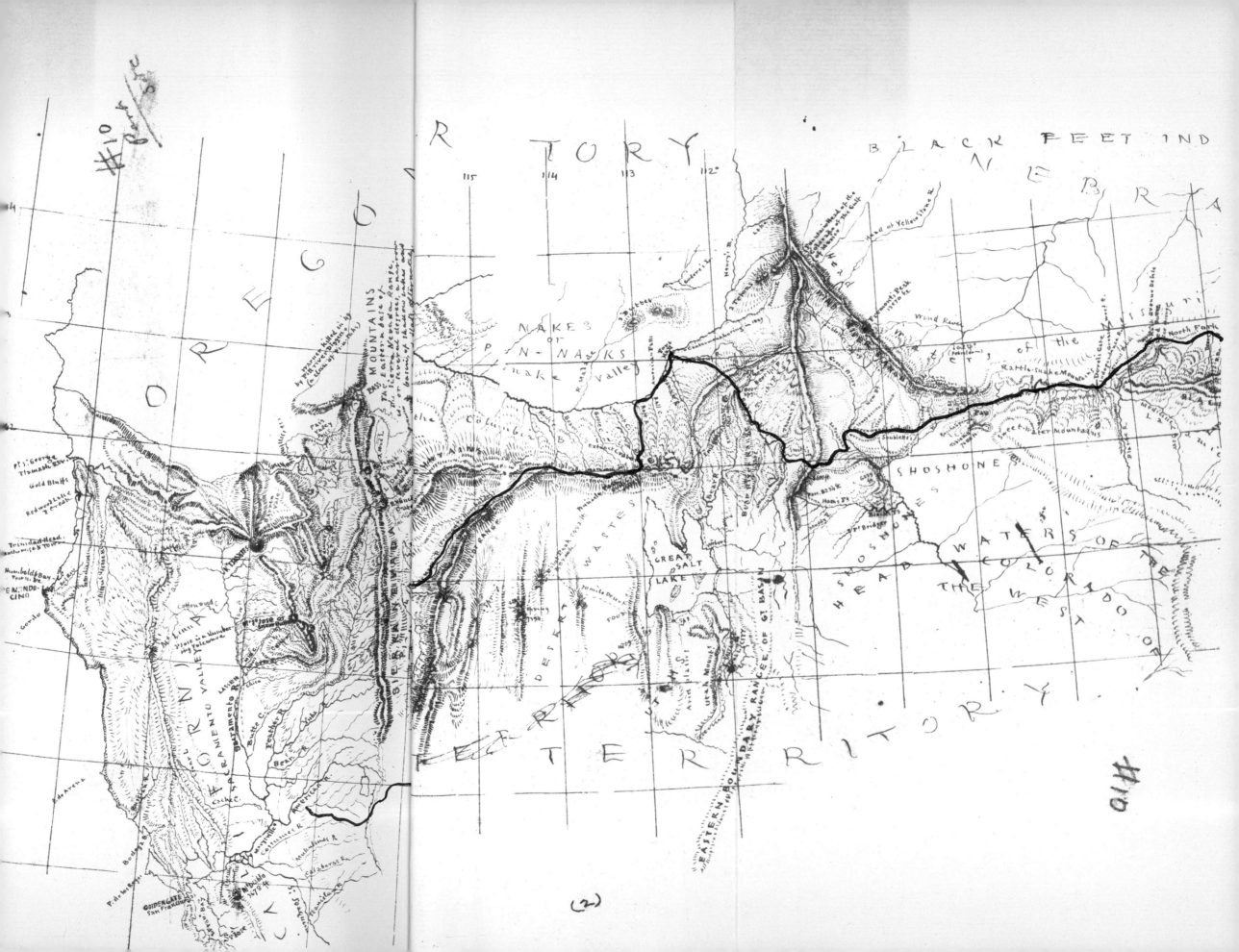

had to turn our mules 1 ½ miles to grass, where we found a small patch in an Obscure bend in the river. We were apprehensive from the appearance of things that we were approaching the sink of Mary's river. And we were therefore desireous to give our mules as much time and rest as possible, haveing as we knew well to cross the great salt dessert immediately after leaveing the Sink. Besides that consideration the weather has been *hot,* the roads heavy, and the grass indifferent—all of which had a direct tendency to pul down and destroy the strength and action of our teams. Distance 14 ms.

Tuesday July 24th It has now become a matter of interest and duty to ourselves, to recruit our animals as much as possible. Our teams are in as good plite if not better than any that I see on the road. It has been and should have been our object from the start to preseve the strength of Our teams as much as the nature of the case would allow. It is an alarming and fearful thing to see as we do every day teams broken down by the mismanagment of their owners in this remote wilderness. The teams that alarmed our boys so much a few days since has not been seen since—and we learn from packers as they come up that they are falling back every day. Our boys are now becoming convinced that we have been and are still, travelling fast enough. About 2 miles from the road today we found good grass, to which we sent Our mules under a suitable guard who remained with them all night. We hearded them in a short bend of the river as it formes a line of protection generally on 3 sides of us. Distance 15 ms.

Wednesday July 25 The Guard brought the mules to camp very early this morning. And in 3 miles after leaveing camp we struck the river.[82] We here watered our mules & filled our Casks with water. At 12 M we reached the slough and in the bottom of it we found a fine cool Spring. The water tasted a little of sulpher. It is 20 miles from here to the point at which we strike the Sink of Mary's River. We nooned before starting across to the Sink. We found grass to the left of the road in a dry ravine. We sunk a well here in the sand and in 5 feet found water that was tolerable good and enough for our selves and Mules.

We took up the line of march at 2 P M and by dark we reached the Sink. Here we found several well[s] that had been sunk. The water in them was barley tolerable; it was so strongly impregnated with Saline & Alkali that we could bearly use it. The grass was so indifferent that our mules would not have touched it except in case of starvation. The Sink is a vast plain Over which the water spreads & gradually sink or looses its self in the sand. It is a vast Quagmire or Marsh of Stagnant Saline and Alkali water mixed, and emits a most offensive and nauseateing effluvia. The Sink proper is about 4 or 5 miles wide & from 12 to 15 in length. It is thickly covered with Bul Rushes. There is nothing of the appearance of Lake about it, as you can only see the water about in spots. It therefore has more the appearance of Ponds than of a Lake. Takeing it all in all, it is one of the most disagreeable and loathsome looking places on the face of the earth.

When we reached here tonight weary thirsty and hungary we could not so much as find a bunch of wild Sage, which before had never failed, to cook a bite of supper. After several unsuccessful attempts the boys all retired to their humble couches to take rest without one bite of any thing to eat. I however felt unwilling to yield the point without first exhausting every means. So Dr Thomas & myself penetrated as fare as we could with safety into the marsh and geathered an armfull each of dead or dry Bulrushes. We kindled a fire of these and held a small tin tea kettle over the fire till it boiled, one feeding the fire all the time with our newly converted fuel, and the other holding the teakettle over the blaze. So far we had done well, we then in like manner broiled a Slice of Bacon—and in a few minutes we had a *good* cup of tea, a Slice of Bacon & a few pieces of heard crackers, which made us a fine supper. This done we laid ourselves down to rest. Distance 24 ms.

THURSDAY JULY 26TH   All hands were called this morning

very early, and a surch was made for grass and about one mile below we found some that was better considerably than that we were upon. We caught up and drove down to it with the view of resting & grazeing Our mules till 3 P M, at which time we intended to commence the much dreaded journey across the 45 mile dessert of Salt, fire, and I had like to have said Brimstone. The Vertical rays of a *full* sun was so oppressive that we were compeled to place our wagons clost togeather spread an orning which we made of our Tents from one wagon to another. The forenoon was spent in telling yarnes, cracking joakes, and bakeing bread &c &c to last us across the dessert. Thus the time was whiled away wateing for the auspicious hour to arrive when we should be relieved from the excrutiateing tortuers of this loathsome & infurnal place.

Our vessels all haveing been filled with water & all necessary preparation made at the appointed hour we took up the line of march. And travelld about ten miles where we struck a large slough in which a number of wells had been sunk—which afforded us pretty fair sulpher water.[83] We here threw away the water that we had put into our Casks, and refilled them. We here ascertained that we had commenced the dessert ten miles to soon. We should have, in the first place come here and spent the day and made our start from this point, which would have saved us ten miles in the Streatch. We however took supper here, and I fed my mules with corn that I had brough with me from the States for this express purpose. Besides filling our vessels with water I filled a Mathurin [?] Duck cloths sack with water that held about 2½ bushels.

At 8 O'clock P M we resumed the line of march & here we struck the dessert, and travelled till daylight. The roads during the night were very good. In 12 ms we struck salt creek a most disagreeable place. We crossed this just before the Moon went down. The water of this place is said to kill stock instantly.[84] Just as day broke we haulted & watered our mules, let them rest

30 minutes & then fed them the ballance of our corn—and ate a bite of breakfast ourselves. It was rather pleasant travelling during the night. Distance 35 ms.

FRIDAY JULY 27TH   After watering & feeding the mules I told the young men who was prepairing breakfast, to let me sleep just 30 minutes as I had driven all night. The boys just droped down on the ground eny where & fell asleep. When the 30 minutes was out (breakfast being ready) I was called. I rose & called the camp & gave ordes to prepair to start in 20 minutes. When the time expired, they had breakfasted and were ready to start. I ate only a cup of tea (that I had prepaired for me) with some crackers crumbled in it. I made a light breakfast in order that I would not be thirsty through the day. And I am of the Opinion that a man can perform one hard march better on an emty stomach than he can on a full one. Just as Aurora's beams began to dawn, & scatter her blushing red along the verge of the fare East, and chase away the gloom of a dismal night and light up the dreary path of weary travellers which lay streached across a place of desolation. We were ready to embrace what to us, seemed to be, an offering of mercy from on high—the rays of the Sun, which were shed upon us by the God of day, clear, bright, and beautifully briliant.

As we began to approach within 15, 12, 10, 8, 6, and so along miles of the river we found scores of wagons that had been left under the protection of a guard and the teams taken on through to grass for the purpose of recruiting them and then returning for their wagons. It took some of them 3 & 4 days to get through in this way. They had to encounter a black sand that admitted the wheels of the wagons from 6 to 10 inches for the distance of 15 miles before reaching the river. A great number of mules horses & cattle had been left on the dessert unable to get t[h]rough. And many had to abandon their wagons all togeather in order to get through.[85]

About 8 A M I came to a place that seemed, at one time to

have been covered with an incrustation of saline—crystalized or rather a kind [of] chrysolite. I found peaces from the smallest particles up to 12 and 15 inches in diameter & from one half to one and a quarter inches thick. To strike them togeather they would fly like glass. I found my sack full of water this morning which furnished a full supply for Our mules and we had left all that we had in our other vessels. I gave my mules a few swallows occasionally through the day, which kept them revived. And when ever I came across a pore fellow who was out I gave him water. The day was oppressively hot, and the burning sands reflected the rays of the sun to such a degree that it appeared like suffocation at once. The Sight of the timber that skirted the river seemed to inspire the men with new life. They at once left the wagons & lead off to water, and the best Pedestrian reached there first. The teams arrived at the river about 11 O'clock A M. One of our teams however found that they could not get clear through without injureing their mules & they left their wagon about 6 miles back & brought their mules in. Our mules were so much exhausted that they would not drink when they got to water. On the oposte side of *Carson River* (the one we were then upon) we found splendid grass and turned our mules across to it. We placed a guard with our mules & commenced getting dinner after which we all done some tall sleeping. Distance 20 ms.[86]

SATURDAY JULY 28TH   When a guard was called for last night to cross the river with the mules, the boys all considered themselves unfit for duty. I volunteered my services & Dr. Thomas J N Hoover & W W Abbott followed the example. We stood 2 on duty at a time and half of the night each. But for the little nap that we got in the evening we never could have stood it. We were just 15 hours crossing from the Slough 5 miles below the Sink to Carson River. Our time across has not been beaten by any train that have pre[c]eded us—nor in all probability will it be. There has been but 3 wagons so far as we have been able to ascertain that have (previous to ours) [been] enabled to make the trip clear across without leaveing their wagons & bring their teams through, resting & returning for their wagons. Every few minutes through the day you can see men come stagering in in search of water, and those of them who are able return with their canteens filled to meet their famishing friends.

I witnessed a most singular incident this afternoon. It was a Lady who came in 12 or 15 miles on horseback in advance of her party to procure water for her husband who was unwell himself, besides he had no one to leave in charge of his team. She came in company with several Gentlemen who were also going to return. She was a stout robust looking woman about 22 years of age. Her Husband was a Dr his name I did not learn. She borrowed several canteens of men at the river & when I saw her last she had 4 filled with water & swong across her sholders. My train was just in the act of moveing up the river to give place to those who were constantly arriveing.[87]

This forenoon was spent by our boys in washing & drying cloths batheing in the river Etc Etc. We moved 4 miles up the river where we found a first rate camping spot with fine splendid grass from 10 to 24 inches high. We stoped our wagons under some large Cotton wood trees that stood immediately on the bank of the river which afforded us a cool pleasant Shade. This of its self was a luxury that we have not enjoyed since we passed Fort Hall—And it is one that is indeed, truly gereatful to Our feelings. Carsan River is about one hundred and twenty feet wide with a strong bold current, and can only be forded in places along here. It takes its rise in the Siera Nevada and emties into a Lake of the same name. Its general course is from West to East. This River and Lake took their name from the famous Kit Carson the Old Mountaneerer. Distance 4 miles.

DESERTS, CATARACTS & CHASMS
Carson River to the Diggings

SUNDAY JULY 29TH   We remained in camp today for the purpose of resting & fixing up a little. We concluded however as the days were very warm to start at 6 P M. and make a night march across a streatch of 20 miles, where we strike the river again. Soon after starting this evening in going over a suddent pitch I broke one of the fore hounds of my wagon. I lashed it with ropes and it lasted me across to the river. Our rout lies now up this river to its head. We reached the river again at 2 A. M. and tied our mules to the wagons & gave them some grass that we had brought from our last encampment [for] the purpose. Distance 20 miles.

MONDAY JULY 30TH   We remained in camp today to make up for night travelling. I have all ways been opposed to that mode of doing business except in cases of necessity, and Our boys are getting pretty well tired of it. By and with the assistance of my Old Friend & fellow traveller Jacob Hoover of Ind. I made and put into my wagon a hound as good if not better than the Origional one. It was made of a good tough white Oak cupling pole that I had picked up a few days previous. We turned our mules across the river to grass & placed a guard over them. We cannot leave them alone one minute along this river on account of the Indians (Diger) who are stealing all the horses mules & cattle that are left unguarded. We can here of stock's being stolen all around us every day. And we see the pore fellows trudgeing along on foot every day with their packs on their backs. We have plenty of wood on this river to bake bread boile Bacon & Beans & make soup, Which is truly a luxury in these remote regions. We enjoy frequent batheings in this river which conduces much to our healths. The day has been spent in loungeing & naping, and talking of our safe & speedy journey across the great Salt dessert. Indeed it is with us, a matter of general & universal congratulation to think that the greatest barier that interposed its self to our march to the land of our promise had been subdued and overcome with such ease.

Tuesday July 31st   We have today to make another 25 mile drive across a dessert before we reach the river which makes a tremendos bend just here. The road has been heavy all day. Nevertheless we made the distance by 2 P M without stoping, When we struck the river. On the oposite side we found good grass again. The reason why we have to cross the river is this, the grass has been eaten down by the trains that are ahead of us. We found at this place several wagons thrown away and the men fixing up pack saddles. Nothing of not[e] occured today. Distance 25 ms.[88]

Wednesday August 1st 1849   In 8 miles from where we started this morning we came to the point where the road leaves the river to cross a spur of mountains. We here nooned, and then commenced the ascent. After gaining the summit we continued across ridges and uneaven ground till we struck the river again a distance of 12 ms. Across these ridges we found the road to be very stony & sandy. The bottom where we struck the river this evening is broad and handsome & covered with a luxuriant groth of Grasses of the most nutritious qualities. This vally is walled in with high and lofty mountains whose summits are covered with eternal snows and evergreen pine. It is a strange contradiction that winter & summer should stand upon the same spot of earth, but it is nevertheless true. Distance 20 ms.

Thursday Aug 2nd   The road lay this morning across a handsome little vally [Eagle Valley] covered with a fine heavy carpet of exelant grasses, and through which a small stream passes rise-

ing in the western mountains.[89] We passed from this vally through a defile, that led out, into, another small, tho as before handsome vally [Jacks Valley], after crossing which we struck a sand plain and travelled upon it about 8 ms, when we came to the River again in what is called Pleasant [Carson] vally. This is a most Spacious vally and abundantly fertile. And covered with various kinds of the most nutritious Grasses, and amongst the rest we found larg *fields* as it ware, of a most luxuriant groth of Red Clover to which our mules did ample justice during the 3 hours we gave them at noon.

The road leads round on the west side of the Vally & River, near the base of the Mountains [Sierra Nevada]. There are quite a number of small streams & spring branches puting in from the base of the mountains all round this vally. The waters of which are fresh from the melting snows on the mountans side, and as clear as the limped stream that gushed from the flinty rock when smote upon by the wand of the Prophet; and as cold, as melted Ice. We nooned upon one of these little streams in company with a train from the State of Ohio who started across the country with fine large Ohio horses, nearly all of which had given out & out of 5 or 6 teams that they started with they only had enough fit for service to draw one wagon & a cart that they had made of one of their wagons. The men all on foot, and driveing before them 25 or 30 head of horses.[90] The men were compelled to force their wagon up the hills by manuel labour.

In six miles from w[h]ere we nooned we came to the hot Springs [Walleys Hot Springs]. The temprature of the water was nearly boiling hot. It bursted out of a ledge of stone so near the base of the mountains that ther was bearly room for Our teams to pass between.[91] I diped up some of the water and cooled and tasted it. I found that it was slightly impregnated with Sulpher, tho not unpleasant to the tast. The Mountains (the Siera Nevada) that wall in this Vally rear their snowy peaks to a very great elevation, So much so that the largest and tallest Pine &

Furr trees appear to be nothing more than stinted seeder. Nor were we undecived untill we climb to the tops of some of the tallest peaks to gratify a vain curiosity. This vally is considerably intesperced with Sloughs & marshes. This vally is from 50 to 60 miles in length, and an average wedth of 10 miles—Some places much wider. We encamped this evening with the Ohio horse train on one of these small streams. At this place one of our mess W. W. Abbott being Qite unwell the Dr gave him an Emetic, which produced a very happy effect. Distance 22 miles.

FRIDAY AUG 3RD   We commenced our march at an early hour in order to reach the mouth of the canon,[92] the outlet from this vally to the top of the Siera Nevada Mountains. We were happy to know that our friend Abbott was considerably better and had recovered enough to travel on horseback this morning. The road for severel miles before reaching the mouth of the Canon runs across high broken ground, considerably sandy. At 1 P M we reached the desired Spot—And I may add, the desireable spot. It was certainly one of the grandest and most sublimely picturesque Scenories that I ever beheld. We pitched our tents [in] a beautiful grove of tall & stately Pine with no underbrush to obscure the sight. But scattered promiscusly along the margin of the stream which (Carson River) came rushing through this Canon, from the mountains in perfect cataracts, lay massive piles of granite that [had] broken off the vertical Wall, which stood on either side reareing their leofty summits to and elevation that seemed to stager human calculation. Many of these Pine trees will measure 7 & 8 feet in diameter and 200 feet in length.

We found just below our selected sight for the camp a handsome litt[le] bottom of green fresh grass where we turned our mules. After all the business of the day (intending to remain here till morning) was over I took my fishing line and tried my luck amongst the stone and roaring waters. I caught two fine Mountain trout, and we had a kind of feast for supper. Several of the party tried it but met with no success. We have just before us now what the emegrants generally call the Elephant. We are resting our teams this afternoon in order to give him a fair tryal in the morning. Distance 20 ms.

SATURDAY AUG 4TH   All hands being ready this morning at an early hour, we commenced the trying ascent through the Canon. And in about One mile we began to meet and brave the difficulties. We have the River to cross 3 times, the first and second time it was bridged by falling two large trees across and then laying puncheons & poles on them, which made a tolerable safe bridge.[93] There being no chance to bridge the 3rd & last place where the road was forced across it, we were compelled to ford it. The water was about to the wast of a man and the bottom filled with large stone over which the Mules would frequently fall—without great care was taken to prevent it. The principal obstructions that interposed themselves to our march was the large piles of granit that had broken off the walls of the Mountains which stood on either side thousands of feet above us—and over hanging us as it ware—and rolled down into the gorge, forming piles from 1 to 300 feet high. These we were compelled to find our way through by circuitous routs and winding ways, Ascending and descending over steep cragy cliffs and precipices. We were compelled to force our wagons over, around, and through, many of these places by manuel labour the turnes being too short to be made with the team hitched on. But by a heard and loborious deys work, to our selves and animals we suceeded in getting through by 5 O'clock P. M. At the top of which, we found a handsome vally of grass [Hope Valley], Where we encamped for the night.

About half way through the Canon we met a family train returning from California to Salt lake. Part of them were Mormans & returning to their Peop[l]e at Morman City. The ballance were families who had emegrated to this county sevral years since—From the East around Cape Horn—and intended to spend the winter at Salt Lake, and go on to the States next

Spring. Amongst the rest there was a very intelligent young Lady with one or 2 others in advance of the train (On horsback) who gave us as much information with regard to the road & country as any person that it had been our good fortune to meet with.[94] After camping this evening dinner being over young Hoover & myself took a hunt up the river & killed severel Ducks & a Sage Hen. Distance 6 miles.

SUNDAY AUGUST 5TH   Our corse this morning was still up the river & branches, tho we were on the river but little the road running over the high broke hills or bluffs which lay between the different forks of the river. The road was rough, hilly & stony. At noone we had reached Reed [Red] Lake, One of the fountan heads of Carson River. This Lake is about one half mile long and about one forth wide And lies immediately at the base of the Mountain [Carson Range] that we have to ascend. This Mountain by the road is about one mile high and appearatly perpendicular. We have to go nea[r]ly (that is the general direction) strait up it winding first to the right & then to the left, gaining by gradual approaches. Large trees have been fell to the ground & a kind of road made above it by throwing brush & dirt on it, to gain the upper side of some large stone which formes a kind of road again untill another turn can be effected. We have to lift our wagons round frequently and make a square tact to the right or left. Many of the places have such perpendicular falls, that, if a mule were thrown off or wagon & team they would fall from 50 to 100 feet without touching anything. One of the party started the fore wheal of a new wagon that had been left without the hind wheels down this mountain and after runing several hundred yards it leaped from one large pile of stone to another, and when it struck upon the last its velocity was so great, that it bounded with such force that it touched nothing for several hundred yards and in its erial flight it cleared the tops of some of the tallest Pine trees that grow upon the mountains—and here it is not rare to see them 8 & 9 feet in diameter, and of the tallest character. This wheel continued to roll and bound untill it run so far that had we not known what it was, we could not have told. About 3 P. M. we commenced the ascent with 14 mules hitched to one wagon and all the men of the train pushing chocking & holding on, & by sunset we had suceeded in takeing 2 of our wagons to the top of the *hill* Mountain [Kit Carson Pass] where we found good water & in 2 miles good grass for our animals. Distance 5 miles.[95]

MONDAY AUGUST 6TH   This morning Our mules being brot into camp by the Guard who stayed with them last night, We commenced bringing up our other wagon & by 9 A. M. we had it with the others at what might properly be called the top of this ridge of the mountains. And pretty soone thereafter we resumed our march across rough stony hills & through an occasional marsh for a distance of 4 miles where we struck lake Vally. This is a handsome Vally with several beautiful little streams puting in from the mountains and running through it, emtying they waters into a beautiful Lake which is found at the lower part of the Vally a mile or mile & one half long & from ½ to ¾ wide. Here we found good grass & encamped for the day[96] at the foot of the next high ridge of Mountains that we have to ascend [culminating ridge of Sierra Nevada].

After haulting & whilst at dinner I opened a poll Book for our precinct and Dr Wm L Thomas & W. W. Woodworth of Pendleton & J A Pritchard of Boone Counties voted for Maj John P Gaines for Congress. And for Delegate to the Convention from Boone Co J A Pritchard voted for Ch Chambers, & for Gabrie J Gaines to the Lower branch of the Legislature of Ky. While at dinner L W Hastings of California rode up. I invited him light and take Dinner which he did. He was on his way to meet his Brother who was in one of the back trains. We told him that we passed his Brother 20 ms above the Sink of Mary's River, & that he told us that he would go the Truckey rout. He remained with us all night and returned next morning. He was very communicative & seemed not to tire in answering the many Questions that were put to him by the party. He gave us all satisfaction with regard to our mineing prospects & provisions &c &c.[97] Distance 4 miles.

TUESDAY AUG 7TH   It was very cold & chilling last night, and this morning the grass was perfectly white & stiffined with frost & ice of ¼ of an inch thick was found on our water Buckets. We commenced the ascent of this last high or large mountain at 5 A. M. & by noon we had all of our wagons up. This mountain is (or ridge of Mt) about 2 miles in length. About half way up we haulted and put all the team to one wagon & in that way we suceeded without difficulty. Near the top is a large snow bank, the melting of which makes the ground very swampy just below it. After we had gained the summit we were then in the region of perpetual snows. We were forced to drive our teams across one of these bank of snow that must have been 20 or 30 feet deep. We travelled one mile from the top of the Mt, where we nooned. We turned Our Mules down to the right of the road, and about 2 or 300 yards we found a flat with a small Lake about 200 yards in diameter; it was fed by the melting snows all round. The waters were so cold that we could not bathe in it, its waters were so clear & transparent that we could have seen a pocket knife in 10 or 15 feet water. Away on down the Mountain we could still see other Lakes, into which this enters & so on down. These Mountain Forests are covered with a very large & heavy groth of Pine & Furr timber & the decidedly the largest that I ever saw. At 3 P M we resumed our march, the road this evening has been rather rough & stony. At 7 we struck Rock vally & encamped for the night, the grass tolerable. Distance 10 miles.

WEDNESDAY AUG 8TH   We did not leave camp this morning until the sun rose from behind the Eastern mountains and shed her warm & gentle rays through mountain, forrest, and dell. We are now upon the topmost ridges of the Sierra Nevada Mountains. Language is inadequate to describe, the strikeing contrast between this grand and magnificent Alpine and Elysian Scenery. Nothing in nature I am sure can present Scenery more wild, more rugged more bold, more grand, more romantic, and picturesquely beautiful, than this mountain scenery. The tall craggy rocks that would discover themselves as walls on either side of the deep Canons & Gorges that would lead off, from the snowy peaks (in which we would frequently discover small Laks or basons, into which the waters teemed) Would present an interest to the admirer of nature which he would scearce get tired of dwelling upon. While upon the other Slope of the mountain: the umbrageous foliage of the tall and stately pines, furrs and cedars, deepening in verdue, and density as the forest approaches the more gentle and grassy sloaps, presenting a most liveing landscape untill they gradually recede from the view. The tops of thise mountains are Carpted with a heavy coat of fine bladed green Blue Grass. And along the small branches many kinds [of] wild flowers are to be found. These contri[b]uted in calling to mind assosiations which melted the sensibilities blunted as they were by long exposier heardships and privations, and forced upon the memory the endearments of home, & the pleasures of civilization.

At 11 A M we haulted a few moments at the cold springs, this water is as cold as melted Ice. At this spring last fall 3 Morman Pioneers in looking out this road were killed by the Indians. Their Graves were near by the spring [Tragedy Spring].[98] We came 2 or 3 miles farther to a spring which was found to the left of the road. At this spring we found Leeks or Unions, towards which the boys did ample justice. We had fine grass. We halted about 4 P M. at what is called the leek springs[99] & turned our mules some ¾ of a mile to the left of the road on a branch to grass. The roads have been tolerable good this afternoon. Distance 20 miles.

THURSDAY AUG 9TH   This morning Dr Thomas killed a Black tail Deer which furnished our little party with a tolerable supply of venison. We made an early start this morning in order to make a 25 miles march, the nearest place that we could find grass. The road today has been remarcably rough & hilly. It runs on the high ridges of the mountains with deep chasms on either side. We haulted the train at one of these places, and pried up some large round stone the size of a Flour barrell & started them down the precipices. They would run until they would loose themselves to the sight, bounding for hundreds of feet at times without touching any thing. In this way we amused ourselves for 20 minutes. We found some of the largest trees today that we have met with. The pine furr & Arbo[r]vita[e]. The boys measured on of the last named trees that was 36 feet round; it forked out in about 5 or 6 prongs some 15 feet above the ground.

At 10 A M we reached Camp creek [and] watered our mules. There being no grass at this point we continued our march— And reached our destined camping place for the day at 7 P M. We here found a large number of teams resting & the men cuting grass & cureing it to last them into the vally. We were compelled to turne our mules 4 miles down a branch where we found a vally that furnished plenty of grass. Our drinking water &c we carried ½ mile all the way up hill. After starting the mules with a suitable guard the ballance of us commenced prepairing supper of our venison, which was by all hands amply discussed. Distance 25 ms.

FRIDAY AUG 10TH   Breakfast being over all hands (save the cooks) started to the Meadow to cut and cure hay to last us into the Vally. We found the grass to be of an exelant quality and nearly wast high, we cut and cured all that we wanted and in the evening caught up our mules & packed it to the wagons, and made preparations for an early start next morning. There was a good many trainnes encamped at this place recruiting their teams.

SATURDAY AUG 11TH   I had the mules brought to camp at an early hour this morning in order to get the start of the large number of teams that were to leave this camp. Those of us who were at camp prepaired breakfast for the guard. And before the sun rose we were on the road. The roads have been down hill pretty much & compairitively good all day. We nooned in the neighbourhood of the diggins [Pleasant Valley], then came on to the forks of the road—the left hand leading to Sutters Fort [Sacramento] & the right hand to the mills or Coloma. It is 50 miles from this point to the Fort—and 15 to the Mills. We here took the right hand road and went down wever Creek through Wevervill [and] came on three miles farther to hang Town, where we encamped for the night.[100] We here met with Our New York friends who packed from fort Hall. They had been in 6 or 8 days. Distance 25 ms.

SUNDAY AUG 12TH   We left this place & came 3 miles to what is called the Cold Springs. We here haulted for the day. After sending our mules to grass I took one and rode down to Coloma 6 miles to see what discoverys I could make. I found it to be a miserably [hot?] place with high mountains all round it reflecting the rays of the sun down into the vally makeing it 3 times as hot as it would otherwise be. This Town is located on the South fork of the American River. It was at this place that the gold was first discovered by Mr. [James W.] Marshall who built the mill for Capt [J. A.] Sutter.[101] I travelled two mile down the river & found several more of our boys who packed through. They were at work, but had done but little. In the evening I returned to our camp.

MONDAY AUG 13TH   This morning we hearnessed up our teams and drove to Coloma—put our mules 1½ miles below town on a small branch, to graze. I then purchased a ¾ inch pland [plank] at the Saw Mill which measured 12 feet at $7.20 cents & set to work to make me a Gold washer. In 2 days I had it, fit for use. Meantime A W Harrison and myself divided out what provisions &c we had left and he took his things Out of my wagon. He and his brother went across to the middle fork.

I made my commencement in the California [diggings] on the

Sand bar just below the Saw mill or Coloma on the South fork of the American River about 50 miles from the mouth of sd River, at which place the City of Sacramento is built. This is the former Embarcadary of Capt Sutter.[102] On this bar I remained for 10 or 12 days, during which time I was employing my time in prospecting, and in informing myself with regard to the mineing operations of the country.

Wishing to push my enquirys still farther and make myself still better acquainted with the country, on the 23rd of August Abbott Hoover & myself harnessed up our mules & started for the City of Sacramento where we arrived on the 25th. Upon my arrival there I found a vast concourse of people all in the hurry of business as it ware. I sold our wagon & three mules for $550.00 an purchased an interest in a boarding house where I continued for some 10 or 12 days.

Not likeing the business I sold out to Capt Basye one of the partners on the 6th of Sept and joined in with Wm. H. Nuttall P. P. Youell and W. W. Abbott, and purchased an Ox teame and waggon and loaded it with provisions & grocerys. And on the 10th day of Sept started to the upper mines on the upper Sacramento at what was called Redding's diggins.[108] We arrived at Kelsey's trading post on Clear Creek 13 miles this side of the diggins proper on the 26th, where we soald out our loading at a proffit of about $1000. Our intention was to sell out our loading & commence mineing, but we were detered from this on account of the vast amount of Sickness among the miners in that vecinity. At Cotton wood Creek 12 miles before reaching the trading post we came up to the Boys from Fleming County Ky—the first time that we had met since we started. On the 28th We commenced a retreat back down the River. We sold out at prices such as these Flour at 60 cts pr lb   Sugar Do 65   Pork Do 75 heard bread Do 75   Molasses $4.00 pr Gal   Whiskey Do $4.00   Brandy's Wines & Surups &c by the case at from $45 to 65   Coffee 55 cts   Tea by the Caddy $4 to 6 pr lb &c &c. These are about a fair avrage of the prices.

On our way up we fell in with 2 young men Francis Hackney & John Elsney, one from Arkansas & the other from Texas who came by Santa Fe & Salt Lake. On Mary's River the Indians stold all their horses & mules and left them on foot to walk in & pack their provisions & blankets or perish on the desert. They however had footed it in & when they arrived at Lawsons (130 ms above Sacramento City)[104] they had not one cent of money nor anything to eat. I took them to my camp & fed them up to the trading post without chargeing them one cent for it. When we got there I proposed to the boys to let's give them an outfit for the mines which was agreed too. I had mineing implements of my own in which the other boys were not concerned. I let them have the tools of mine and then we furnished them with a lot of provisions and took their joint note for $81.80 the amount of the provisions &c. The other boys feeling it was just that much gone sold out to me at $5.00 each—Except Abbott. I Kept the note and in Decr they came down to the city with their pockets full of the precious mettle & lifted their note like Gentlemen. These other boys were all present at the time and requested that I should not say anything about their haveing sold out to me at the mear nominal sum of $5.00.

After leaveing the trading post we met waggons in crouds & a vast number of men going to Trinity w[h]ere it was our intention to have gone if we mined at all. This River heads in the same range of Mountains that the Sacramento River does, and almost directly opposite to, and very near each other. Trinity river emties into Trinity Bay some 300 or 350 ms above the Bay of San Francisco. And to get from Sacramento River to Trinity you have to cross the Cascade or cost Range of Mountains. It is called 300 ms from Sacramento City across to Trinity River. It is said that small vessels can enter into the mouth of Trinity Bay & ascend the river for some distance. At least this is the account as given by some. Others however say that there is no such Bay and that Trinity River emties into another River on the west side of the mts called Tlimax River and it has a small Bay which leads out into the Pacific. I have not been able to ascertain which of these are correct. But probably I shall and if so will correct the statement and incert it.[105]

As we went up we ascended the West side of the River, and as we returned we came back on the East side, so that we had a view of both sides. The vally are generally wide & continue to the bluffs or slopes of the mountains. The Sacramento River from its junction with Feather River is a very rapid stream & is a nulity so far as successful Navigation is concerned. It is a very crooked stream and has a great number [of] riffles & fall. On the West Side of the River there was no streams put into the Sacramento untill we get to Cottenwood creek. But on the East Side there are small streams putting in every few miles of pure clear cool waters just from the melting snows. Among these are Deer Creek Big Butte and little Butte Feather River, Uba [Yuba] River Bare [Bear] River & a great many more that I never learned the name of.

On our return we were all taken sick at Lawsons 130 ms. above Sacramento city & we had to hire a man to drive our wagon for us. On the 12th day of Oct we reached Sacramento City & sold our team. We applyed to Drs Ormsly [Ormsby?] & Warnock for medical aid and by the 20th we were all on our feet again. Here our partnership seased. I joined in partnership with Wm. H. McGrew of Frankfort Ky & purchased a team & commenced hauling to the mines in which business we did well, makeing in the short space of 6 week about $2500. The rainy season set in much arlier this year than usual which operated very much against us. The rain commenced on the 9th of Nove[mber] and continued for several week without intermission. We had 2 week of fair weather in Decr. When the rain commenced we were compelled to ceace our hauling & to put our cattle on a ranch for the winter. Meantim we purchased hay & sold, rented a house &

lot & started an auction which did us but little good as the rainy season put a stop to business generally.

We continued in our house till the 9th of January 1850, [when] about 4 O'clock P. M. the water broke over the banks & temporary leavies [levees] of the Town & before midnight The water was from 4 to 7 feet deep in the houses, destroying every thing perishable in its way, Not giveing the merchants a chance to save any thing in the shape of goods. So raped was the rise that men only thought of safeing their own lives. Flower, Salt, Sugar, d[r]ied Beans & Fruits, in fact every thing that water would spoile was lost. Stock of every description was swept away & drowned. In this general loss we sustained our share. Out of 14 head of cattle we lost 7 head, 7 Tones of hay worth $250. pr ton and a veriety of other things—Makeing our losses not less than $2500, which broke McGrew & myself flat and left us just where we commenced—with nothing. Such is the fate of fortune.

Our not being the only sufferers was no consolation to us. Others lost as much or more than we, yet that did not recompence us atal. The water continued in Town till in February, when it gradually receded.[106] In Feb we had some very pretty pleasant weather. But in March it made up for it all—it rained stormed & blowed nearly the whole of March through. In Decr we had the cold weather, in Nov & Jan the wet weather, in Feb the plasant weather, in march the stormy unpleasant weather. We had some hot days about the last of March the Themometer stood at 85 in the house.

Being still unwell about the first of March I took my wagon & put into it my cot & beding & such provisions as was suitable for me to eat & drove out into the country & encamped with Hawkins & co, about 9 ms from Town. Upon leaving the stench and disagreeable smell in Town & getting out where I could enjoy pure air I commenced recovering & my health improved rapedly. Some time in march Hawkins moved his stock down on the river (west side) at a place called the Island. I took mine down there too and at the same time took charge of Thos McKarney's for which he paid me $7.00 pr day, at the same time superintended the stock of Hawkins & co. Some time about the last of March the River commenced raiseing from the recnt heavy rains and it bid fare for another overflow and we were afraid that we would be hemed in with our stock. So we recrossed the river and located 4 miles below the City. Whilst there, I was employed by Hawkins & Davis, at $10.00 pr day, who became the owners of all the stock to assist Mr David McKarney to take care of the stock he being acquainted with the San Deago cattle & I being acquainted withe the old stock makeing in all about 180 head. At this place we continued for several weeks and in the last week of May we moved our stock down on the San Cosemice [Cosumnes] some 15 ms from Town in consequence of the Grass's becomeing short where we were. On this river which is about 60 feet wide, with a bold strong deep current we found most exelant grass, with an abundance of wild Oats & Red Clover. Here our cattle did finely. We at the same time took in some stock to ranch for other men at one dollar pr head per week which was to us an additional fee.

Some time in March I proposed to McGrew to desolve our copartnership, which was as redily agreaed to by him. We divided off our stock & other property and then divided out our liabilities and each fellow commenced for himself. This was done because we wished to pursue different businesses. I regard McGrew as one amongst the few pure minded Gentlemen in this Country. He is to my mind clearly an honest *Man* & when I say this I mean all that I say—& I say all that can be said of a *man*. We were both poore unfortunate fellows & have to do all of our first work over again. But so the World Wags—

NOTES ON THE DIARY

1. The Ithaca Company reached California by a remarkable route, taking the Santa Fe Trail to Pueblo, as recorded in Ralph P. Bieber, ed., *Southern Trails to California in 1849* (Glendale, 1937), pp. 364-367, thence going via the Cache la Poudre, Laramie Plains, Browns Hole, and Fort Uintah to Utah Valley, from which they took the southern road to Los Angeles. See Charles V. Stuart to H. H. Bancroft, August 4, 1872, in Bancroft Library MSS. (C-E 65, No. 30). Stuart gives the names of many of his fellow travelers and adds that they were guided from the Arkansas by a mountain man, Kinney, and from Utah Valley by a half-breed Cherokee, Charley Macintosh. For other accounts of travel by this route, see the dictations in the Bancroft Library by Harvey S. Brown (C-D 54), W. C. Randolph (C-D 143) and J. H. Widber (C-D 174), as also George Wither to Robert Miller, Great Salt Lake City, August 12, 1849, in Miller Papers, Missouri Historical Society.

2. Pritchard, Burrall and Tate are the only diarists who describe a journey across Missouri from St. Louis by land in 1849; Tate varied in going to St. Joseph from Lexington. Compare, however, the letters of Mifflin (George Mifflin Harker) to the St. Louis *Reveille*, reprinted in Missouri Historical Society, *Glimpses of the Past*, vol. 6, April-June, 1939, pp. 35-76. Having set out five days after Pritchard, Mifflin wrote from Rocheport on April 26: "The roads have been excellent, except in a few narrow strips of timber, where we have found some horrid, ugly places. Grain is abundant and cheap, and by going a short distance each day, we are quite confident that our mules will be in much better plight when we arrive at Independence, than they would have been had they been kicked and cuffed around by inhuman deck hands, crowded together in a narrow compass, uncurried, half-fed, and nearly starved to death, on board a steamboat. Hundreds have wisely pursued the same course that we have."

3. Mifflin called Columbia "the prettiest village that I have seen in the State . . . the county-seat of Boone county—where is situated the University of Missouri—one of the finest edifices of the kind in the State. The other towns along the road are small and unimportant."

4. Having crossed at Rocheport "in a miserable horse ferryboat," Mifflin termed the conveyance "a very small clumsy affair—one wagon with six mules, another wagon with four yoke of oxen, and three or four horses, were all crowded into it, and I thought we would never get across."

5. Dr. John Sappington (1776-1856) was born in Maryland. In 1804 he married Jane Breathitt, daughter of a Kentucky governor, and in 1817 settled in Missouri, afterwards building a home near Arrow Rock. One of the pioneers

in administering quinine for malaria, in an age of "bleeding and purging," he began the wholesale manufacture of "Dr. John Sappington's Anti-Fever Pills" in 1832, and 12 years later published *The Theory and Treatment of Fevers*, the first medical text printed west of the Mississippi. See articles by Thomas B. Hall in the *Dictionary of American Biography* and *Missouri Historical Review*, vol. 24, January, 1930, pp. 177-199; vol. 37, April, 1943, pp. 336-341. A striking description of Sappington was written in 1850 by Joseph Price: "he is a man a bout 75 years of age   his hed is very white thoug not bald   his beard is a bout 6 inches long and he is a very Masterly looking man polite in his address but profanely wicked   he has a very extencive farm and a great many slaves." See Thomas M. Marshall, ed., "The Road to California: Letters of Joseph Price," *Mississippi Valley Historical Review*, vol. 9, September, 1924, pp. 237-257.

6.   Pritchard's description of Independence in 1849 has been quoted by most recent writers on the Gold Rush. Since 1828 an outfitting point for Santa Fe traders, later for Oregon and California emigrants, the town was now entering a period of decline. St. Joseph, on the east bank of the Missouri 100 miles to the north and more than 70 miles farther west, had been found a convenient point of departure for plains travelers since its founding in 1843, and in 1849 many more emigrants set out from St. Joseph than from Independence. Westport and Kansas Landing, situated immediately west of Independence, were also about to boom, and the older town soon ceased to be a factor even in the Santa Fe trade.

7.   Western historians have assumed that the Hudspeth who figures so prominently in the history of 1849 was James M. Hudspeth, best known for his association with Lansford W. Hastings in the opening of the Hastings Cutoff in 1846. However, Thomas Lorraine Campbell (Mrs. Paul Campbell) of Minden, Louisiana, has established that the Forty-niner was Benoni Morgan Hudspeth. She informs me that he was born in 1816 and died in California in 1850, having been a voyageur with Frémont in 1845-1846, and later an officer in the California Battalion. Four brothers, Robert Nicholas, George Washington, Thomas Jefferson, and Silas Bourke Hudspeth took the trail with him in 1849, as did J. J. Myers. It was this company from Jackson County, Missouri, that opened the Hudspeth Cutoff in Idaho the following July; see Note 59.

8.   The Lone Elm stood on Cedar Creek. The area early became a place of note as Round Grove, later as Elm Grove, but by 1843, as observed by Theodore Talbot, in his Journal, only two elms remained, "their fellows having fallen by the axe of the cold and hungry traveller." Fifteen days after Pritchard, D. Jagger (who sketched its forlorn aspect) expressed the opinion that "the old tree will never put forth its leaves again," being nearly stripped of its bark. A letter from William Brady in *Kansas Historical Collections*, vol. 11, 1909-1910, pp. 459-

460, recalls a visit to the Lone Elm camp ground in 1854. "The old tree was lying on the ground: the greater part of it had been burned up." A commemorative marker was placed by the Kansas State Historical Society in 1906 at the N.W. corner of the N.W. quarter of Section 23, Township 14 South, Range 23 East.

9. Pritchard's Bull Creek seems to have been present Captain Creek, which flows north into the Kansas River. Present Big Bull Creek, which flows south into the Osage, he had crossed near the junction of the Oregon and Santa Fe trails.

10. One of the steep-banked creeks crossed during the day was the Wakarusa, usually accorded more attention by the Forty-niners. Coons Point, where Pritchard camped for the night, is located by the Kansas State Historical Society in Douglas County, about 8 miles west of Lawrence and 3½ miles south of Lecompton, approximately Section 10, Township 12 South, Range 18 East. William Kelly also describes the road past Coons Point.

11. Shonganunga Creek flows into the Kansas at present Topeka.

12. The Pottawatomies were one of the tribes of the Old Northwest who by the Chicago treaty of 1833 agreed to remove west of the Mississippi. Some were finally settled in southwestern Iowa, near Council Bluffs, others in Kansas on the Osage River. Wishing to locate the whole tribe together, the U. S. government in 1846 persuaded the Pottawatomies to settle on lands formerly a part of the old Kansas Reservation. The Indians moved to the new reservation between September, 1847, and November, 1848, the united band numbering 3,235. See William Elsey Connelley, "The Prairie Band of Pottawatomie Indians," *Kansas Historical Collections*, vol. 14, 1915-1918, pp. 488-570.

13. The ferries were at Topeka and present Rossville. The lower ferry was operated by the Papan brothers as early as 1842; the other is said to have been carried on for three or four years from 1849 by Charles Beaubien and Lewis Ogee. Its primary function was to connect the Pottawatomie settlements on the north and south banks of the Kansas River. See George A. Root, "Ferries in Kansas," *Kansas Historical Quarterly*, vol. 2, November, 1933, pp. 363-365; vol. 3, February, 1934, p. 3.

14. "Potiwatimi" is better known as Uniontown or Union Village, where the government located traders to the Pottawatomies. A Baptist school previously conducted in Iowa was now situated on Mission Creek, 9 miles below Uniontown. Although most of the Michigan Pottawatomies did not come to the reservation until 1850, then settling around the Catholic mission at St. Marys, it appears from Pritchard that a half-breed, and an enterprising one at that, had come in advance of his people. Other interesting accounts of Uniontown and its environs

are by Kelly, Jagger, and Batchelder. Pritchard's night camp was on Cross Creek, the site of Rossville.

15. The bridged stream was called by Hixson two days later "Mill Creek," with the further observations: "Peter Bullbony, a half-breed, Indian and French, resided here.... He owned, or at least claimed and exercised authority over thirty miles square of as fine land as a crow ever flew over. He had a number of comfortable hewn-log cabins, a circular sawmill, etc." When on the 10th Hixson's party crossed on Bullbony's bridge, they contributed "fifty cents each to his already well filled purse." On May 13 Buffum got across "Crooked Creek" at a somewhat better rate, "1 dime per waggon."

Several emigrants describe the newly founded St. Mary's Mission, including Kelly, Hixson, and Buffum. The site for the mission was selected in the summer of 1848 by Father Felix L. Verreydt, and it was given into the charge of a Swiss Jesuit, Father Maurice Gailland, whose diary, translated from the Latin by James M. Burke, S.J., has been published as "Early Years at St. Mary's Pottawatomie Mission," *Kansas Historical Quarterly*, vol. 20, August, 1953, pp. 501-529. This diary details his coming to Uniontown on September 7, 1848, ten days later erecting "a cross on the hill of our residence." A chapel, begun next month, was completed in the spring of 1849. On May 8, the day Pritchard passed, the priest noted in his diary: "From the beginning of this month innumerable wagons, horses, and men have passed by on their way, intent upon going into New California. They are lavishly squandering their counterfeit money and stealing horses."

16. Buffum wrote on May 13: "This [the Vermillion] is the boundary between the Kaws and Pawnees. Here is a village from which the Kaws were driven by the Pawnees lately.... We now keep a sharp lookout for the Pawnees who are represented as savage...." Trains joined up for mutual protection on arriving at the Vermillion, where the trail turned sharply northwest, away from the Kansas toward the Big Blue.

17. What Pritchard calls Captain Fash's train from Indiana was possibly built up around a party from Peoria, Illinois, listed in an April 19 Independence dispatch in the *Missouri Republican* of April 25, 1849. Said to have three wagons, with six mules to each, the members were J. E. Carter, J. Fash, William E. Gunett, A. H. Fash, Robert Taylor, J. Clegg, D. A. McConnell, George Scott, and [M.] Peck.

Jacob Hoover, mentioned earlier in Pritchard's entry, is listed in an April 17 dispatch in the *Republican* of April 23, 1849; he was one of a company declared to hail from Indianapolis, Indiana, which included A. W. Harrison, Samuel Dunlop, M. Alford, T. P. Harrison, A. A. Ackley, W. B. Greer, George Baker,

R. C. Grogdon, William L. Morris, John Culley, B. F. Ringland, H. H. Ohr, W. Bradon, E. R. Myers, J. Latimore, J. Hoover, J. Hoover, Sr., and G. W. Larimore, "organized into four messes, each mess being provided with a wagon, tent, and necessary equipment and provisions." The senior Hoover, as noted in Samuel Harden, *Early Life and Times in Boone County, Indiana* (Indianapolis, 1887), p. 292, and in *A History of the State of Kansas* (Chicago, 1883), p. 664, was born in Tennessee in 1808, lived at Eagle Village, Boone County, "from 1814 to October 1857," and from 1858 lived in California Township, Coffey County, Kansas (his California adventures entirely passed over!). He was married in 1829 to Sarah Lowe, and had 13 children. If the younger Jacob was his first-born, he would have been not yet 20 years old in May, 1849. Later, on the Carson River, Pritchard refers to "young Hoover," but does not otherwise differentiate father and son.

18. Independence Crossing, about 8 miles south of present Marysville, Kansas, near which the road from St. Joseph crossed the Big Blue.

19. This withdrawal, just six days after Pritchard's party joined Fash's for mutual safety, foreshadows the disintegration the Boone County company, like so many others, underwent on the trail. By the time Pritchard reached the diggings, he had separated from all of his original traveling companions, while joined by others met along the way.

20. Andrew W. Sublette, second youngest of five brothers celebrated in the history of the early West, was born in Kentucky about 1813, and went to the Rockies as early as 1830. After an active but unsuccessful career in the fur trade, in 1847 he was elected captain in an Oregon Battalion enlisted by the State of Missouri to protect the road to Oregon. He commanded the escort when a site for Fort Kearny was selected at the head of Grand Island that fall, and was stationed at the new post next spring. Late in 1848 he guided Lieutenant E. F. Beale to Santa Fe, but then turned back to Independence. Not he but his younger brother, Solomon, gave to Joseph E. Ware the information which led Ware in his *Emigrants' Guide to California* (St. Louis, 1849) to "take the liberty" of renaming the old Greenwood Cutoff west of South Pass the "Sublette Cutoff." Like many other Forty-niners, Pritchard carried a copy of Ware's *Guide*, and it was a simple misidentification that led him to call Andrew "the discoverer of the Sublett or Greenwood cut off." William G. Johnston on May 7 made a similar mistake. There are few later allusions to Andrew Sublette's company, but Bennett C. Clark, below the great bend of the Humboldt, on July 26 and 27 mentions "Subletts ox train." After reaching California, Andrew settled in the Los Angeles area, where he died late in 1853. Many documents pertaining to him are preserved by the Missouri Historical Society, St. Louis.

21. Respecting A. W. Harrison, see Note 17.

22. As to Hamline I have no information, but James Croslin may have been one of the five young men mentioned by Pritchard on May 15 as from "Pendleton County, Kentucky." The *Missouri Republican*, April 25, 1849, lists a company made up of E. W. Hayes, Kenton County; C. K. Snyder, W. H. Childers, B. B. Mullons, Pendleton County; James Croslin, Campbell County; J. Frizzland, H. Shelton, Woodford County; D. W. Thorpe, Grant County; and G. Young, Jackson County, "provided with a wagon, six mules, necessary provisions, &c. . . . fitted out by Mr. R. Mullens, upon conditions that he receives, as compensation, a certain portion of their findings for a specified period." The names of Mullins, Hayes, and Snyder subsequently appear in Pritchard's diary.

23. The site of Fort Kearny (for a time called Fort Childs) was selected by Lieutenant Daniel P. Woodbury in the fall of 1847. Next spring the Oregon Battalion, which had wintered at "Old" Fort Kearny (present Nebraska City) marched up the Platte to begin a desultory job of fort building. In October, 1848, the volunteer Battalion was relieved by two companies of regular troops who wintered at the new fort, officially named in December for the recently deceased Stephen W. Kearny. According to the annual report of the Chief of Engineers, in the fall of 1848 three temporary buildings were erected for officers and men, a bakery, temporary stables, and a large adobe storehouse. During 1849 a hospital, temporary magazine, and two-story barracks were added. Fort and garrison did not impress most Forty-niners; the brightest feature of the place was described by Niles Searls, "a family of Mormons who keep a boarding house, & with whom a large number of our men made an excellent supper of bread, milk, fresh butter doughnuts & all the little etceteras." Peter Decker adds that this Mormon family "lost their stock last year on way to 'the Brethren' at Salt Lake & stopped here and expect to go on next year." Louis Nusbaumer, stranded at the fort for a while, tells of going on to Salt Lake on July 6 with "the keeper of the boarding house, Knowlton," and later gives his name as G. Knowlton (evidently Quincy Knowlton).

Captain Charles F. Ruff was in command when Pritchard went by, but from May 29 to July 16, while the great stream of emigration passed, the commanding officer was Lieutenant Colonel B. L. E. Bonneville. (Most of the military facts above are derived from a history by Lillian Willman in Nebraska State Historical Society, *Publications*, vol. 21, 1930, pp. 211-326, which includes Lieutenant Woodbury's official correspondence, 1847-1851, and the map which accompanied his report of November 10, 1847; see also Lyle E. Mantor, "Fort Kearny and the Westward Movement," *Nebraska History*, vol. 29, September, 1948, pp. 175-207.)

24. A Fort Kearny dispatch of May 18, published in the *Missouri Republican*, June 4, 1849, observed that up to that morning 476 wagons had passed

since the first gold digger arrived on May 6. A postscript on May 19 added, "Yesterday 180 wagons [including Pritchard's] passed here, making in all 656." Hence there were plenty of wagons to pass.

25. In a St. Joseph letter of April 25, in the *Missouri Republican*, May 2, 1849, no less than 12 companies were listed from Cincinnati, almost all equipped with mules.

26. The constitution-making on the plains in 1849 speaks volumes for the political and legalistic traditions of the emigration, but as long as one emigrant could punch another in the nose and walk out, their provisions were unenforceable.

27. Edwin Bryant in *What I Saw in California* (New York, 1848), p. 81, described a prairie-dog village seen in 1846 on the Platte.

28. Three major fords of the South Platte used in 1849 are described by Major Osborne Cross. The lowest was near the point where the first highlands lift between the forks of the Platte, the highest near present Brule, this latter being the ford used by Pritchard. It is evident, however, that the Forty-niners crossed wherever the whim took them, from just above the forks on up, congestion of the trails and availability of grass being major considerations. Cross noted wagons ascending both banks of the South Platte, as well as along the bluffs between the two forks; and had he been able to see over the bluffs, he would also have observed wagons moving up both banks of the North Platte. The chart gives a rough indication as to whether a higher or lower crossing of the South Platte was employed, evidenced by whether it took more than one day to reach Ash Hollow.

29. The Sioux first moved south into the valley of the Platte in force during the 1830's. They were generally friendly to the whites till 1854, and their nomadic villages on the two forks of the Platte gave the Forty-niners much to write about. French-Canadian fur traders, often half-Indian themselves, had dwelt among them for a generation or more.

30. All the emigrants, regardless of where they crossed the South Platte, passed through Ash Hollow, the most convenient place to descend the bluffs after a high crossing, and a necessary detour from bluffs obstructing the south bank of the North Platte if emigrants came up that river after a low crossing.

31. M. M. Basye was named a delegate to the Illinois State Whig Convention at a meeting of the Shelby County Whigs in Shelbyville, May 26, 1840, but no further facts about him have appeared. Information about his party in 1849, however, is afforded by a diary kept by a Dr. T. (see Bibliography). On commencing this diary on May 20, 60 miles west of Fort Kearny, Dr. T. wrote: "Our company consists of eleven teams 6 mules each and 42 men. New Yorkers

Kentuckians mostly Kentuckians first rate fellows as you ever saw. our captain Mr. Basye a Kyn. is much of a gentleman and well qualified to conduct a company to California—we joined his Co. at Fort Childs that was, but now is Fort Kearney."

32. Coming in rapid succession, Court House Rock, Chimney Rock, and Scotts Bluff excited the wonder of the Forty-niners. Court House Rock was given its name for its resemblance to the St. Louis court house; it was sometimes also called Lone Tower or Church Rock.

33. Dr. T's diary for May 31, which first mentions Pritchard's party as "a Company from Boone County Ky," also says: "Yesterday being a rainy day and most trains laying by having nothing else to do, a general destruction and devastation appeared to take Place—in almost every train—I thought I had before seen destruction of property but this morning beat anything I had ever seen. To attempt an enumeration of what was thrown away would be useless as it could not be done. Trunks, clothes, Matrasses, Quilts, Beef, Bacon, Rice Augers, Handsaws, planes, Shoes, Hats, Thread, Spools, Boss [?] Soap mowing sythes etc. These are a few of the items I saw this morning. They were thrown out yesterday by one train in order to make their loads lighter."

34. An illuminating article on Chimney Rock is Merrill J. Mattes' "Chimney Rock on the Oregon Trail," *Nebraska History*, vol. 36, March, 1955, pp. 1-26. Mr. Mattes, who reproduces 15 sketches of the Rock made between 1841 and 1874, observes that "The Camp Clarke Quadrangle of the U. S. Geological Survey, based on a survey of 1895, shows its summit about five hundred feet above the river and perhaps three hundred feet from the base of the cone. No present scientific measurements of the column or spire are available, but it appears to rise about one hundred feet above the peak of the cone."

David Cosad, on May 26, 1849, tells of measuring the height of the rock by comparing its shadow with that of a man 5 feet 9 inches tall, thus found to be 360 feet from base to top. Many Forty-niners inscribed their names on the rock, but erosion of the soft shale has left no traces.

35. Pritchard adds another to the innumerable tales respecting the origin of the name of Scotts Bluff, a topic judiciously examined by Merrill J. Mattes in "Hiram Scott, Fur Trader," *Nebraska History*, vol. 26, July-September, 1945, pp. 127-162. Continuing research has confirmed Mr. Mattes' conjectural identification of the unfortunate fur trader as Hiram Scott, but the date of the tragedy is still uncertain, whether 1827 or 1828. The tale that his journal was found, with "a full account of the whole transaction," is unsubstantiated.

36. Dr. T. also encamped at this spring: "I suppose there must have been 200 teams encamped contiguous . . . Singular as it may appear we found here a

blacksmith shop—Carried on by 3 Frenchmen—They live by trading with the Indians. I suppose that Emigration induced them to adopt Blacksmithing." A great many other Forty-niners noted this establishment at Scotts Bluff, run by a member of the ubiquitous Robidoux clan. If one of the well-known brothers, it was most likely Michael; the other brothers, Joseph, Antoine, Louis, Francois, and Isidore, are otherwise accounted for in 1849. It may well be, however, that Joseph E., the eldest son of Joseph, born in 1801, was the Robidoux concerned, for several of the Forty-niners noted that the man at Scotts Bluff had a Sioux wife or two, alliances of 13 or 14 years' standing, and Orral Messmore Robidoux, *Memorial to the Robidoux Brothers* (Kansas City, Missouri, 1924), pp. 226-227, records that Joseph E. raised two Indian families, retired from trading about 1857, and died on a reservation near White Cloud, Kansas, about 1888. Perplexingly, Charles Darwin, who had a considerable visit with the Scotts Bluff Robidoux on June 26, 1849, gives his name as Antoine (thus confirming George Gibbs's observation of a sign, "Tinware by A. Rubidue") and also refers to his uncle, Joseph Robidoux of St. Joseph. This would identify him as a cousin of Joseph E.—but no such Antoine is recorded by Orral Messmore Robidoux unless he was "Louis," son of Isidore, baptized August 12, 1820, and nothing more said of him. The elder Antoine, who had no children of record, was born in 1794 and in 1828 married Carmel Benevides in Santa Fe; he guided a party from St. Joseph to California in 1849; he was encountered along the trail by McCall and others, and mentioned by Burbank as far west as Green River. McCall raises the possibility that Antoine had one or more children by an Indian wife, for he says Antoine was accompanied west in 1849 by "a son, a lad of eighteen, dusky in hue." As a final note, Austin on July 6, 1849, said the Robidoux post at Scotts Bluff "was established last spring."

Merrill J. Mattes, who has made a specialty of the North Platte landmarks, writes informatively of "Robidoux's Trading Post at 'Scott's Bluffs,' and the California Gold Rush," in *Nebraska History*, vol. 30, June, 1949, pp. 95-138; the Robidoux post was maintained until 1851.

37. Dr. T. gave Fort Laramie a far more appreciative notice. He also wrote: "We found a number of emigrants here—many with broken down teams, some preparing to pack, others turning back, not being able to procure the necessaries for packing, and less able to proceed farther with their present teams. This appears to be a place of general renovating amongst travellers. Most stay a day or two for the double purpose of resting their mules and repacking their loads—Good waggons here bring from 4 to 30 dollars, Mules from 100 to 150 dollars. —That is you sell your waggons to the traders at the Fort and buy from them their mules—Everything you buy cost four times as much as it is worth and every thing you sell bring perhaps one tenth its value."

One of the Indianans attached to Pritchard's party on June 4 wrote to the Indianapolis *Indiana State Journal* a letter reprinted in the New York *Tribune*, July 31, 1849; after describing the fort, wagons, provisions, and mode of travel, and mentioning the expectation of reaching California about the middle of August, he said: "From all that we can learn about 300 wagons are ahead of us, some of them ox teams, and probably 3,500 or 4,000 behind us." The Pritchard and Basye trains visited Fort Laramie during its last weeks as a private trading post. On June 26 it was purchased by Lieutenant D. P. Woodbury for $4,000, and thereafter converted into one of the most famous of U. S. military establishments.

38. From Fort Laramie there was, in 1849, a choice of two principal routes. A "river road" kept up the bank of the North Platte to the mouth of Warm Spring Canyon, then up that canyon to the Warm Spring, some 14 miles altogether, while a shorter and rougher hill road made directly west from Fort Laramie to the Warm Spring. As did most others during the season of high water, Pritchard seems to have chosen the hill road, afterward going on to camp on Bitter or Cottonwood Creek; his warm spring next day is not that mentioned above. The Black Hills, an early name for the Laramie Mountains, were so called for their dark growth of pine and juniper; in crossing them, Pritchard found the going difficult and was happy finally to reach the North Platte bottoms near Deer Creek. Next year a wagon road was worked out on the north side of the Platte above Fort Laramie, an especial convenience to emigrants from Council Bluffs who previously had had to cross the North Platte at or below Fort Laramie. and follow one or another of these south-bank trails through the Black Hills.

39. Basye's train had been in company with Pritchard's all this day, and Dr. T. writes: "A hunter [at the noon halt] ran a large buffalo into our camp— I never saw so excited a mass of men in all my life. Our mules took affright and came near making a stampede,—This, however, attracted not the slightest attention from the chase—A number of shots were fired at him but, without effect, we were so completely surprised that we were unprepared for him, and before we could mount our horses he had gotten away."

40. Dr. T. gives a more extended account of events at the Upper Ferry from June 10-12:

"Sunday, 10th. Was on our Journey at ½ past 4 this morning and at 15 minutes after 6 arrived at the Ferry—on the North Fork of the Platte river— This ferry is owned by a company of 11 Mormons. Here there is a blacksmith shop—We found 150 wagons in ahead of us. About 50 can be crossed in a day— Just before we arrived a young man by the name of Brown from Missouri was drowned in attempting to swim his cattle across—This accident appeared not in the least to produce more excitement than if he had been a dog although he was represented to be a young man of fine abilities, and esteemed by all who knew him.—We found for our mules good grass, about 3 miles from camp to which we drove them, where they remained until the [next day? Placed?] a guard over them—This evening Shepherd [?] arrived, his company being broken up—He is now packing one mule and walking.

"Monday 11th. As soon as I breakfasted this morning I walked over to where our mules were grazing in order to let Heaton return for Breakfast, remained herding mules until 3 oclock when I was again releived by Heaton, brought them in and tied them to the wagon tongue Traded mules with one of the [   ] Company who had left and was going with an ox team—got a first rate mule—Dr. Bower from Missouri arrived this evening—He is the old gentleman with whom I roomed on the Steamboat last Spring from Cin[cinati?] to [   ] city. Spent a pleasant evening with him.

"Tuesday 12th. Nothing of importance occurred to day every Person attending to his own affairs. Business here is quite brisk, wagons unloading, repairing, getting mules and oxen shod, &c. A general renovating takes place here, washing up [?] For shoeing a horse $3.00 an ox $6.00. Our riding horse wanting shoes, and as I had seen a great many shoes nailed on, concluded I could do it as well if not so neat as any person thereby save a dollar. An important item, as we are getting tolerably scarce of the needful—I went to work, shod our horse, and when completed the Job was pronounced very good."

On the 13th, after crossing the river, Dr. T. added, concerning the Mormon Ferry: "The boat is made by framing cross pieces across 3 canoes—over which sufficient width of plank is pinned down for the wagons to stand on. Forming a very simple and safe boat—We paid for crossing $3.00. They cross on an average 60 wagons daily for which they get $180.00 This I think is better than gold digging."

The Mormon Ferry had been established in 1847, as described in Dale L. Morgan, "The Mormon Ferry on the North Platte," *Annals of Wyoming*, vol. 21, July-October, 1949, pp. 111-167. Each year thereafter, through 1852, it was operated during the season of high water, a company coming out from Great Salt Lake City for the purpose. In 1849 the Mormon ferrymen reached the river on May 27 and began ferrying, 3½ miles east of Casper, next day. They continued until late July. For a fuller account, see a study by Dale L. Morgan commencing in *Annals of Wyoming*, April, 1959.

41. Pritchard did not take the usual route of the Forty-niners after crossing the North Platte. That trail left the river almost immediately, went nearly west 8 miles, then southwest across Emigrant Gap Ridge some 5 miles to a

"mineral spring and lake" in the valley of Poison Spider Creek. Pritchard kept near the winding Platte some 9 miles, then turned northwest up the valley of Poison Spider Creek to the same mineral spring, afterwards going on to encamp in the valley of Poison Spring Creek. A somewhat variant route is described by Breyfogle and Geiger, among others.

42.   Pritchard evidently went hunting northwest of Poison Spring Creek, only to find that the road had veered southwest toward Willow Creek and Willow Spring. He overtook the train while it was nooning on Fish Creek, some 8½ miles beyond the Willow Spring. Dr. T., in Basye's train, tells of passing some 53 ox teams during the morning's travel.

43.   It seems certain that Independence Rock was so named after William L. Sublette's mountain-bound party of fur traders celebrated the Fourth of July there; the year could only have been 1829. Pritchard was an exception among the Forty-niners in taking a distasteful view of inscribing his name on the already famous rock; others, in every accessible space, carved their names or splashed them on with tar and paint. Charles Kelly's Emigrant Register, MS. in the Bancroft Library, reports that few inscriptions from 1849 still survive, because of exfoliation of the granite; paradoxically, inscriptions in this "hard" rock do not last like those made in sandstone, usually thought of as a "soft" rock.

Independence Rock and the nearby Devils Gate were the two outstanding landmarks situated along the Sweetwater River, which would now conduct Pritchard to South Pass.

44.   These "ice springs," which have given name to "Ice Slough," a southern tributary of the Sweetwater, were enjoyed by most of the Forty-niners as a pleasing novelty. Dr. T. says, "We gathered several buckets full [of ice], from which we have had Mint Juleps in abundance."

45.   Dr. T. remarks at this point: "about 3 oclock we came to an old Indian encampment, where the trail leaves the river—This village we were informed by a mountain Trader, was before the emigration, inhabited by the Snakes who, in consequence of the traders' telling them the Small pox was coming left the road on sight of the first Waggons—We passed through the Crow Nation without seeing one single Indian—There are a number of traders in these mountains whose policy it is, to prevent the Emigration and Indians from coming in contact they well knowing if they did their trade would be done, as the emigrant could get from the Indian, everything he wanted and that too at the smallest minimum price."

46.   Another omission in Pritchard's diary is supplied by Dr. T., who says of the noon encampment on the Sweetwater: "Here a number of Frenchmen, mountain Traders, had erected their lodges for the purpose of trading with the

emigrants. They must, I think, have had 300 head of horses and mules, a good mule or pony here is worth $100 to $150. They are from Fort Bridger bound for Fort Laramie—We could exchange almost any kind of a horse with them by giving $30. difference   two trades were made."

Many other Forty-niners commented on these traders at the last crossing of the Sweetwater, including Johnston, Kelly, Boyle, Decker, Hixson, Tinker, Chamberlain, Mann, Hackney, and Kirkpatrick, the range of dates being from June 9 to July 1. Several, like Breyfogle, mentioned Louis Vasquez among the traders; Mann on July 1 "saw Jim Bridger to day the mountaineer who owns a fort on west of us," but this must have been a brief visit, for others before and after this date encountered Bridger at his fort on Blacks Fork of Green River. On July 2 Hackney remarked the passage of the traders, en route back to Fort Bridger.

47. Pritchard's data come from Ware's *Guide*, copied (with one mistake, as corrected in brackets) from Frémont's observations, August 7, 1842. Frémont did not state the altitude, and Ware's figure is too low, the altitude of South Pass being now reckoned as 7,550 feet above sea level. Beyond South Pass the first westward-flowing water rises at Pacific Springs.

48. Of the 12 earliest diarists who reached this first major road junction west of Fort Laramie only five took the Salt Lake Road, doubtless as Dr. T. says, "to save 85 miles (according to our guide)." The disadvantage of this route was the long, waterless stretch of more than 50 miles from the Big Sandy to Green River.

Pritchard uses both the old and new names for the cutoff. Bruff's map disallows the propriety of calling the Greenwood Cutoff the Sublette Cutoff, applying the latter name to a route approximating what became the Lander Cutoff (*cf.* p. 175). Bruff says in his diary on August 2, "It is call'd by the emmigrants, very improperly, 'Soublette's Cut-Off,' but it was discovered by another Mountaineer,—Greenwood [in 1844]; and should be called 'Greenwood's Cut-Off.' [William L.] Soublette had discovered and traveled a short cut higher up, from near the base of 'Fremont's Peak,' to Fort Hall, which is only practicable for mules, and now probably nearly obliterated."

49. In Basye's train Dr. T. says: "After nooning we travelled on expecting to make Green River—About dark we met 2 men who informed us that we were 17 miles from the river, consequently we encamped forthwith without wood or water. We traveled 31 miles today." And on the 21st: "Started at 5 oclock this morning, traveled over some high mountains [bluffs] and reached the river at 11 oclock—There we encamped for the day ... 150 Waggons had crossed before us." This indicates that Pritchard and his traveling companions had materially improved their position in the emigration.

50. As yet the ferry across the Green operated by mountain men was the only one. Mormons who this year manned ferries both on the Salt Lake Road and on the Sublette Cutoff had not yet arrived; they set out from Great Salt Lake City June 12, but seem unrecorded at this upper crossing before June 30. So far as known, there had been no commercial ferry on the Green River in 1848, but mountain men supplied from Fort Bridger and associating with the Snake Indians saw the possibilities; when David Cosad reached the river on June 15, 1849, he wrote: "There are about 40 French men that came thare in A. D. 1814 they ware drove from canida they keep a ferry which we had to pay $3.00 for Each Wagon, they live in Indian stile with the Squaws for Wives & many half Bloods children & the hansomest horses I ever Saw, they handle a large quantity of money, & manage the Indians to Suit themselves." None of the "French" ferrymen is named in 1849, but next year John Steele found Jim Baker and one McDonald owners of a ferry. The Green was high and swift in 1849, and no one seems to have forded before Samuel McCoy on July 29.

51. Dr. T. may be this Dr. William L. Thomas, but his journal just fails to establish the fact. The last entries in the Bancroft Library transcript read:

"Friday 22nd. Crossed the river this morning without any difficulty—Sold 100 lbs Bacon for $7.00   Bought some mockasins etc—This ferry is kept by some French traders. They have squaw wives and a portion of the Snake tribe of Indians are also encamped with them—This tribe of Indians are the most honorable and civilized I have seen—If you make them presents they will thankfully receive them, but begging they detest. They are a fine looking race of beings. We only traveled 6 miles today over a winding road through mountain after mountain. Encamped on a small creek, found good grass, water and wood.

"Saturday 23rd. Remained in camp yesterday mending or rather altering Harness, our mules resting" [and here, still describing events of the day before, the transcript breaks off].

52. This was perhaps the James Roach mentioned in a St. Joseph letter of April 17 in the *Missouri Republican*, April 23, 1849. The "Albany Overland Association" was made up of James Roach, D. R. Haswell, B. F. Post, J. A. Becker, Henry Steele, Dr. E. Toker, N. Gazaway, Charles S. Perry and A. S. Brayton.

53. It would have been a service to history had Pritchard named this "Old Chief," who was not Washakie, soon to be the best known of all Shoshoni. General John Wilson, "Salt Lake Indian Agent," writing from Fort Bridger on August 22, 1849, said, "The principal chiefs of the Sho-sho-nies are *Mono*, (about 45 years old) so called from a wound in his face or cheek from a ball,

that disfigures him; *Wiskin*, (Cut-hair) *Washikick*, (Gourd Rattle) with whom I have had an interview; and *Oapiche*, (Big man.)" See Dale L. Morgan, "Washakie and the Shoshoni," *Annals of Wyoming*, vol. 25, July, 1953, p. 146.

54. William H. Russell's party, enumerated in the *Missouri Republican*, April 23, 1849, had set out on April 21. He had first gone out to California in 1846, traveling with Edwin Bryant. The Monroe, Michigan, company which included Delos Ashley was still with Russell's party at this time. The Russell party was one of the very few in 1849 which traveled the Old Oregon Trail via Fort Bridger; John F. Lewis heard from Jim Bridger on July 11 that only 15 wagons had gone that way. Another who went by this route in 1849 was David Pease; and part of the Regiment of Mounted Riflemen, including Dr. Moses, marched thus to Bear River.

55. Below Thomas Fork the Bear dips to the south. The emigrants of 1849, like the modern highway, climbed across this bend.

56. Bruff on August 15 "Saw a grave on the 3d hill side on left [after crossing Thomas Fork], about 3 ms. from creek. On the head was a rude wooden cross, on which was pencilled:—'An Indian Squaw; June 27th, 1849, Kill'd by a fall from a horse, near this place: Calm be her sleep, and sweet her rest. Be kind to the Indian.' "

57. The mountain man Thomas L. (Pegleg) Smith enlivens the diaries of many Forty-niners. Born at Crab Orchard, Kentucky, in 1801, he went to Santa Fe in Alexander LeGrande's caravan in 1824, and for the next several years was active in the fur trade of the Southwest. In 1827-1828, while a member of Pratte and St. Vrain's party trapping the North Platte and the Green, his leg was shattered, and he performed the necessary amputation himself, recovering to get about afterwards on a cork or wooden leg. From 1845 his name often occurs in the area between Fort Bridger and Fort Hall; it is evident that he had been living among the Shoshoni for some years. His trading post on the Bear dates from 1848. In April of that year Joseph L. Meek, eastbound with dispatches from Oregon, was given a letter in which Pegleg announced his intention of establishing at the Big Timbers on Bear River just such a trading post as Pritchard and others came upon in 1849; this appeared in the St. Joseph *Adventure* of May 19, 1848. Parke on July 17, 1849, referred to "Ft. Smith" as being "at '*Big Timber*' "; and Isaac Lord on August 3 observed: " 'pegleg Smith' . . . who lives in a log house four or five miles east of camp, conceived the idea in the spring of '48, of raising vegetables and grains, and packed a plough, tools and seed from Salt Lake, bringing a Mormon to assist him. From various causes he failed in every thing except a few messes of peas. The wheat which promised fair and had reached eighteen inches in height, 'Had

not yet filled its husk, when from the hills A swarm of fierce black crickets rushing down Swept it away.' At Salt Lake, when they make a descent, the Mormons meet them with the whole population and drive them back or kill them. I give all this on the authority of Smith and his Mormon, not vouching for the truth, for Smith is a '*customer*' and they are ready now, to shoot each other—indeed did threaten it only day before yesterday."

Contrary to a story Wistar tells, Pegleg did not engage in an Independence saloon brawl in the spring of 1849; in the Latter-day Saints Church Historian's office is some correspondence Pegleg had with Brigham Young in May and June, 1849, which shows that he had wintered on Bear River and had been far from well at the time. Corroboratively, William E. Chamberlain on July 8 remarked that during the preceding severe winter Pegleg had "fed a great many Indians on his beef and horses and saved them from starvation."

The earliest diarists to mention Pegleg and his post, which was near present Dingle, Idaho, were Boyle and Decker on June 24. Dr. Boyle wrote, "Smith is a jolly but one-legged man commonly known as Peg-legged Smith. . . . I here got a bowl of bread and milk from a Mormon woman. It was quite good. Prescribed for a Frenchman who lives here with a squaw. Saw a Delaware Indian, Jim Hill, a fine-looking fellow. He is married to a Nez Perce squaw. He had not been home for eight years. Smith has many horses and cattle." Decker added that Smith was making $100 a day by his trading activities. Jasper M. Hixson on June 25 said the trading post "consists of four log cabins and some Indian lodges." Chamberlain on July 8 observed that Pegleg had "a cabin across the river," and "a squaw for a wife & is quite rich," "a man of about 50 to 55 years of age, rather portly, round headed. . . . has a large no. of cattle & horses & 2 pigs." Israel Hale on July 16 added, "His squaw is about sixteen, rather bulky than otherwise. She has one child, a boy, and a spoiled child." Bruff, the last to mention Pegleg in 1849, does so on August 15. After that, he vanishes from Bear River. His post was prosperous enough in 1849, yet no diarist of 1850 records his presence. Perhaps he hied himself to California with the tail end of the emigration, or went down to Great Salt Lake City and afterwards to California. He was there in 1852, and is next heard from early in 1854, when he turns up in California at the head of a party searching for the never-yet-found "Pegleg's Lost Gold Mine." By the early sixties he was living in San Francisco, and he died there in October, 1866.

The Mormon with Pegleg, Isaac Brown, received considerable attention from the Forty-niners, but only Osborne Cross names him; Brown had been associated with Pegleg at least from the summer of 1848. Among others, Boyle, Geiger, Mann, and John E. Brown refer to the Mormon, his wife, and his children on Bear River in 1849. (There are some references to Mormons in the plural; it would seem from Joseph A. Stuart's account that the other was Elijah [Barney] Ward, the only mountain man ever converted by the Saints.) Brown is definitely known to have been in Salt Lake in the fall of 1849, and he accompanied Parley P. Pratt on an exploration of southern Utah the following winter. By the summer of 1850, as recorded in Albert K. Thurber's journal, he was in Mormon service in California. He was evidently killed by Paiutes the same year, while returning to Utah on the southern road; see *L. D. S. Millennial Star*, vol. 14, January 15, 1852, p. 19.

58. Soda or Beer Springs are described by nearly every diarist. The springs now lie beneath the waters of the Soda Point Reservoir. Pritchard's latitudes and longitudes, as before, come from Frémont via Ware's *Guide*.

59. Here, at the great bend of the Bear, was the point of departure for the Hudspeth Cutoff, opened just 20 days later by a company of Missourians captained by Benoni M. Hudspeth and guided by John J. Myers. As early as 1845, in his *Emigrants' Guide to Oregon and California*, Lansford W. Hastings had argued for a road to California that would cut off the long northward bend to Fort Hall, and in 1846 he opened the Hastings Cutoff west from Fort Bridger as his own answer to the need. The formidable Salt Desert, among other disadvantages, militated against the acceptance of the Hastings Cutoff, but the logic of a shorter route persisted. Perhaps the first direct forecast of what became the Hudspeth Cutoff was by Levi Scott, who in 1846 had helped pioneer the Applegate Cutoff to Oregon; in a letter of October 25, 1847, printed in the Oregon City *Oregon Spectator*, November 11, 1847, he expressed belief that a cutoff could be made from the end of the Greenwood Cutoff to the head of Raft River. Jesse Applegate himself, in a waybill printed in the *Spectator*, April 6, 1848, similarly said, "From where Greenwood's cut-off enters the Bear river valley on a direct course (nearly E. & W.) to the head of Cajeux creek is less than 100 miles, by the road it is 225. There is nothing to prevent wagons from making this cut-off, but some 6 or 7 miles of rough road in descending into Cache valley; this might be examined, and its practicability determined in a day or two." He added, "Mr. Anderson and many other mountaineers you will meet with on Bear river are well acquainted with this route and would conduct a party through for a trifle. I would advise emigrants to examine, and if practicable to make this cut-off, it will avoid some bad roads and save seven or eight days travel."

Bear Lake, and the mountains which wall it in, prevented any such easy access to Cache Valley from the west end of the Greenwood Cutoff, but from Soda Springs a practicable route was subsequently found, which saved a day or two of travel. It is interesting that Holt and Applegate correctly foresaw that the cutoff would strike upon Raft River, for Henry R. Mann, writing on July

24, 1849, of the emergence upon Raft River of "Messrs. Hedspeth and Myers of the Jackson Co. Mo. Co.," said, "They intended to come out at the head of Mary's River, but not understanding their true latitude have struck the old road before it crosses the dividing ridge to the Basin. They would have made some 200 miles on the old road had they succeeded, but as it is they have made nothing. They were almost thunderstruck, when upon emerging they found they were only 70 miles from Fort Hall." Small though the saving in distance was, the opening of the cutoff pinched off travel via Fort Hall, instantly and almost completely. After the opening of the cutoff on July 19, a theme developed by J. S. Holliday in a forthcoming book on the Gold Rush, of all the diarists reported on the chart, only Tate and Caldwell traveled to Fort Hall as members of a company; Bruff visited the fort seeking information, but his company meanwhile traveled the cutoff. As remarked in Note 7, Mrs. Paul Campbell has established that it was Benoni Morgan Hudspeth, rather than James M. Hudspeth, who made this contribution to overland travel.

60. After turning north the previous day along the western edge of the Soda Spring Hills, Pritchard had gone on to Tenmile Creek and Tenmile Spring. This day he veered more westerly to the upper Portneuf River — which, because here it flows southward, many Forty-niners supposed was an affluent of the Bear. Pritchard actually crossed the Rim of the Great Basin in traversing the low plain in upper Gem Valley. He then continued up the Portneuf and encamped at the foot of the divide between the Portneuf proper and Ross's Fork, which he and many others conceived to be the Rim.

61. The Bannock Indians, closely related to the Shoshoni, ranged widely through Idaho and neighboring States. When, a few lines farther on, Pritchard mentions "Senika's," he possibly refers to some Flatheads.

62. Established on the Snake a few miles above the mouth of the Portneuf by Nathaniel J. Wyeth in 1834, and sold to the Hudson's Bay Company three years later, Fort Hall was the farthest outpost of the British fur trade in the old Oregon country, still maintained though this part of Oregon had passed under United States sovereignty in the boundary settlement of 1846. The factor was Richard Grant. Cosad, the first diarist to arrive, said on June 24, "bought beef at 8d butter at 2p cheese 2p. . . . Saw Some white woman the first we had Seen in over two months." The woman was one of a Mormon family, or perhaps several families, who attracted the attention of Forty-niners starved for a little civilization. Boyle on June 29 wrote: "We halted at the fort for a couple of hours to regale ourselves on bread and milk. . . . A Mormon family had moved hither from Salt Lake City for the purpose of supplying emigrants with articles of this kind and had brought a large number of cows. Butter was

very scarce as they sold it as fast as they could make it. Cheese brought 25 cents per pound, [milk] 12½ cents per quart. . . . I here saw and smoked with some Flat-Heads . . . and saw some Mexicans and French Canadians, who had Indian wives. Snake Indians were plenty here and so were Pamaches [Bannocks]. . . ."

Similarly, Hixson commented on June 30, "A man by the name of Grant had charge, but there were a lot of Mormons here who appeared to have charge of the cattle, of which there was a herd of some 300 head, as fine fat animals as one ever saw in the best stock farms in the Western States. They made plenty of good milk, butter and cheese. We had a feast of white biscuits with no sand in them, good milk and fresh butter. . . . We found a fine supply of buckskin and mountain sheepskin clothing, and moccasins, etc., much cheaper than at Peg Leg Smith's. . . . There were a few Mormon women and children who seemed to be happy and contented. They were evidently making money, for they had quite a large number of cows to milk, and between making butter and cheese and preparing meals for the emigrants, they had enough to do. . . ."

Bruff, the last Forty-niner to visit the fort, on August 24 described it and its commander in extraordinary detail. He also described Cantonment Loring, established 5 miles from Fort Hall by the Regiment of Mounted Riflemen, and garrisoned until the spring of 1850, when the troops went on to Oregon.

63. These developments mark the final break-up of the party from Boone County, Kentucky; not one of his original companions accompanied Pritchard the rest of the way to California.

64. The ferocity of the wild life in the Snake River bottoms universally impressed the Forty-niners; Buffum on July 9 spoke for all when he wrote that he "breathed, fought, bled, and died almost with mosquitoes."

65. At American Falls a great dam has been built to impound the waters of the Snake. Much of Pritchard's trail from Fort Hall was across land now flooded by the American Falls Reservoir.

66. Pritchard was well ahead of the foremost Oregon train of 1849, with which David Pease traveled; Pease did not arrive at this road junction for another ten days. Thereafter came William Watson on July 22, Lewis Baldwin on July 30, and the military diarists, Osborne Cross and Israel Moses, on August 11.

67. The name Cash—or Cassia or Cashier or Cassue; there are several dozen variants—derives from the term *cajeux* long ago applied by French peasants to small rafts. Thus it is simply a translation of the name of Raft River, applied during the era of the North West Company in the Snake Country, 1818-1821. See the note by Crawford Lindsay in R. G. Thwaites, ed., *The Jesuit Relations and Allied Documents* (Cleveland, 1898), vol. 31, p. 313,

where in connection with a usage of 1648 it is explained that the term *cajeul* or *cajeux* is "not found in the dictionaries [but is] used by the peasants to mean 'a small raft,'—probably a diminutive of *cage*, the French-Canadian term for large rafts of logs or square timber. *Cage* is used by the voyageurs and lumbermen in place of *train-de-bois*, the proper French term." For examples of the persistence of the word, see the *Original Journals of Lewis and Clark* (New York, 1904), vol. I, pp. 34, 36, 40, 44, 48; other examples are found among the Chouteau Papers in the Missouri Historical Society. The name Cassia is now applied to a western fork of Raft River and to an Idaho county.

68. Although Pritchard well describes the mountainous character of the City of Rocks area, and later the valley leading out of the basin, Cosad on June 28 had a better eye for some details: "Passed several trains   went up a Small stream   travled over rocks So large that the wagon would hardly pass over them nooned at rock Citty a place surounded by verry high rocks of the limestone order hardly a place left for the wagon to pass out." The name City of Rocks emerged next year, but Jagger, referring to "the Monumental Rocks or the City Rocks," like Cosad closely anticipated the name.

Cosad at this time was in advance of all the diarists who traveled via Fort Hall, and on reaching the junction with the Salt Lake Cutoff beyond the southern exit to City of Rocks, he added, "Squire Curl overtoock us with several other packers that left us at Fort Larymy & had been to Salt Lake   Joined our train again." A comparison of Cosad's travel time with Johnston's shows the difference it made, going by way of Salt Lake. J. L. Moody of Johnston's party wrote on August 7, 1849, that 70 wagons got ahead of them from this cause.

Johnston's party with their five wagons reached the junction on July 2; these may well have been the first Forty-niner wagons on that route, and Pritchard's information is that in the six days since then, some 25 other wagons had come along. Four would have belonged to Kelly's party on July 4, four to Breyfogle's on July 5, and four to "Captain Lewis' train" which joined Breyfogle's Delaware company on June 29 while northbound from Salt Lake. No diaries by packers in advance of Johnston have appeared, and Cosad's is the earliest mention of them. On the basis of a June 16 arrival at Salt Lake, as set forth in the Introduction, packers might have arrived at City of Rocks from the Mormon settlements as early as June 23. As another point of view, on the emigration as a whole, when Breyfogle reached the junction on July 5 he remarked that there were "about one hundred and fifty waggons ahead of us, and a host close behind us."

69. It appears that one of the returning Mormon companies of 1848 discovered mica on Goose Creek. The tale of this discovery was carried to the world, and most Forty-niners were on the *qui vive* for yellow metal while ascending Goose Creek. Pritchard reached this stream from City of Rocks by a sharp climb up over Granite Mountain.

70. The California Trail followed up Goose Creek to where it bore away to the northwest, then turned southwest across a divide to Thousand Springs Valley, in 1849 usually called Warm or Hot Springs Valley. There were two sub-basins, the first sometimes called Well Springs Valley, the second Hot Springs Valley proper; confusion between them makes for some inexactitude on the chart as to date of arrival. When ascertainable, the date of reaching the Hot Spring is the one reflected on the chart.

71. The sick man is subsequently identified as a Mr. Stuart (a W. G. and a J. J. Stewart had set out in Edwin Bryant's company). Pritchard carried a copy of the book his fellow Kentuckian had published after his journey to California in 1846 and return next year; and indeed Edwin Bryant was one of the notables on the trail in 1849. In December, 1848, and January, 1849, he had published in Louisville newspapers counsel to intending emigrants (reprinted in the *Jefferson* [Missouri] *Inquirer*, December 23, 1848, and March 31, 1849). The *Missouri Republican* on April 17, 1849, listed 48 men then comprising his company; and one of these was Charles F. Dulany, several of whose MS. letters are in the Bancroft Library. Various diarists mention the passage of Bryant's pack train west along the trails. Pritchard is here noting contact only with a detachment from Bryant's party, but beginning July 15 he makes many references to the main company. In the Bancroft collection a letter, H. W. Dulany to Robert Dulany, Louisville, October 16, 1849, quotes a letter Charles had written from Sacramento August 7, saying he had got to Johnson's Ranch on August 3 "after a very long & fatiguing journey of about 85 days. . . . Moor & Murry left our Company at Ft Hall thinking they could travel more expeditiously with a small party."

72. Again Pritchard is not clear on the geography of the Great Basin—no one could be, in 1849. He had re-entered the Great Basin on crossing over from Goose Creek to Thousand Springs Valley. Where Pritchard made this comment, he had a choice of two routes to the Humboldt Valley, one more southerly by way of the Humboldt Wells (which, it would seem from the diary of Jacob R. Snyder, was first traveled by emigrants in 1845 [see Society of California Pioneers, *Quarterly*, vol. 8, December, 1931, pp. 203-260]), or the original wagon road of 1843-1844 down Bishops or Canyon Creek. This latter route Mormons had used eastbound the previous year, and again, it would seem, westbound in the spring of 1849. Pritchard and other early Forty-niners seem to have taken the route via Wells; when Hackney came to the junction on August 2 and took the canyon road, he noted that it had scarcely been traveled this season. Several afterwards, Israel Hale among them, made the same choice; in their diaries the description of the canyon, and of the hot spring in it, is unmistakable. Confusingly, some of the diarists—Burbank, for one—call this canyon road

the "new" road. The two trails came back together again near present Deeth.

73. The North Fork was sometimes erroneously referred to in 1849 as Martin's Fork. Frémont in 1848 had given the Humboldt its name, in preference to the names Ogden's, Mary's, and St. Mary's, previously used by trappers. Pritchard was now descending the north bank of the Humboldt, on which he remained all the way to the Sink. In prior years, emigrants had traveled on the south bank for considerable distances, but as the Forty-niners were earlier on the trail than travelers of the past, they doubtless found the river at a stage which made fording difficult. Those who came along behind tended to follow in the beaten track, but the need for grass exerted a counter-influence for south-bank travel below Gravelly Ford; Hinman on August 18 mentions that some had descended the river on the south side.

74. Osino Canyon, northeast of present Elko.

75. This detour became derisively known as the "Greenhorn Cutoff," but it was not greenhorns only who had to leave the river road when high water prevented the descent of Moleen Canyon. Tappan on August 7 calls the river road the "Mormon" trail.

76. Because the Humboldt could not be followed through Palisade Canyon, from his campsite at present Carlin Pritchard ascended the hills and continued on to present Emigrant Springs (virtually the same route used today by highway US 40), then swung back to the river at Gravelly Ford, near Beowawe. Still keeping to the north bank, during the afternoon Pritchard traveled through the hills parallel to the river, and finally camped on it below Dunphy, where the Humboldt Valley opens out as a wide plain.

77. Some further information on this tragedy is given by D. H. Moss, in a letter of August 17, 1849, written two days after reaching Sacramento (reprinted in Walker D. Wyman, *California Emigrant Letters* [New York, 1952], pp. 63-66). "Mr. Hugh Riddle, late of Baltimore," he says, "received a mortal wound on Mary's river about 100 miles after striking the head of it; he stepped out some ten steps from his pile of packs at a late hour of the night to see about his mules, and was discovered near the mule by a fellow called Kirkwood, a great poltroon and fool doubtlessly, but not knowing whom it was, hailed him three times, (so said) but getting no reply to his question shot him while in a few yards of camp. . . . He was shot on the night of 17th of June, and died on the morning of the 19th."

78. Among those who remarked Bryson's grave were Bennett C. Clark on July 25, Chamberlain on July 27, Biddle on August 6, and Mann on August 10. Biddle, whose journal enables us to locate the site of the grave as near present Redhouse, observed it as that of E. A. Bryson, aged 34, of Louisville, Kentucky.

By September 11, when Bruff came past, the inscription was already nearly obliterated.

79. Pritchard camped this night near the great bend of the Humboldt, north of Winnemucca.

80. These marshes, or meadows, extending for many miles below Winnemucca, became known as Lassen's Meadows. On them teams were recruited for the desert crossings ahead.

81. The "16-mile" stretch Pritchard describes, which cut across the bend of the Humboldt in which Mill City stands today, was termed by Hinman on August 21 "the Mormon cutoff," and not all Forty-niners traveled it. During the subsequent 6 miles of "night travel" Pritchard passed the junction with a southern road to Oregon opened in 1846, the Applegate Cutoff. The previous year Peter Lassen had led a small company of California emigrants west on this trail, turning south toward the Sacramento Valley after reaching Goose Lake, near the Oregon-California border. Beginning August 11, 1849, many Forty-niners chose this route, thereafter known as the "Lassen Cutoff"; they were frightened by tales of the lack of grass farther down the Humboldt, and of the sufferings of emigrants on the desert beyond the Sink, and simultaneously they were excited by reports that via this new route it was only 150 miles to the diggings. Few took the circuitous Lassen Cutoff but afterward regretted it. A superb contemporary map of the Lassen Cutoff is that of J. Goldsborough Bruff, reproduced in the present volume; another map of the Cutoff by him is reproduced in Georgia Willis Read and Ruth P. Gaines, eds., *Gold Rush* (New York, 1944), p. 1222.

The date the first trains entered on the Lassen Cutoff is fixed by B. R. Biddle, who on August 11 wrote: "The Oregon route will be left, a few days after taking it, and a trail taken to the left which was traveled, last season, with thirteen wagons, by a man named Clareson [Lassen], who has since settled on Feather River, and has given Messrs. [Milton] McGee and [J. J.] Myers, two mountain traders, a description of the road, which induced them to take it, this morning, with eleven teams. Others are following them during the day...." Previously it had been thought, from a notation by Josselyn on arriving at the Cutoff August 13, that the date of the event was August 12. It will be seen from the chart that Biddle and Josselyn, on September 10 and 11, are the earliest diarists to arrive at Lassen's via the Cutoff; and it is interesting to note how diarists arriving at the junction after August 11 decided for or against the "new route"; 41 finally went this way, more than took any other single road, though during the entire season 69 traveled the combined Carson-Truckee road to the Sink of the Humboldt.

82.   Pritchard has now reached the vicinity of Lovelock, made a productive agricultural area by the Rye Patch Dam on the Humboldt.

83.   Near present Miriam. Johnston, who reached this point about noon on July 15, says his party found it necessary to dig wells which, "about four feet in diameter and of a trifle less depth, furnished an abundant supply of water, but intensely brackish, bitter with salt and sulphur."

84.   In Pritchard's "salt creek" flowed the dregs of the Humboldt, from the lowermost reaches of "Humboldt Slough" out upon the Carson Sink, where in wet years its waters mingled with those of the decaying Carson River. Just beyond this creek, "excessively salt and utterly unfit to drink," as Johnston noted on the early evening of July 15, "the trail forked, the road to the right leading to the northern pass of the Sierra Nevada, via Truckee River; whilst the other . . . led to Carson River, and a more southerly pass."

This fork in the trail came about 2 miles north of present Parran, on the Southern Pacific Railroad. The road to and up the difficult canyon of the Truckee, pioneered in 1844, offered water of a kind at the Boiling Springs (now Springers Hot Springs on highway US 40), nearly midway in the journey to the life-giving Truckee, but no good water at all could be had on the Carson road, short of the river itself; here the Forty-mile Desert commenced in earnest.

The Mormons of 1848, after opening their road across the Sierra and down the Carson River, had turned northwest from the northernmost bend of the Carson to strike the Truckee at its great bend (the same route used today by the highway from Fallon to Wadsworth), afterwards turning at right angles to head for the Sink of the Humboldt past the Boiling Springs. Joseph Chiles, west-bound with 48 wagons that same summer, having learned from the Mormons of their new road, conjectured that he could cut across the angle of the Mormon trail, and being successful in doing so, established the arduous route across the Forty-mile Desert Pritchard was now following. Knowing only of the intention, and not of the accomplishment, the handwritten Best Guide to the Gold Mines, got out by Ira J. Willis at Great Salt Lake City in the summer of 1849, and sold to many of the Forty-niners, advised at the Sink of the Humboldt, "Here . . . you may find a new track on your left that Childs intended to make last fall which may be nearer & a less distance to do without grass & water." If the Battalion road was taken instead, it was 20 miles to the Boiling Springs, 25 to the Truckee, then 25 miles southeast to the Carson. (See Irene D. Paden, ed., "The Ira J. Willis Guide to the Gold Mines," *California Historical Society Quarterly*, vol. 32, September, 1953, pp. 193-207, in which the Guide is printed from an original MS. in the James M. Hutchings Papers in the Yosemite Museum.)

85. As Pritchard intimates, Forty-niners ahead of him had had some griev-
ous experiences getting across the Forty-mile Desert. All diarists who preceded
him, Cosad, Johnston, Kelly, Hixson, Ashley, Boyle, Decker, and Breyfogle,
have graphic tales to tell. Boyle and Decker remained in the desert with the
wagons of the Columbus company from the night of the 23rd to the evening
of the 25th, while Breyfogle of the Delaware company was stranded from the
23rd to the 26th. Breyfogle's is a particularly arresting account. On the afternoon of the 25th he wrote, "About midnight the trains of emigrants commenced
passing untill daylight or sunrise when they ceased passing as they cannot cross in
daylight on account of the heat of the weather and sand. . . . Two Irishmen
came along this afternoon with one horse. Two of their horses fell into a well
about six miles back and they had to go on with only one and would hardly get
to the river." Next morning he mentioned drinking the last of his water, and
said again, "From twelve o'clock till sunrise the emigrants are passing in crowds,
nearly perishing for water, and are leaving mules, horses and oxen to starve on
the plains for they can't drive them on. I don't know what will become of the
back trains." It was about dark on the 26th that "the boys came out to haul us
in," and Breyfogle reached the Carson about sunrise on July 27, a few hours
ahead of Pritchard; "this was," he wrote, "the most horrid night I ever passed.
The road was strewd with the carcasses of dead mules, horses and cattle, and
most of them with pieces of the flesh cut out by the Indians. . . ."

86. The trail reached the Carson at what became known as Ragtown, about
7 miles northwest of present Fallon. The trail across the desert ran about midway
between the present line of the Southern Pacific Railroad and the modern road
between Fallon and Lovelock.

87. On the 29th Breyfogle of the Delaware company, again taking up the
journey, thought it possible his party might not get a horse across the mountains,
but "still we are well off compared to those behind us. There is about four
thousand wagons behind that will have to pass about three hundred miles with-
[out] any grass and very little water. There must hundreds perish on the plains.
The forty-five mile stretch is now almost impassible on account of the stench
of the dead animals along the road which is literally lined with them and there
is scarcely a single train or wagon but leaves one or more dead animal, so that
it must be getting worse every day."

Such tales were carried back across the Forty-mile Desert all the way to the
Sink. Bennett C. Clark on August 2 encountered a man "who had been through
the lower or new road in advance of his train and returned to advise them to
take the old road. He gives a wretched description of the state of things on that
rout & says many wagons had been deserted on the route as the teams had failed.
What water there was, was saline & unwholesome." Two days later, having

moved along to the sulphur wells, Clark wrote: "We saw a man here who had just returned by the left hand road & he gave a horrid account of the teams that had gone that way. A general panic now seezed upon all & doubt & fear prevailed every where." His party already had decided to take the Truckee road, but the chart brings out an interesting development in the number of diarists who made for the Truckee during the first week of August, Buffum, Tinker, Long, Clark himself, and Chamberlain going that route within a space of four days, while only six diarists are recorded as arriving on the Carson River for nearly five weeks after Pritchard. However, Mann wrote at the Sink on August 26, on taking the Truckee road, "there being no one ahead of us for two weeks all th[e] teams having gone the Southern road for some time past—They have now begun to take this road again."

No known diarist reached the Truckee before Buffum got there on August 2, but the route had been used; from Note 71 above it is apparent that Bryant's party went via the Truckee about the same time that Pritchard made for the Carson. If the sampling from the diaries is representative, more Forty-niners used the Truckee than the Carson route in 1849, as 37 diarists went via the Truckee, 32 via the Carson.

88. Pritchard came back to the Carson some miles east of present Dayton. Next day he left the river at Dayton, and returned to it where Empire later stood.

89. Here Nevada's capital, Carson City, stands today.

90. This was the Delaware company, whose fortunes Breyfogle records. On July 29 he had observed, "We have now twenty horses and a wagon and a half, and if it keeps such roads, we will not get a horse across the mountains. . . ." After nooning with Pritchard on August 2, and camping near him at the mouth of Carson Canyon on the 3rd and again in Hope Valley on the 4th, the Delaware company moved slightly ahead, staying ahead the rest of the way to the diggings.

91. Also noted by Ashley on July 31, these are the springs now called Walleys Hot Springs, 1¾ miles south of present Genoa. At the latter place a trading post called Mormon Station was commenced in 1850, the first settlement in Nevada.

92. Called "Pass Creek Canyon" by the Mormons the previous year, and—in consequence of Willis' Best Guide to the Gold Mines—also so called by many of the Forty-niners, this was Carson Canyon, through which flows the West Fork of the Carson. Reaching its mouth at present Woodford on July 29, 1849, Hixson had noted: "At the entrance to this canon was a register of those ahead with wagons. All told there were eighty-three—our two making to date

eighty-five." William G. Johnston asserts that his party, which entered the canyon with five wagons on July 20, and got through next day, was the first among the Forty-niners to take wagons across the Sierra, those ahead being packers, but Joseph L. Moody of this party wrote on August 7, 1849, that theirs was the 10th wagon to reach the Sacramento Valley.

93. Cosad and Johnston say the bridges had been made by the Mormons. Compare the diary of Henry W. Bigler with the eastbound Mormons of 1848, in *Utah Historical Quarterly*, vol. 6, October, 1932, pp. 148-160.

94. This company of Utah-bound Mormons inspirited many of the Forty-niners, and made a corresponding impact on the diaries; meetings are recorded from July 23 (Cosad) to September 15 (Hutchings and Judge). Some of them had come to California around the Horn with Sam Brannan in 1846, as Pritchard observes; and the company was in charge of Thomas Rhoads. They had left Sacramento July 14, if Kimball Webster is correct. Besides their own gleanings from the gold fields, they carried east over $4,000 in tithing collected by Amasa Lyman from the Saints in California, and sent to Brigham Young in Thomas Grover's care; consequently they traveled in fear of violence, as related by one of their number, William Glover (in a Bancroft Library MS., *The Mormons in California*, edited by Paul Bailey, Los Angeles, 1954). They reached Salt Lake at last on September 28. The diaries of Bruff in particular are rich in information obtained from these Mormons; and of special interest is Lord's comment on September 2 — Rhoads was then, Lord says, 48 days from Sutter's. "Met the first packers the second day, then mule and ox teams together, and the second week met little else than ox trains."

95. Having reached Hope Valley at the head of Carson Canyon the day before, Pritchard turned south to Red Lake, beyond which he began the ascent of Kit Carson Pass, 8,573 feet above sea level.

96. Even next year, emigrants believed Lake Valley to be the source of the South Fork of the American River, but it gives rise to the Upper Truckee, above Lake Tahoe; Pritchard had not yet crossed the main divide.

97. It has scarcely been known that Lansford Warren Hastings had a brother. Born in Ohio in 1819, Hastings went overland to Oregon in 1842, thence to California and back to the States. In Cincinnati in 1845 he published his celebrated *Emigrants' Guide to Oregon and California*, and later the same year returned to California, taking grave risks by a belated journey. Next spring he traveled east to beyond South Pass and persuaded a number of emigrants, including the Donner-Reed party tragically famous ever after, to attempt his new cutoff to the Humboldt. (See J. Roderic Korns, "West from Fort Bridger," published as *Utah Historical Quarterly*, vol. 19, 1951, for a comprehensive

account of these events.) Afterward he served as an officer in Frémont's California Battalion and actively engaged in real estate speculation, politics, and the practice of law. In later years he pioneered in Arizona mining, intrigued for the Confederacy, and was largely involved in Brazilian colonizing activities when he died in the 1870's.

From information furnished by the California State Library, the brother on the trail in 1849 was probably Daniel Ephraim Hastings, listed in the Sacramento County Census, October, 1852, as 23 years old, and Ohio-born. Afterwards he lived at Sutterville, where he was killed by an accidental gunshot wound, September 1, 1867. His obituary, in the Sacramento *Daily Union* next day, mentions a brother then living at Latrobe, California, James Hannum Hastings, who is also listed in the El Dorado County *Great Register of Voters*, 1867, as born in Ohio, age not stated.

98. The tragedy occurred, it was believed, on June 27, 1848. David Browitt, Daniel Allen, and Henderson Cox had gone ahead of their brethren to look out a road. They were slain by Indians, apparently while sleeping. The occurrence gave name to Tragedy Spring and Tragedy Creek, source waters of Bear River, one of the heads of the Mokelumne.

99. Leek Spring rises near the head of the North Fork of the Cosumnes River. The road from this point on was a ridge road, first between the waters of the South Fork of the American River and those of the North Fork of the Cosumnes; afterward between the latter and Webber Creek. The emigrant road of 1849 kept at all times south of highway US 50, which today crosses Echo Summit south of Lake Tahoe and afterward descends the canyon of the South Fork of the American.

100. Weaverville has so completely disappeared from the map that it is sometimes confounded by students with the town of the same name in Trinity County; it was situated on Weaver or Webber Creek at its junction with Ringgold Creek. These names are corruptions of Weber. E. Gould Buffum, *Six Months in the Gold Mines* (Philadelphia, 1850), pp. 92-93, relates: "The diggings upon Weaver's Creek were first wrought by a German, Charles M. Weber, a *ranchero* on the San Joaquin, who went thither in the early part of June [1848]. He carried with him articles of trade, and soon gathered around him a thousand Indians, who worked for him in consideration of the necessaries of life and of little trinkets that so win an Indian's heart. He was soon joined by William Dalor . . . and the two . . . soon realized at least fifty thousand dollars. By this time, individual labourers began to come in, and one of Dalor's men one morning started into the hills for newer and fresher diggings. He struck what was formerly called the 'dry diggings,' but which now goes by the euphonious name of 'Hang-town'. . . ."

Dr. Boyle, who like Pritchard visited Hangtown on August 11, writes that he "encamped under the widespread branches of a beautiful oak tree in the center of a little valley where we found some houses. We soon learned that this was the gallows tree as three men were hanged upon it six months before for robbery and murder, after a fair trial by a jury of miners, as has been the custom in this country." Now better known as Placerville, Hangtown received its name from the lynching in January, 1849, of three men accused of robbery and attempted murder on the Stanislaus River; E. Gould Buffum was an eyewitness.

101. Dr. Boyle, visiting Coloma on August 14, said "the town is small and is built of logs, frames and cloth houses and is populated by Americans and foreigners from all parts of the world." On August 20 he said further that Coloma was "situated on the southeast bank of the South Fork of the American Fork of the Sacramento. This is the place where gold was first discovered in this country. While digging at Sutter's saw mill the discovery was made [January 24, 1848] by a Mr. [James W.] Marshall, who is now as poor as any one need wish to be. The houses are either log huts, or frames; shingled and weather-boarded with cloth." A very early account of the gold discovery was written by Marshall himself from Coloma April 2, 1849, reprinted in the New York *Herald*, June 27, 1849.

102. The "Embarcadero," or landing, lay just below the fort John A. Sutter had founded in 1839 and called New Helvetia. E. Gould Buffum, *op. cit.*, p. 32, comments: "The beautiful plain on which is now located the thriving and populous city of Sacramento, was, when I first landed there [October, 1848], untenanted. There was not a house upon it, the only place of business being an old store-ship laid up upon its bank. . . . [where] after a lapse of only one year, a flourishing city with a population of twelve thousand stands. . . ."

103. Redding is a phonetic rendering of the name of Pierson B. Reading, who had a ranch in the upper Sacramento Valley, and who in 1849 opened up important diggings at old Shasta City, 6 miles west of present Redding.

104. These two young men had traveled a remarkable course to reach Peter Lassen's ranch on Deer Creek, the last stretch of their journey being by the Lassen Cutoff. It would be interesting to know whether they reached Salt Lake by the more usual route north along the Front Range of the Rockies, by a route through the Uinta Basin such as was taken by the Ithaca Company (see Note 1) and by William L. Manly after his abortive effort to get to California down the Green River (see Manly's *Death Valley in '49* [San Jose, 1894]), or by the Spanish Trail. Hosea Stout might have referred to just such a party when, at Great Salt Lake City on August 6, 1849, he wrote in his diary, "Emegrants arrived here direct from Santa Fe across the mountains."

105. The second conception was correct; the Trinity flows into the Klam-

ath. Efforts were made in the winter of 1849-1850 to penetrate to the Trinity by way of its supposed mouth in Trinidad Bay, and prevalent newspaper reports account for these notations by Pritchard.

106. The flood Pritchard describes is one of the notable events in the history of Sacramento, has left a deposit in all the county histories, and still enlivens the pages of the contemporary newspapers. Breyfogle, in Sacramento at the time, wrote on January 9: "This is truly an awful night, now ten o'clock. Yesterday we had quite a rainy day and a very heavy rain all last night. This morning the river commenced rising and at this time the whole city is under water. My house on one of the highest parts of the city is now flooded, about one foot of water on the floor and the water still rising very fast. It is now rain-[in]g and likely to rain all night. We can hear the boats in every direction and around us carrying people from and too their houses. The lower part of the City must be in a deplorable state as the river, as we learn, has broken over the banks and inundated the whole lower part of the city. . . ." Next morning he wrote further, "we have about five feet of water in our house. We hailed a boat and moved across the street in the upper story of a wooden house, some fifteen of us. the whole town is from two to ten feet under water and in fact the whole country as far as the eye can reach is under water, nothing but a wild sea all around. Hundreds of families have had to leave their houses in boats and go out on the high land."

After a series of melancholy reports beginning on January 12, the San Francisco *Daily Alta California* was at last able, on February 4, 1850, to quote the Sacramento *Placer Times* of February 2 as saying, "A week of sunshine has changed the condition of the city very materially. The principal streets in the vicinity of the levee are now nearly dry, and business has commenced in most parts of the town. . . . The river is falling very rapidly. . . ." As a parting note, however, Breyfogle wrote on February 7, "Well here we are again afloat bound for the mines. . . . and we are now sailing over ten foot water over the very ground that I traveled over in October in ox teams nearly perishing for water [up the Sacramento], and now as far as the eye can extend, east, west, north and south, a ten foot sea of water."

A NOTE ON THE MAPS

The two previously unpublished maps attributed to J. Goldsborough Bruff are reproduced by courtesy of The National Archives, where they are preserved in Record Group No. 75, filemarked CA 477A and CA 477B. Although appearing as two sheets of a single map, obviously they were drawn separately, and are the east and west halves of two largely similar maps. Neither is signed, but the character of the information they contain is such that no one but J. Goldsborough Bruff could well have drafted either.

The uniquely valuable feature of the maps is that they represent the trail situation on the road to California as it was in 1849. When they were actually drawn is problematical; one at least has additions to 1850, when Humboldt Bay was explored, and Utah Territory created; and it may be that neither was constructed in this form until Bruff returned to Washington, D. C., in July, 1851. The maps were unknown to the Misses Read and Gaines when in 1944 they published their monumental edition of the Bruff papers, *Gold Rush*, though they did include in that work a reduced portion of a "Map of the United States and Their Territories between the Mississippi and the Pacific Ocean," compiled by the Corps of Topographical Engineers in 1850, a copy of which has MS. additions by Bruff; they also reproduced a sketch map by Bruff showing the Lassen Cutoff, and a good many of the small detail maps made by Bruff in his trail notebooks.

Since Bruff traveled by boat up the Missouri River to St. Joseph, then went up the river to cross at Lake House (Indian Point), Missouri, afterwards going on to the Platte via Old Fort Kearny, his map has superior detail along this line of travel. Though placenames up the Kansas River are lacking, he does show with general correctness the trails heading west from Independence and St. Joseph. Bruff gives the Little Blue geographical priority over the Big Blue, calling it Blue Fork and not naming the latter river at all. Also, as may be seen by reference to Stansbury's map, he is mistaken in showing the Independence-St. Joseph road proceeding up the south bank of the Little Blue. The Mormon Trail, on the north bank of the Platte from Council Bluffs, Bruff makes no effort to depict at all.

Trails up the Republican Fork of the Kansas, and down the Kansas proper, represent Frémont's outbound trail of 1843 to Oregon, and inbound trail of 1844 from California; these were not used by Forty-niners, so far as known. Bruff does, however, depict the Santa Fe Trail with its two principal branches from the Arkansas, used by many Forty-niners taking southern routes to California. Trails from Pueblo again are renditions of Frémont routes, but a number of goldseekers used one of these routes to enter the South Pass road at Fort Laramie.

173

The main south-bank trail would best have shown the Independence-St. Joseph road meeting that via Old Fort Kearny about 11 miles east of (New) Fort Kearny, though Howard Stansbury's map shows two slightly variant routes from the head of the Little Blue.

Afterward, up the Platte and South Platte, Bruff might have rendered more amply the complex situation presented by the several fords of the South Platte. But once on the North Platte his map is attractively detailed, showing Ash Hollow and Creek, Cathedral Rock (also so called in his journal; by others termed Castle Rock), Fort Washington Rock (not mentioned in his journal, and more usually called Jail Rock in the diaries), as well as Courthouse and Chimney rocks. A little farther along, Scotts Bluff and the (Robidoux) trading post are located, though the legend is misleadingly set back too far from the river; Horse Creek; and the grave of (Charles) Bishop, a member of Bruff's company who died of cholera on July 8, 1849. From Fort Laramie the hill road west is similarly well depicted, and Bruff's place of crossing the North Platte, just above the unnamed Deer Creek.

On the western sheet which completes the Bruff map of 1849, Deer Creek is named, and R. (or Fourche) Boise as well. A generally more complex map, this sheet shows the influence, in particular, of two other maps. It was chiefly indebted to—sometimes betrayed by—the "Map of Oregon and Upper California, from the Surveys of John Charles Frémont and other Authorities," drawn for the U. S. Senate by Charles Preuss in 1848. Bruff's rendition of the Snake Valley, the Great Salt Lake country, the desert wastes to the west, the Humboldt Valley generally, the Sierra Nevada, and the adjacent western reaches of the Great Basin, all markedly reflect this map; and some of Bruff's worst errors, reflecting country he had not seen, come from following this model, as when he makes the Old Oregon Trail from Fort Bridger ascend upper Hams Fork, places Salt Lake City on Utah Lake, and accepts the disorientation of all the south-bank tributaries of the Snake. The other map by which Bruff was influenced was T. H. Jefferson's great "Map of the Emigrant Road from Independence Mo. to St. Francisco California," published in New York in four sheets in 1849, a copy of which Bruff seems to have carried with him on the trail. Jefferson, whose map was constructed on the basis of an overland journey of 1846—going via the Hastings Cutoff from Fort Bridger to the Humboldt—principally contributed place name conceptions, his "Rock Defile" beyond the North Platte becoming "Rock Avenue Defile"; his "Saleratus Pond" coming through intact; and on the Humboldt his "Wall Defile" becoming "Rock Defile or Wall Pass" (Moleen Canyon), and his "Pauta Pass" through the "Blue Mountains" also coming through intact (this being the passage of the present Hot Spring Range, east of the great bend of the Humboldt). Bruff did not follow

Jefferson in depicting the emigrant road as it ascended the Truckee River from the great bend of that river, north of where it enters Pyramid Lake; his would have been a better map had he done so.

But Bruff's was no slavish copy of any map; it was a highly original production, and nowhere more so than for the region west of South Pass. For some reason he did not trouble to show the emigrant trail east of this point on this western sheet of his map, but he does depict from first-hand observation the course of "Greenwood's Cut-off, erroneously Soublette's" from South Pass to the Bear River; and also, quite accurately, "Soublette's Cut-off" northwest along the base of the Wind River Mountains, and on to the upper Snake below Jackson Lake. Just such a route was traveled by William L. Sublette in going to Rendezvous in 1832; and the first part of it, to Green River, after 1858 became established as a part of the Lander Cutoff. (A one-time fur trader, Joseph Thing, guiding the party in which Batchelder, Stuart, and Webster traveled in 1849, attempted to go by that very route to the Snake Valley, but west of the Green missed Lander's later route over to Salt River, and finally had to descend Smiths Fork to reach the Bear and the known trail.)

From the great bend of the Bear River at Beer or Soda Spring Bruff shows the course of the new Hudspeth Cutoff, by him called "Emigrant Cut-off," to City of Rocks, by him termed "Rock City" and "Pinnacle Pass." Here his map is most grievously damaged by Frémont-Preuss geography, with the course of the Portneuf River badly conceived, and the critically important courses of the Raft River and Goose Creek set at the wrong slant, so that the road around by Fort Hall is badly out of whack, and its course to City of Rocks not even shown (the road up the Bannock or "Pannack" River as depicted is simply Frémont's north-bound trail of 1843 after his exploration of Great Salt Lake; but Bruff does show the course of the [here unnamed] Salt Lake Cutoff around the north shore of Great Salt Lake to City of Rocks, possibly the first map to do so).

On the basis of Frémont geography, it was impossible for Bruff to show the trail ascending Goose Creek after crossing Granite Pass west of City of Rocks, and he merely leads it west into "Hot Sp. Valley" (Thousand Springs Valley), after which the Humboldt Valley offers plain sailing. Farther south, Bruff also shows what was essentially the course of the Hastings Cutoff, used intermittently from 1846 to 1850, but he renders it as Frémont's trail, westbound in 1845, and thus leaves it hanging in mid-air some distance southwest of the head of the South Fork of the Humboldt—down which stream the Hastings Cutoff took emigrants to the semi-security of the Humboldt Valley.

Marvelous as is the detail in Bruff's map for the Lassen Cutoff, west of the great bend of the Humboldt, for purposes of illustration in the present book it is sadly lacking in not showing either the Truckee or the Carson roads to the diggings—the Truckee River itself is barely indicated, and the Carson not shown at all. To supply this deficiency, a section is reproduced of a superb map by George H. Goddard, "Britton & Rey's Map of the State of California," published in San Francisco in 1857, a copy of which has been placed at my disposal by Francis P. Farquhar. With a wealth of detail found on no other map of its period, this map shows the country and the trails from the Humboldt to the Sacramento. The entire map, with many others dating from this period, has been reproduced by Carl I. Wheat in his *The Maps of the California Gold Region, 1848-1857* (San Francisco, 1942).

As one additional feature of Bruff's map, he clarifies the geography of the Trinity and Klamath river basins which leaves a deposit of confusion in the last few pages of Pritchard's journal; he also shows much of interest in the Sacramento Valley, including under variant names Mounts Shasta and Lassen; he has misplaced Marysville, however, and does not show Sacramento at all; properly it would be placed across the American River from where Marysville is shown, and that town should stand at the junction of the Feather and the Yuba.

In preference to showing Pritchard's routes on a modern map, I have projected them in red on the Bruff maps and the section from Goddard. Where Bruff's geography is a bit askew, as from Soda Springs to the Humboldt Valley, an area of fantasy gets into the depiction of the routes, but it is hoped no one will be led seriously astray; the prime importance of the Bruff maps as source documents for the history of the Overland Trail in 1849 outweighs all other considerations. The maps, without overlay, will hereafter be reproduced by Carl I. Wheat in Volume III of his monumental *Mapping the Transmississippi West, 1540-1861*.

DIARIES

Kept on the South Pass Route in 1849 by Overland Travelers bound for California, Oregon & Utah

Every known diary kept on the northern overland trails in 1849 is listed in this bibliography. It and the chart of travel are complementary; in general, information reported in the bibliography is not repeated on the chart, and vice versa. Most of the diaries I have been able to examine personally, but for reports on those in the Yale University Library I am primarily indebted to Mr. J. S. Holliday and Mr. Archibald Hanna. An immense number of diaries had been collected by the Bancroft Library before I began this investigation, and through the courtesy of individuals and other libraries, copies of many more were obtained while research was in progress; nothing else made this work possible.

As a seasoned laborer in the field, I am aware that finality is never possible in a bibliography, and I would not have it otherwise; it would be a dull world in which no fresh discoveries could be looked for. I shall be grateful if persons who come upon new diaries will write me at the Bancroft Library, University of California, Berkeley. It has not been practicable within the limits of the present book, and of my own time and energy, to report on diaries kept on southern routes to California in 1849, but I hope some interested student will hereafter do the job; meanwhile most of the printed accounts of travel across Arizona in 1849 have been listed by Glen Dawson as an appendix to his new edition of Lorenzo Aldrich's *A Journal of the Overland Route to California & the Gold Mines* (Los Angeles, 1950).

Necessarily, a number of fragmentary journals are included, some beginning west of South Pass. Travel on the southern road from Salt Lake to Los Angeles has presented special problems. I have included Shearer's journal, which begins at Salt Lake as what must have been the last stage of a journey from the Missouri River, but I have omitted Mormon journals by that route

—the more willingly in that most such records have been printed by LeRoy R. and Ann W. Hafen in their *Journals of Forty-niners, Salt Lake to Los Angeles* (Glendale, 1954). Those who traveled the Santa Fe Trail as the first stage of a southern route started from the same place and for a few miles traversed the same country as those bound from Independence to South Pass, hence much that is illuminating will be found in Ralph P. Bieber's *Southern Trails to California in 1849* (Glendale, 1937).

Diaries kept by eastbound travelers have been excluded, but in any event are few in number. The only non-Mormon record of the kind is Captain L. C. Easton's diary from Fort Laramie to Fort Leavenworth, August 2-September 17, 1849, edited by Merrill J. Mattes in *Kansas Historical Quarterly*, vol. 20, May, 1953, pp. 392-416. Because Easton was directed to make an exploration of the Republican River, only the last few entries of his diary have much bearing on the overland emigration of 1849. Two MS. diaries by Mormons traveling from Salt Lake to the Missouri River are in the L. D. S. Church Historian's Office in Salt Lake City. Of these Lorenzo Dow Young's diary, May 3-June 1, with one further entry of June 12 after leaving Fort Laramie, was published in *Utah Historical Quarterly*, vol. 14, 1946, pp. 167-170, with supplementary information on the same trip in a biography published with the journal. The unpublished diary of Curtis E. Bolton in considerable detail describes the eastward journey of the Mormon missionary party under John Taylor and Erastus Snow which left Salt Lake on October 18 and reached Kanesville, Iowa, on December 11, 1849, too late to report effectively on the year's overland emigration. However, John D. Lee, who went out from Salt Lake on a scavenging expedition which took him in July and August as far east as the Sweetwater, made some striking observations; see *A Mormon Chronicle: The Diaries of John D. Lee, 1848-1876*, edited by Robert Glass Cleland and Juanita Brooks (San Marino, 1955, 2 vols.), vol. 1, pp. 110-114. No journal has yet been found, kept by a Forty-niner who started the journey, then turned back. However, interesting encounters with returning "Californians" are recorded in the journals of Laura A. and Julius Barnes, June 25-September 9, 1849, while migrating from Princeville, Illinois, through Iowa to Oregon, Holt County, Missouri (edited by Joe H. Bailey in *Annals of Iowa,* 3d Series, vol. 32, January, 1955, pp. 576-601).

The "diaries" include eight groups of letters individually entered in the bibliography (and two others incidentally mentioned in connection with Thomas N. Eastin's journal). (A few other letters are mentioned in the "Notes on the Diary.") The descriptive notes call attention to published and unpublished letters by the diarists that have come to my attention, and in some instances to collateral reminiscent narratives by other writers not eligible for inclusion among the diaries. The diarists are listed alphabetically in the bibliography, with a bracketed number to facilitate cross-reference to the diarist's place in the chart, which is organized in accordance with the date of arrival at Fort Laramie.

As in the case of manuscripts, notably rare printed diaries are located in the possession of at least one library. When no location is stated, it is to be understood that any mentioned edition of a printed work may be seen in the Bancroft Library.

Appleby, William I. [132] Diary, July 4-October 27, 1849. Kept as the camp journal of George A. Smith's company, the last of 1849, of the Mormon emigration from Council Bluffs to Utah. Original MS. in L. D. S. Church Historian's Office, Salt Lake City. Letters by Appleby written prior to and on the journey are published in the Kanesville, Iowa, *Frontier Guardian,* June 27, July 25, and September 19, 1849; and *L. D. S. Millennial Star,* vol. 11, November 15, 1849, pp. 346-350, two additional letters he wrote as clerk appearing with one reprinted from the *Guardian.*

Arms, Cephas [98] Diary, May 20, 1849-January 23, 1850. Begins at Council Bluffs in the Knoxville, Illinois, Company; ends on arrival at Mission San Gabriel. As six letters dated Fort Laramie, June 29; Deer Creek, July 4; Sweetwater River (and Big Sandy), July 18 (and 27); Great Salt Lake City, August 15 and 17, September 26 and 29; Lower California, January 14 (and 23), 1850, printed in *Knoxville,* Illinois, *Journal,* October 17-

November 7, 1849, January 23-February 6, May 29-June 12, 1850. This diary I am preparing for publication. A fragmentary diary for the same company, kept by Asa Haynes, begins on leaving Knoxville but has dated entries only to about April 22, 1849, when in Iowa; during later travels through Death Valley, entries are made daily, but not dated; this is printed in part in John G. Ellenbecker, *The Jayhawkers of Death Valley* (Marysville, Kansas, 1938).

Armstrong, J. E. [61] Diary, April 9-September 14, 1849. Begins on leaving Hebbardsville, Athens County, Ohio. Original MS. in Ohio Historical Society, Columbus, Ohio; photocopies in Nebraska State Historical Society and Bancroft Library.

Ashley, Delos R. [3] Diary, March 6, 1849-April 16, 1850. Begins on departure from Monroe, Michigan. MS. transcript in Bancroft Library (C-B 101, pp. 271-324). Also see entry for Monroe Company.

Athearn, Prince Allen [49] Diary, April 24-September 14, 1849. Begins on leaving St. Louis Mills, Switzerland County, Indiana. Original MS. in College of the Pacific Library; printed in *The Pacific Historian*, beginning May, 1958.

Austin, Henry [121] Diary, April 13-November 14, 1849. Begins on leaving Baltimore. Austin was a member of the same company as Bruff, *q.v.* Photocopy of original MS. in Bancroft Library.

Backus, Gurdon [47] Diary, March 14, 1849-May 1, 1851. Begins on leaving Burlington, Vermont; only occasional entries after August 18, 1850. Original MS. in Yale University Library.

Badman, Philip [95] Diary, April 14-October 2, 1849. Begins on leaving Warren, Pennsylvania. Original MS. in Yale University Library.

Baldwin, Lewis [62] Diary, April 28-September 11, 1849. Begins on leaving Marion County, Missouri; ends on arrival at The Dalles. Unique as the record of an emigrant who started for California, but changed his mind in the Bear River Valley and went to Oregon. Original MS. in collection of Fred A. Rosenstock, with a letter written from Vancouver, May 20, 1851.

Batchelder, Amos [117] Diary, April 17, 1849-December 13, 1850. Begins on leaving Boston as a New Hampshire member of the "Granite State and California Mining and Trading Company," of which Stuart and Webster, *q.v.*, were also members. (Another account of this party is by R. C. Shaw, *Across the Plains in Forty-nine*, first published in the Farmland, Indiana, *Enterprise*, 1895; published in revised form, Farmland, 1896; and republished, edited by Milo M. Quaife, Chicago, 1948.) Batchelder's diary has only occasional entries after October 20, 1849. Original MS. in Bancroft

Library; typed transcripts in Utah State Historical Society and California Historical Society.

Benson, John H. [76] Diary, May 6-September 23, 1849. Begins on crossing the Missouri at St. Joseph. Typed transcript in Nebraska State Historical Society; photocopy in Bancroft Library.

Biddle, B. R. [28] Diary, May 7-19, June 11-September 13, 1849. Biddle was a member of the "Illinois and California Mining Mutual Insurance Company" of Springfield, Illinois, which set out March 27, 1849. Two instalments of his diary, May 7-13 and May 14-19, appeared in letters of May 13 and 30 published in the Springfield *Illinois Journal*, June 6 and 8, 1849. The entries from June 11 were serialized in the *Journal* for December 6-7, 10-15, 17-20, 1849, preceded in the *Journal* of December 3 by an undated letter from "Gassonis, Sacramento River." See also under B. A. Watson.

Boggs, John [8] Diary, May 3-August 20, 1849. Begins on crossing the Missouri near Old Fort Kearny; the first two pages of the diary are described as illegible, but showing that he was from Howard County, Missouri, and had wintered at Council Bluffs. Photocopy of original MS. in Bancroft Library, which also has some MS. recollections by Boggs (C-D 341).

Bond, Robert [25] Diary, March 1-July 17, 1849. Begins on leaving Newark, New Jersey; he is said to have died at Salt Lake, where this sketchy diary ends. Original MS. in Yale University Library.

Bowman, E. L. [36] Diary, March 2-May 6, 1849. Begins on leaving Jerseyville, Illinois; ends three days after crossing the Missouri at St. Joseph, before beginning the Plains journey. Bowman was one of the "Green and Jersey County Company" which included Hackney, Kirkpatrick, Page, and Tappan, *q.v.* Printed in Elizabeth Page, *Wagons West* (New York, 1930), where his initials are given both as E. L. and as E. I.

Boyle, Charles Elisha [9] Diary, April 2-August 26, 1849. Begins on leaving Columbus, Ohio, as a member of the "Columbus and California Industrial Association," as was Decker, *q.v.* Printed in the *Columbus*, Ohio, *Dispatch*, October 2-November 11, 1949, with some entries after June 17 omitted, and those after July 19 summarized.

Breyfogle, Joshua D., Sr. [1] Diary, April 2, 1849-December 7, 1850. Begins on departure from Delaware, Ohio, in the "Delaware Mining Company." Original MS. in Baker Library, Dartmouth College; photocopy in Bancroft Library. Mimeographed edition published at Denver, 1958.

Brown, John Evans [100] Diary, March 15-August 31, 1849. Begins on departure from Asheville, North Carolina; entries summarized after entering on

Lassen Cutoff August 22. Edited by his daughter, Mrs. Katie E. Blood, in *Journal of American History*, vol. 2, January-March, 1908, pp. 129-154.

Bruff, Joseph Goldsborough [120] Diary, April 2, 1849-July 20, 1851. Begins on leaving Washington, D. C., as captain of the "Washington City and California Mining Association," and ends on return to Washington; another member was Austin, *q.v.* There are two collections of MS. notebooks and diaries by Bruff — in the Henry E. Huntington Library and in the Yale University Library. The whole record is edited by Georgia Willis Read and Ruth P. Gaines in *Gold Rush* (New York, 1944), 2 vols. A condensed and revised version, with the same title, was published at New York in 1949.

Bryarly, Wakeman. See under Geiger.

Buffum, Joseph Curtis [23] Diary, September 13, 1847-ca. January, 1855. Unusual as a diary begun before the Gold Rush and showing the evolving idea. Buffum set out from Keene, New Hampshire, March 1, 1849, with the "California A. T. & M. Company," which broke up at Independence. He made the journey with some Missourians, and returned via Nicaragua in December, 1851. Original MS. in California State Library; photocopy of typed transcript in Bancroft Library.

Burbank, Augustus Ripley [81] Diary, April 12, 1849-August 22, 1880. Begins on departure from Naples, Scott County, Illinois. Entries intermittent after September 25, 1849, describing his return to Illinois via the Isthmus in 1851, voyage to Oregon, 1853, and life there and in Washington. Original MS. in Library of Congress; photocopy in Bancroft Library.

Burrall, George P. [24] Diary, March 5-June 28, 1849. Begins on leaving Battle Creek, Michigan, as a member of the Battle Creek Mining Company and ends at the Little Sandy on the Salt Lake Road; he is said to have gone on to Salt Lake and thence Sacramento, arriving October 15, 1849. Typed transcript in Newberry Library; photocopy in Bancroft Library.

Caldwell, Dr. [T. G.?] [67] Diary, May 25-October 23, 1849. Begins on the Little Blue River. Caldwell apparently was from Missouri. MS. transcript by J. Goldsborough Bruff, printed by Georgia Willis Read and Ruth P. Gaines in *Gold Rush* (1944 ed.), pp. 1250-1269. See also McLane.

Castleman, P. F. [101] Diary, May 2, 1849-May, 1851. Begins on leaving Larue County, Kentucky; summary to arrival at St. Joseph; intermittent entries after October 27, 1849, describing life in the diggings and an overland journey to Oregon in April and May, 1851. Photocopy of typed transcript in Bancroft Library.

Chamberlain, William E. [43] Diary, April 11-August 20, 1849. Begins on leaving Iowa City [?] ; no entries, April 13-May 17. Original MS. in California State Library; photocopy of typed transcript in Bancroft Library.

Chapman, W. W. [41] Diary, May 5-July 25, 1849. Commences with a summary of events since March 13, when he left his home in Illinois, perhaps in Jersey County. Chapman's date of entrance on the Hudspeth Cutoff, July 18, suggests that his chronology got askew, as it appears definite that the Cutoff was first opened July 19, 1849. Hackney's diary shows that Chapman reached California via the Truckee. Original MS. in Henry E. Huntington Library; entries from June 8 printed in Wyoming Historical Department, *Quarterly Bulletin*, September 15, 1923; reprinted in *ibid.*, August 15, 1924, with prior entries added.

Churchill, Stillman [107] Diary, March 27-September 30, 1849. Begins on leaving Lowell, Massachusetts; he was in the same company with Sedgley, *q.v.*, though afterwards they separated. Original MS. in collection of Fred A. Rosenstock. Typed transcript in Minnesota Historical Society; photocopy in Bancroft Library.

Clark, Bennett C. [22] Diary, April 10-August 10, 1849. Begins on leaving Cooper County, Missouri. Original MS. in the Yale University Library; edited by Ralph P. Bieber in *Missouri Historical Review*, vol. 23, October, 1928, pp. 1-43. A narrative of a company from Pleasant Hill, Cass County, Missouri, with a list of members, is W. J. Pleasants, *Twice Across the Plains, 1849 . . . 1856* (San Francisco, 1906).

Clark, Jonathan [104] Diary, April 25, 1849-June 29, 1850. Begins on leaving Maquoketa, Iowa. As published in *The Argonaut*, vol. 97, August 1-22, 1925, excerpts [?] to August 20, a full diary afterward. Letters Clark wrote about the journey were printed in the Dubuque *Miners' Express*, February 13, 1850, and the Andrew *Western Democrat*, March 1, 1850.

Clark, Sterling Benjamin Franklin [54] Diary, March 11-September 1, 1849. Commences on departure from Hollidaysburg, Pennsylvania, though Clark was a Vermonter. Original MS. in Society of California Pioneers; edited by Ella Sterling Mighels as *How Many Miles from St. Jo?* (San Francisco, 1929). Letters Clark wrote from St. Joseph, April 11; Fort Laramie, June 23; Great Salt Lake City, July 19; and Sacramento, August 25, were printed in New York *Herald*, May 3, September 11, October 8, and November 12, 1849.

Cone, G. C. [102] Diary, April 23, 1849-July 16, 1850. Begins on departure from Waukesha, Wisconsin; ends on return home via the Isthmus and New York. Original MS. in collection of Fred A. Rosenstock.

Cosad, David [6] Diary, March 13-October 18, 1849. Begins on leaving Junius, Seneca County, New York. Original MS. in California Historical Society; photocopy in Bancroft Library.

Cross, Osborne [85] Journal, April 25, 1849-May 20, 1850. Describes a journey, with the Regiment of Mounted Riflemen, from Philadelphia to Oregon, and return by sea. Daily entries are for the period May 21-October 4, 1849. Printed in 31st Congress, 2nd Session, *Senate Executive Document 1* (Serial 587), and in the corresponding House serial (595), with a log of the route. Reprinted with other documents (see Gibbs and Moses), but excluding the log, in Raymond W. Settle, ed., *The March of the Mounted Riflemen* (Glendale, 1940). Settle calls attention to letters by Cross written en route, now in the War Department records, National Archives: June 14, 24; August 8; September 1, 9, 14, 23, 28; and October 11, 12, 1849.

Darwin, Charles [99] Diary, May 5, 1849-August 14, 1850. Darwin came from Paris, Tennessee. Some pages are missing at beginning; first complete entry made near Kanesville, Iowa; diary ends at Brownsville, Texas. Original MS. in Henry E. Huntington Library.

Decker, Peter [10] Diary, April 4-November 5, 1849. Begins on leaving Columbus, Ohio, in the same company with Boyle, *q.v.* Other diaries describe mining on the Yuba River, 1850-1855, trips to Oregon, Yosemite and Los Angeles in 1857, and a trip to Yreka and Siskiyou County in 1871. Original MSS. in Society of California Pioneers. Photocopy in Bancroft Library. Excerpts from the overland diary are printed in the Society's *Annual Publication*, 1953, pp. 12-33.

Delano, Alonzo [33] Diary, April 5, 1849-February, 1851. Begins with a summary concerning his departure from Ottawa, Illinois; diary proper commences May 3. Reworked MS. in Yale University Library. Entries for July 18-September 16, 1849, were printed in the Ottawa *Free Trader*, February 2-9, 1850. The entire journal was published in his *Life on the Plains and Among the Diggings* (Auburn and Buffalo, 1854; another issue in 1857; and new edition, New York, 1936). Delano's letters of April 19, 1849-August 1, 1852 to the Ottawa *Free Trader* and the New Orleans *True Delta,* including letters relating to the overland journey dated St. Joseph, April 19 and 21, English Grove, April 30, Harney's Landing, May 2, Lawson's Settlement, September 18, and Sacramento, September 30, 1849, were edited by Irving McKee in *Alonzo Delano's California Correspondence* (Sacramento, 1952).

Dewolf, David [115] Diary, May 2-October 16, 1849. Diary begins at Lexington, Missouri; Dewolf set out apparently from Springfield, Ohio. Typed transcripts in Newberry Library and Henry E. Huntington Library; printed in Illinois State Historical Society, *Transactions*, 1925, pp. 185-222, with letters from Cincinnati, April 12, West Port, May 15, Platt River, June 17, [Fort Laramie] July 7, and Weaversville, December 12, 1849; as also four later letters, to November 2, 1850.

Doyle, Simon [79] Diary, April 2, 1849-January 1, 1852. The overland diary from Rushville, Illinois, April 2-October 4, 1849, with summary for 1850-1851, is supplemented by a letter from Fort Bridger, July 19, 1849; a diary of a second overland journey in 1854 and return voyage via Panama in 1856; and by ten later letters of 1849-1853. Doyle was a member of the same company as Tolles, *q.v.* Original MSS. in Yale University Library.

Dundass, Samuel Rutherford [64] Diary, March 24-September 6, 1849, with summary to January 9, 1850. Begins on departure from Steubenville, Ohio, with the "California Mining Company." Printed as *Journal of Samuel Rutherford Dundass* . . . (Steubenville, Ohio, 1857).

Eastin, Thomas N. [103] Diary, May 1-August 19, 1849. Begins at Independence; Eastin was one of a company from Henderson, Kentucky. Original MS. in library of The Filson Club, Louisville, Kentucky. In the Yale University Library is a collection of 12 letters by or pertaining to Thomas Lyne, also a member of the Henderson company, April 22, 1849-July 25, 1850, chiefly describing the journey from the departure at St. Louis, April 3, to the arrival at Fort Bridger, July 22. In the California State Library is a collection of 13 letters by Edwin G. Hall, likewise of the Henderson company, February 13, 1849-May 29, 1851, which show that the party reached California by the Lassen Cutoff; the Hall letters pertaining to the overland journey were written from Henderson, February 14, St. Louis, April 14, Independence, May 11, "75 miles Southeast of Platte River," June 2, "near Fort Laramie," June 30, and Sacramento, October 26.

Evans, Burrelle Whalen [46] Diary, May 2-September 19, 1849. Begins on departure from Oregon, Holt County, Missouri. Photocopy of original MS. in Bancroft Library.

Everts, F. D. [73] Diary, March 15-June 30, 1849. Begins on departure from Kingsbury, La Porte County, Indiana; breaks off beyond the Willow Spring. Original MS. in Yale University Library.

Fairchild, Lucius [92] Letters, April 3, 1849-May 2, 1855. The letters describing the overland journey from Mineral Point, Wisconsin, were written from Mineral Point [April 3]; Dubuque, Iowa, April 8; Mississippi River,

April 10; St. Joseph, April 23, 24; May 2, 5, 11, 13; Ten miles west of Fort Childs, June 5; and Sacramento, October 13, with an abstract of his diary, June 3-October 10. Later letters describe life in California. Original MSS. in Wisconsin State Historical Society; edited by Joseph Schafer as that Society's *Collections*, vol. 31, 1931.

Farnham, Elijah Bryan [63] Diary, April 2-September 23, 1849. Begins on departure from Cumberland, Ohio. Entries from April 19 edited by Merrill J. Mattes and Esley J. Kirk in *Indiana Magazine of History*, vol. 46, September, December, 1950, pp. 297-318, 403-420.

Foster, Isaac [65] Diary, March 26, 1849-October 4, 1850. Begins on leaving Plainfield, Illinois; ends en route home via the Isthmus. From May 16 to June 9, Foster traveled in the same company with Jewett, *q.v.* The diary is supplemented by 13 letters, April 4, 1849-September 23, 1850; those relating to the overland journey were written from Elmira, Illinois, April 4; Madison, Iowa, April 15; Council Bluffs, May 9; "Upper Fork Platte," June 23; Big Sandy, July 6, with postscript of July 17; Salt Lake, July 23, and "De Cosma [Cosumnes River]," December 2 and 10, 1849. Originally printed in *The Foster Family* (San Jose? 1889), copy in Library of Congress; republished (Santa Barbara? 1925) with an overland diary of 1852 and other documents added.

Geiger, Vincent E. [44] Diary, February 8-June 23, 1849; same diary continued by Wakeman Bryarly to August 30, 1849. Begins with Geiger's departure from Staunton, Virginia. He and Bryarly were members of the Charlestown Company, as were Hoffman, *q.v.*, and Edward McIlhany, who published *Recollections of a Forty-Niner* (Kansas City, Missouri, 1908). Original MS. in Yale University Library. Edited by David M. Potter as *Trail to California* (New Haven, 1945).

Gelwicks, Daniel W. [7] Diary, April 13-June 16, 1849. Begins on leaving St. Joseph; ends on starting for the Sublette Cutoff. Gelwicks was one of a company from Belleville, Illinois. MS. transcript in Illinois State Historical Library; typed copy in Bancroft Library.

Gibbs, George [87] Diary, May 8-June 25, 1849. Begins on arrival at Fort Leavenworth (from New York?); ends at Fort Laramie. Written as two letters published in the New York *Journal of Commerce*, July 25 and September 1, 1849; reprinted with the Cross journal, *q.v.*, by Raymond W. Settle in *The March of the Mounted Riflemen*. Further data on the march were set down by Gibbs on a Frémont map on which he also copied Jedediah Smith's routes of 1822-1830; reproduced in Dale L. Morgan and Carl I. Wheat, *Jedediah Smith and His Maps of the American West* (San Francisco, 1954).

Gould, Charles [113] Diary, April 16-September 27, 1849. With a further diary of a return voyage via Panama, 1852. Gould was a member of the "Boston and Newton Joint Stock Association," as was Staples, *q.v.*, and the diary begins on departure from Boston. Original MS. in Minnesota Historical Society; photocopy in Bancroft Library. Typed transcripts in Bancroft Library, Newberry Library, Nebraska State Historical Society, Indiana University Library, and American Antiquarian Society; some of these from a mimeographed edition ca.1947, said to have been limited to 15 copies.

[Granville Company, Ohio] [55] Diary, April 3-September 18, 1849. Kept by an unidentified member of this company, beginning at Zanesville, Ohio. Original MS. in Yale University Library.

Gray, Charles [26] Diary, February 26-November 19, 1849. Begins at New York (?) as itinerary; diary proper begins May 1 at Independence. Apparently Gray was from New York. Original MS. in Henry E. Huntington Library.

Gunnison, John Williams [124] Diary, April 11, 1849-November 13, 1850. Begins at Detroit; intermittent entries until May 17, 1849, when Lieutenant Gunnison left St. Louis with Captain Howard Stansbury, *q.v.*, on their exploration of the Great Salt Lake country. Ends at St. Louis. Original MS. in Records of the Topographical Engineers, War Department records, The National Archives; photocopy in Bancroft Library. MS. letters by Gunnison to his wife and his mother, written on the overland journey, [St. Louis, May 21?]; Steamer Kansas, Missouri River, May 21-22; Fort Leavenworth, May 26; near Fort Leavenworth, June 2-3; Big Blue River, June 10; Fort Laramie, July 13-14; on the Sweetwater, August 4; Camp Grist, Jordan River, Utah, October 7, October 9, 1849; with two others dated Great Salt Lake City, February 2 and March 1, 1850, are among the Gunnison Correspondence in the Henry E. Huntington Library.

Hackney, Joseph [38] Diary, May 1-September 12, 1849. Begins at St. Joseph. Printed with the fragmentary diary of Bowman and the letters of Page, *q.v.*, in Elizabeth Page, *Wagons West* (1930). See also Kirkpatrick and Tappan, members of the same party.

Hale, Israel Foote [52] Diary, May 5-September 14, 1849, with a summary to October 22, 1849. Begins on leaving St. Joseph. Original MS. in Society of California Pioneers; printed in that Society's *Quarterly*, vol. 2, June, 1925, pp. 59-130.

Hale, John [127] Narrative, April 18, 1849-October, 1850. Describes an overland journey from North Bloomfield, New York, and return via

Panama. Published as *California As It Is* (Rochester, 1851); copies in Yale University Library and the collections of Everett D. Graff and Fred A. Rosenstock. Republished, San Francisco, 1954.

Hall, Edwin G. See under Eastin.

Hall, O. J. [116] Diary, May 2-ca.October 25, 1849. Begins on leaving Nauvoo, Illinois; from July 15 entries are intermittent, and journey is summarized after October 11. Typed transcript in California State Library; copies in Bancroft Library and Utah State Historical Society.

Hamelin, Joseph [93] Diary, April 12, 1849-April 12, 1850. Begins on leaving Lexington, Missouri, as a member of the Pomeroy mercantile train; ends at Sacramento after taking the southern road from Salt Lake to Los Angeles. (Diary also kept in 1856-1857.) Original MS. in Yale University Library.

Haynes, Asa. See under Arms.

Hester, Sallie [82] Diary, March 20, 1849-October 5, 1871. Begins on leaving Bloomington, Indiana; ends with her marriage in Nevada to James K. Maddock; she was a 12-year-old girl in 1849, and entries are intermittent. Printed in *The Argonaut*, vol. 97, September 12-October 24, 1925, the overland diary appearing in the issues of September 12-19.

Hinman, C. G. [66] Diary, April 2, 1849-March 29, 1850. Begins on departure from Groveland, Illinois, in the "Groveland Belle" company. Original MS. in Denver Public Library. In the collection of Everett D. Graff are eight MS. letters written by Hinman to his wife, from St. Joseph, May 3 and 8; Fort Childs, May 27; en route, June 7, mailed via mail carrier from Salt Lake; Fort Laramie, June 17; City of the Lakes [Great Salt Lake], July 20; Reading's Diggings, October 7; Sacramento, October 18, 1849; with two others from California, 1850.

Hixson, Jasper Morris [14] Diary, May 1-August 6, 1849. Begins on leaving Liberty, Missouri. Original MS. reportedly destroyed in the 1890 Los Angeles flood, but the diary had been published in the Los Angeles *Herald*, January 13-April 30, 1890; typescript of that version in California Historical Society; photocopy in Bancroft Library. Extracts printed in Owen Cochrane Coy, *The Great Trek* (Los Angeles, 1931). A MS. letter by Hixson to Robert Miller, Fort Kearny, May 20, 1849, with other letters by Forty-niners, is in the Miller Papers, Missouri Historical Society.

Hoffman, Benjamin [45] Diary, March 27, 1849-October 15, 1850. Begins on leaving Charlestown, Jefferson County, [West] Virginia, in the same company with Geiger, *q.v.* Extracts printed in the Shepherdstown, West Virginia, *Register*, January 31-February 4, 1901; portions of the diary from June 4-September 1, 1849, edited by C. H. Ambler in *West Virginia History*, vol. 3, October, 1941, pp. 59-75.

Howell, Elijah Preston [89] Diary, May 6-September 25, 1849. Begins on leaving Athens (now Albany), Gentry County, Missouri; "written out more than twenty years after the notes were taken down on the road," with some interjections of later date. Original MS. in State Historical Society of Missouri; typed transcript in California State Library, with photocopy in Bancroft Library.

Hutchings, James Mason [125] Diary, May 16-October 7, 1849. Hutchings was an Englishman; his diary begins at New Orleans. Original MS. in Library of Congress; photocopy in Bancroft Library. A transcript by Hutchings' daughter is in the Yosemite Museum.

Isham, G. S. [11] Journal, April 26-August 12, 1849. Begins on departure from St. Joseph; daily entries end on arrival at Coloma; includes a summary of return voyage to Lyons, Michigan, via the Isthmus and New Orleans. Printed as *G. S. Isham's Guide to California, and the Mines, and Return by the Isthmus, with a General Description of the Country* (New York, 1850), copies in Yale University Library and American Antiquarian Society.

Jagger, D. [91] Diary, August 18-31, 1846; April 5, 1849-January 10, 1850; with intermittent further entries to February 29, 1860. The 1846 diary describes a voyage on the Great Lakes; the overland diary of 1849 begins on leaving Warren, Ohio. Original MS. in California Historical Society; photocopy in Bancroft Library.

Jewett, George Enoch [75] Diary, April 19, 1849-July 20, 1850. Begins near Knoxville, Iowa. From May 16 to June 9, 1849, when the "Iowa Company No. 1" separated as three detachments, Jewett traveled with Foster, *q.v.* Photocopy in Bancroft Library.

Johnson, John A. [34] Letters, March-December, 1849. Apparently 22 letters to his wife, describing the journey from Cincinnati and life in California; letters en route were written from Cincinnati [March 10?]; St. Louis, March 16; Independence, March 23, April 1, 8, 15, 16, 22, 23, 29, 30, May 1-2, 3; Kansas River, May 10; Fort Kearny, May 23; Sacramento, August 19; North Fork American River, August 26, 1849. Printed with the unrelated McCoy journal, *q.v.*, in *Pioneering on the Plains* (Kaukauna, Wisconsin, 1924).

Johnston, William G. [5] Journal, March 1-July 29, 1849. Begins on departure from Pittsburgh in the "Diamond K Company"; continues in description of the mines and a voyage home via the Isthmus early in 1850. Printed as *Experiences of a Forty-Niner* (Pittsburgh, 1892); republished as *Overland to California* (Oakland, 1948). See also a letter by Joseph L. Moody of Johnston's party, Sacramento, August 7, 1849, in *California Historical Society Quarterly*, vol. 13, March, 1934, pp. 84-85.

Josselyn, Amos Piatt [35] Diary, April 2-September 11, 1849. Begins on leaving Zanesville, Ohio. Original MS. in California State Library, with five MS. letters, Fort Kearny, May 23; Salt Lake, July 15, 1849; and January 29, May 12, and May 19, 1850. The second letter is printed as one of eight "Letters by Forty-Niners written from Great Salt Lake City in 1849," edited by Dale L. Morgan in *Western Humanities Review*, vol. 3, April, 1949, pp. 98-116. A typed transcript of the journal is in the Newberry Library, and a photocopy in the Bancroft Library.

Judge, Timothy [126] Diary, September 6, 1849-January 26, 1850. Begins on leaving Salt Lake. Only intermittent entries after October 22. Original MS. in Bancroft Library.

Kelly, William [2] Narrative of a journey to California from Liverpool via New York and Independence. Commences January 20, 1849. Very few dates are given, but the overland narrative is written day by day, and its chronology can be worked out; however, as his date of arrival at Salt Lake can be fixed as June 22, there is a three-day discrepancy between Fort Laramie and Salt Lake, depending on whether one works forward from the former place or backward from the latter; also Kelly says he reached Weaverville July 26, at least four days too early. It may be that the name Kelly is a pseudonym. His narrative was first published in two vols. as *An Excursion to California* (London, 1851); republished in London next year as two separate volumes having the titles, *Across the Rocky Mountains, from New York to California*, and *A Stroll Through the Diggings of California*. The latter volume was republished at Oakland, 1950.

Kirkpatrick, Charles Alexander [39] Diary, April [8], 1849-January 27, 1850. Begins on leaving Grafton, Jersey County, Illinois; includes prefatory autobiographical notes and a concluding summary of experiences in California, 1850-1851. Kirkpatrick's weekdays are correctly entered in his journal until July 15, but his days of the month are one day off, as shown by the diaries of his fellow members of the Jersey County company, Bowman, Hackney, Page, and Tappan, *q.v.* On the chart his dates before July 15 have been corrected. MS. transcript (in Kirkpatrick's own hand?) of original diary in Bancroft Library.

Krepps, Bolivar G. [83] Letters, May 11, 1849-December 17, 1850. Apparently from Brownsville, Fayette County, Pennsylvania, Krepps set out with a St. Joseph company. Eight letters before he died at Mathenys Creek, January 14, 1850, include five describing the journey, St. Joseph, May 11; Big Blue, May 20; Little Blue, May 27; Chimney Rock, June 14 (with postscripts to June 19); and Cosumnes River, October 15. Two more letters to Krepps's family by Joseph Troth, 1850, tells of his death. Original MSS. in Denver Public Library.

Lewis, Elisha B. [84] Diary, April 5-September 30, 1849. Begins on departure from Turtleville, Rock County, Wisconsin. Typed transcript in State Historical Society of Wisconsin; photocopy in Bancroft Library.

Lewis, John F. [70] Diary, May 12-December 31, 1849. Begins at St. Joseph, after his departure from Huntsville, Randolph County, Missouri; a second diary, 1852-1854, describes life on his farm in Howard County, Missouri, after his return. Original MS. in Yale University Library.

Lindsey, Tipton [30] Diary, February 20-September 7, 1849. Begins on departure from South Bend, Indiana; some letters of February, 1850, are written into the back of the diary. Lindsey was a member of the "South Bend California Joint Stock Mining and Operating Company." Original MS. in Bancroft Library. Another party from South Bend included David Rohrer Leeper, who published his reminiscences as *The Argonauts of 'Forty-Nine* (South Bend, 1894; republished, Columbus, Ohio, 1950); Leeper compiled a roll of 122 St. Joseph County, Indiana, Argonauts, including Lindsey, from the 1849 files of the *St. Joseph Valley Register*. His own party took the Lassen Cutoff.

Long, Charles L'Hommedieu [19] Diary, March 10-August 14, 1849. Begins with his departure from Cincinnati, Ohio; includes an entry of September 1, 1850, concerning his departure for Panama. Original MS. in Yale University Library.

Lord, Isaac S. P. [96] Diary, May 6, 1849-April 3, 1851. Begins en route up the Missouri River; ends at Aurora, Illinois, after return voyage via Panama. Partially MS. and partially clippings, undated, from the (1849-1850?) Elgin, Illinois, *Western Christian;* in the Henry E. Huntington Library.

Love, Alexander [17] Diary, March 20, 1849-March 5, 1852. Begins on leaving Leesburg, Pennsylvania; also describes life in California and return voyage via Panama in 1852. Original MS. in Yale University Library.

Lyne, James. See under Eastin.

McCall, Ansel James [77] Journal, March 14-September 18, 1849. Begins on leaving Bath, Steuben County, New York; includes letters dated 150 miles west of St. Joseph, May 21; North Fork of Platte, June 10; and Sacramento, September 18. Originally printed in the Bath *Steuben Courier,* and reprinted as *The Great California Trail in 1849* (Bath, 1882). McCall continued his story in *Pick and Pan* (Bath, 1883), the text of which had also been first printed in the *Courier;* this contains his journal for September 19-November 25, 1849, but no letters.

McCoy, Samuel Finley [108] Diary, May 19-December 17, 1849. Begins on leaving Independence, after emigrating from Chillicothe, Ohio. A letter from Fort Laramie, July 2, is incorporated into the diary. Printed with the unrelated Johnson letters in *Pioneering on the Plains* (Kaukauna, Wisconsin, 1924).

McLane, Allen [68] Diary, September 5-15, 1849. A fragment, transcribed by J. Goldsborough Bruff, *q.v.*, which describes experiences on the Lassen Cutoff by a messmate of Caldwell, *q.v.*, while separated from him. McLane died on the trail October 9, 1849, identified as from Platte County, Missouri. Printed in Georgia Willis Read and Ruth P. Gaines, eds., *Gold Rush* (New York, 1944), pp. 1247-1250, 1269-1271.

Maddock, Sallie (Hester). See Hester.

Mann, Henry R. [53] Diary, June [21]-September 18, 1849. Entries prior to that for June [21] are missing; diary begins near Deer Creek. Photocopy of original MS. in Bancroft Library.

Markle, John A. [31] Diary, April 18, 1849-January 6, 1850. Begins on leaving St. Joseph. Original MS. in Auburn Parlor, Native Sons of the Golden West; photocopy in Bancroft Library. Entries for August 12-September 2 printed in *The Grizzly Bear*, vol. 55, December, 1934, pp. 7, 9, 11; reprinted in the Auburn, California, *Donner Trail Rider*, vol. 6, July 25, September 29, October 27, 1936.

Merrill, Joseph Henry [32] Diary, March 1-September 25, 1849. Begins at Boston; Merrill was from New Hampshire. Typed transcript in the State Historical Society of Missouri.

Middleton, Joseph [112] Diary, May 26, 1849-April 5, 1851. Begins north of the Kansas River; ends at San Francisco. Original MS. in Yale University Library.

Miller, Reuben [129] Diary, June 4-September 24, 1849. Kept as the camp journal for the "second division of fifty" in Orson Spencer's company of the Mormon emigration of 1849. Original MS. in L. D. S. Church Historian's Office, Salt Lake City; photocopy of typed transcript in Henry E. Huntington Library.

Mitchell, Lyman [88] Diary, April 21-October 5, 1849. Begins at Iowa City, Iowa. Photocopy of original MS. in Bancroft Library.

[Monroe Company, Michigan] [4] Diary, March 6-June 28, 1849. Begins at Monroe; ends after leaving Soda Springs. The identity of the diarist has not been established, but he was one of the following: George Withington, Milton Sweeney, Horace Bisbee, H. Bulkley, William Wilson. The diary was retained among the papers of Delos R. Ashley, *q.v.*, and transcribed for the Bancroft Library (C-B 101, pp. 327-352).

[Morgan, Jesse] [131] Diary, May 24-October 12, 1849; April 22-July 4, 1850. Begins on departure from St. Joseph; but Morgan went up to Council Bluffs and traveled to Utah with the Mormon emigration. Thus far the diary is unique for the further journey on from Salt Lake in the spring of 1850, ahead of that portion of the emigration which started from the Missouri River. Morgan was killed at Sacramento August 14, 1850. Printed in Martha M. Morgan, *A Trip Across the Plains in the Year 1849, with Notes of a Voyage to California by way of Panama* (San Francisco, 1864); copies in California State Library, Henry E. Huntington Library, and Harvard College Library. Her former husband is identified as the author of the diary in Mrs. M. M. Graham's *The Polygamist's Victim* . . . (San Francisco, 1872), in which she gives a slight account of the same journey and much background information. A narrative by M. S. McMahon printed as Chapter XIV of William L. Manly's *Death Valley in '49* (San Jose, 1894) tells of going on to California with the Morgans in 1850.

Moses, Israel [86] Odometer record, May 10-October 13, 1849. Begins on departure from Fort Leavenworth; ends on arrival at Oregon City, Oregon. Although not a diary, included here as a record of the daily marches of that portion of the Regiment of Mounted Riflemen which went via Fort Bridger and the Old Oregon Trail; it is supplemented by the narrative report of Colonel W. W. Loring, October 15, 1849. Both MSS. in War Department records, The National Archives; printed with the Cross and Gibbs diaries, *q.v.*, in Raymond W. Settle, ed., *The March of the Mounted Riflemen* (Glendale, 1940).

Nevins, Julius Martin [72] Diary, ca. March 28-October 11, 1849. Begins on departure from Wisconsin. Typed transcript in California State Library, with three MS. letters of December 2 and 26, 1849, and March 8, 1850; photocopy in Bancroft Library.

Nusbaumer, Louis [128] Diary, March 20, 1849-March 10, 1850. A very fragmentary record, with daily entries chiefly from December 11, 1849-March 10, 1850, while Nusbaumer was with one of the parties struggling through Death Valley. He started from New York in the same company with Hermann B. Scharmann, who is my source for Nusbaumer's date of departure from Independence and of arrival at Fort Kearny. (Scharmann contributed a narrative of his experiences to the *New Yorker Staats-Zeitung*, vol. 18, April 10-May 1, 1852; reprinted as *Scharmann's Landreise nach Californien* [New York? 1908?]; subsequently translated by Margaret Hoff Zimmermann and Erich W. Zimmermann as *Scharmann's Overland Journey to California* [New York, 1918], copy in Library of Congress.)

Photocopy of original MS. in Bancroft Library; also a typed transcription of the German MS., and a typescript copy of a translation by Nusbaumer's daughter. Some of the Death Valley entries are quoted in Read and Gaines, eds., *Gold Rush* (1944 ed.), pp. 1227-1233.

Orvis, Andrew M. [74] Diary, March 12, 1849-June 8, 1850. Begins on leaving Lake Maria, Marquette County, Wisconsin; events summarized from July 10-November 30, 1849. Original MS. in Yale University Library, with a letter to his wife, Sacramento, February 15, 1850.

Page, Henry [37] Letters, April 13, 1849-December 29, 1850. Page became a member of the Jersey County, Illinois, company with Bowman, Hackney, Kirkpatrick, and Tappan, *q.v.*, but set out from Woodburn, Macoupin County. Of 26 surviving letters, those describing the overland journey are dated St. Louis, April 13; 15 miles below St. Joseph, April 22; St. Joseph, April 24; 6 miles north of St. Joseph, May 2; 30 miles from St. Joseph, May 8; Big Nemahah, May 13; Fort Kearny, May 24; Fort Laramie, June 13; South Pass, July 2 (with postscript of July 22, west of Fort Hall); and Sacramento, November 22, 1849. Printed in Elizabeth Page, *Wagons West* (New York, 1930).

Parke, Charles R. [59] Diary, April 8, 1849-January 1, 1851. Begins at Como, Illinois; ends at St. Louis. Original MS. in Henry E. Huntington Library.

Pease, David E. [15] Diary, April 28-September 5, 1849. Written from Astoria, Oregon, in the form of a letter to his father in Illinois, dated at beginning February 5, 1850, at end April 21, 1850. He probably came from Jersey County, as Bowman mentions him. From May 6 to June 19 Pease traveled with the Green County detachment of what had initially been the "Green and Jersey County Company"; for the Jersey detachment, see under Page, *et al*. Pease traveled the Old Oregon Trail via Fort Bridger, and afterward journeyed on to Oregon with the first company of the year. Typed transcript in Nebraska State Historical Society; photocopy in Bancroft Library.

Perkins, E. Douglas [105] Diary, May 9, 1849-February 23, 1850. Begins on leaving Marietta, Ohio; intermittent entries after reaching Sacramento. Original(?) MS. diary in Henry E. Huntington Library; revised MS. in University of Kentucky Library; photocopy of typed transcript of this version in Bancroft Library.

Pond, A. R. [90] Diary, August 24, 1849-June 18, 1852. Begins on arrival at the Lassen Cutoff; ends on the Feather River. Original MS. in Henry E. Huntington Library.

Pratt, James [111] Letters, March 10, 1849-February 5, 1850. One of the "Wolverine Rangers," Pratt wrote nine letters to the Marshall, Michigan, *Statesman* which in part quote his diary. The dates in brackets are those of publication in the *Statesman:* Independence, March 19 [April 11], 20 [April 4—*sic*]; April 9 [May 2]; May 5 [May 23]; On the Trail, May 17 (including entries for May 17, 18, 20, 25 [June 20]; Kansas Ferry, May 28 [July 4]; Little Blue, June 10 [July 18]; 56 miles east of Fort Laramie, July 1 (including entries for July 1-4) [September 12]; and San Francisco, February 5 [April 24], 1850 (entries for October 14-November 15, 1849). In general, these describe Pratt's journey from St. Louis to Fort Laramie, and from the summit of the Warner Range on the Lassen Cutoff to Lassen's Ranch. Most of the time he was in company with William Swain, *q.v.* A narrative by one of the Rangers is Oliver Goldsmith, *Overland in Forty-Nine* (Detroit, 1896), a copy in Library of Congress; and two letters by yet another Ranger, James D. Lyon, July 4 and December 24, 1849, were printed in *Detroit Advertiser*, September 10, 1849, February 22, 1850.

Prichet, John [57] Diary, March 21, 1849-February 18, 1851. Begins on departure from Wayne County, Indiana; ends on return home via the Isthmus and New Orleans. Original MS. in Indiana State Library; photocopy of typed transcript in Bancroft Library.

Pritchard, James Avery [12] Diary, April 10, 1849-May, 1850. Begins on departure from Petersburg, Boone County, Kentucky; events summarized after August 13. Original MS. in collection of Fred A. Rosenstock. Printed herewith; excerpt, April 10-May 12, 1849, printed in *Missouri Historical Review*, vol. 18, July, 1924, pp. 535-545.

Ramsay, Alexander [29] Diary, March 21-October 14, 1849. Begins on leaving Park County, Indiana; after September 24 has only an entry for October 14 and a cover letter of November 25, sent with the diary. Edited by Merrill J. Mattes in *Pacific Historical Review*, vol. 18, November, 1949, pp. 437-468.

Robinson, Zirkle D. [20] Diary, March 20-August 26, 1849. Begins on departure from Virginia, Cass County, Illinois. Typed transcript in possession of Francis Coleman Rosenberger, 509 Fontaine St., Alexandria, Virginia.

Royce, Sarah Eleanor (Bayliss) [122] Narrative, April 30-October 24, 1849. Begins on departure from Iowa; as a record of an overland journey ends on arrival at Pleasant Valley, but continues to describe life in California afterward. The narrative was elaborated about 1885 from a skeletal diary kept on the trail; its dates, though few, are valid. Edited by Ralph Henry

Gabriel as *A Frontier Lady* (New Haven, 1932), after publication in part in *Yale Review*, vol. 20, Summer, 1931, pp. 754-777. A letter by her husband, Josiah Royce, dated Weaverville, October 27, 1849, is in 31st Congress, 1st Session, *Senate Executive Document 52* (Serial 561), p. 106.

Searls, Niles [97] Diary, May 9-October 1, 1849. Begins near Independence, after a brief summary. Searls was from Rensselaerville, Albany County, New York, and took passage from Independence with Turner & Allen's "Pioneer Line." Original MS. in Bancroft Library; edited by Robert M. Searls as *The Diary of a Pioneer and Other Papers* (San Francisco, 1940).

Sedgley, Joseph [106] Diary, March 29-November 28, 1849. Begins on departure from Lynn, Massachusetts, as a member of the "Sagamore and California Mining and Trading Company," of which Stillman Churchill, *q.v.*, was a member until May 24. Printed as *Overland to California in 1849* (Oakland, 1877).

Senter, Riley [130] Letters, April 25, 1849-[   ], 1853. Senter began his journey at Perry, New York, but wrote his first letter from Chicago. Others were written on the trail from Council Bluffs, June 20; 300 miles west of Council Bluffs, July 24; near Fort Laramie, August 23; Fort Laramie, August 24; near Fort Laramie, August 25; City of the Great Salt Lake, October [   ] and ca. October 10; and [Los Angeles, ca. February, 1850]. These describe a late journey on the plains, continued by the southern road from Salt Lake; other letters describe life in California. Printed, with some excisions, in the *Exeter*, California, *Sun*, and separately as *Crossing the Continent to California Gold Fields* (Exeter, 1938).

Shearer, – – – [94] Diary, September 16-December 16, 1849. Begins on departure from Salt Lake, by the southern road, and ends on the Mohave River. MS. transcript by Benjamin I. Hayes in Bancroft Library (C-E 92), with which are some notes Hayes recorded in January, 1850, of the journey Jacob Grewell made via the Hastings and Lassen cutoffs while his family was traveling the southern road to Los Angeles; and a waybill of the southern road obtained from [H.] Stickney, who traveled with the Pomeroy train.

Shombre, Henry J. [58] Diary, March 19-June 17, 1849. Begins on departure from Hagerstown, Indiana; ends on arrival at Fort Laramie. Original MS. in Kansas State Historical Society; photocopies in Indiana State Library and Bancroft Library.

Spooner, E. A. [42] Diary, March 15, 1849-April 23, 1850. Begins on departure from Adrian, Michigan. Original MS. in collection of Fred A. Rosenstock; photocopies in Kansas State Historical Society and Bancroft Library.

The Rosenstock collection also includes 14 letters, March 11, 1849-August 28, 1850. Those relating to the overland journey were written from Adrian, March 11 and 13; Tiffin, Ohio, March 22; Cincinnati, April 1; Kansas River (n.d.); June 12 (with postscript, June 22, at Mormon Ferry on North Platte); Mormon City, July 19; and California, October 20.

Stansbury, Howard [123] Diary, June 4, 1849-October 1, 1850. Begins after departure from Fort Leavenworth, en route to map the Great Salt Lake country; ends on the return journey. No entries made, September 26-October 18, November 6, 1849-April 8, 1850. Stansbury's subordinate was Lieutenant J. W. Gunnison, *q.v.* Original MS. in Records of the Topographical Engineers, War Department records, The National Archives, with other documents pertaining to the expedition; photocopy in Bancroft Library. Considerably revised, the diary as written up in a formal journal, and with preliminary entries for May 31-June 3, 1849, added, was published in Stansbury's *Exploration and Survey of the Valley of the Great Salt Lake of Utah* . . . (Philadelphia, 1852; reissued in 1853; and also issued as 32nd Congress, Special Session, *Senate Executive Document 3* (Serial 608).

Staples, David Jackson [114] Diary, April 16-September 1, 1849. Begins on departure from Boston as a member of the same company as Gould, *q.v.* Original MS. in Bancroft Library. Edited by Harold F. Taggart in *California Historical Society Quarterly*, vol. 22, June, 1943, pp. 119-150. The Bancroft Library also has a MS. Statement written by Staples in 1877 (C-D 158), which gives additional details as to his experiences in Salt Lake and further journey on to California; and some extended MS. Recollections (C-D 288).

Starr, Franklin [21] Diary, March 22-August 24, 1849. Begins on departure from Alton, Illinois; ends at the Boiling Spring on the Truckee route. Original MS. in Illinois State Historical Library.

Steck, Amos [80] Diary, May 27-October 7, 1849. Pages are missing before the opening entry, but notations on the inside front cover give some details as to prior route and dates. Steck emigrated from Pennsylvania. Original MS. in State Historical Society of Colorado.

Stuart, Joseph Alonzo [118] Diary, April 17, 1849-December 6, 1853. Begins on departure from Boston in the "Granite State Company," which united with the "Mount Washington Company"; he traveled with Batchelder and Webster, *q.v.* Published as *My Roving Life* (Auburn, California, 1896, 2 vols., of which the second volume is a record of experiences at sea, 1864-1867). A MS. account of Stuart's overland journey, differing somewhat from the published version, is described in *The Month at Goodspeed's*, February, 1957.

Swain, William [110] Diary, April 11-October 31, 1849. Begins on departure from Youngstown, New York. Swain traveled with the "Wolverine Rangers," of which Pratt, *q.v.*, was a member. The original MS. is in the Yale University Library, with 30 letters written en route to and in California until his return via Panama, April 11, 1849-January 31, 1851. The Swain papers are being edited for publication by J. S. Holliday.

Swan, Chauncey [109] Letters, June 1, 1849-July 27, 1851. Swan was from Iowa City, Iowa, a member of the "Sacramento Mining Company." His letters en route are dated from Council Bluffs, June 1; Pacific Springs, July 27; Utah Lake, September 2, 1849; and San Francisco, April 25, 1850; he took the southern road from Salt Lake. Original MSS. in State Historical Society of Iowa; edited by Mildred Throne in *Iowa Journal of History*, vol. 47, January, 1949, pp. 63-77. A member of Swan's company was Jacob Y. Stover, whose reminiscences were edited by John W. Caughey in *Pacific Historical Review*, vol. 6, June, 1937, pp. 143-181; reprinted in part in LeRoy R. and Ann W. Hafen, eds., *Journals of Forty-Niners, Salt Lake to Los Angeles* (Glendale, 1954), pp. 273-291.

T――――, Dr. [13] Diary, May 20-June 23, 1849. Begins some 60 miles west of Fort Kearny; breaks off on Fontenelle Creek, west of Green River. The MS. transcript in the Bancroft Library (C-B 383: 1) was made at Coloma about 1934 by George Johnson, from the original which afterward disappeared. Apparently Johnson copied the whole journal, but only this portion remains in his papers. According to Johnson's note, the journal was that of a Dr. Taylor or Thomas (hence perhaps that of the Dr. William L. Thomas, of Augusta, Kentucky, mentioned in Pritchard's journal). Johnson also noted: "It is written in the same book in which he kept his medical accounts. Some of them written in ink, dated 1848 and early 1849 in Marcelline, Illinois. Others late 1849 & 1850 written in pencil in California. His Journal breaks off abruptly on his arrival at Hangtown."

Tappan, Henry [40] Diary, April 27-September 7, 1849. Begins on arrival at St. Joseph from Jerseyville, Illinois. Tappan was one of the same company as Bowman, Hackney, Kirkpatrick, and Page, *q.v.* Edited by Everett Walters and George B. Strother in *Annals of Wyoming*, vol. 25, July, 1953, pp. 113-139.

Tate, James [61] Diary, April 5-October 7, 1849. Begins on departure from St. Louis. Typed transcript in Missouri Historical Society; photocopy in Bancroft Library.

[Taylor, Dr.? See under T――――, Dr.]

[Thomas, Dr. William L.? See under T――――, Dr.]

Tiffany, P. C. [18] Diary, April 17-August 29, 1849; January 1, 1850-March 13, 1851. Begins on leaving Mount Pleasant, Iowa; ends at Chagres while returning via Panama. Entries are intermittent after reaching California. Original MS. in Yale University Library.

Tinker, Charles [16] Diary, March 20-August 19, 1849. Begins on departure from Kingsville, Ashtabula County, Ohio. Edited by Eugene H. Rose-boom in *Ohio State Archaeological and Historical Quarterly*, vol. 61, January, 1952, pp. 64-85.

Tolles, James S. [78] Diary, April 3, 1849-March 11, 1856. Begins on departure from Rushville, Illinois, in same company with Doyle, *q.v.* The diary continues with fairly regular entries to describe Tolles' life in California, chiefly in the Marysville area. Edited by his granddaughter, Miss Doris Beard, in Marysville *Appeal-Democrat*, February 5-March 11, 1930; file in California State Library. The overland journal is printed in the nine issues, February 5-14, 1930. The Great Salt Lake City *Deseret News* of May 29, 1853, reprints from the *St. Louis Intelligencer* a communication from J. D. Manlove, captain of the Rushville company, on the subject of the 1849 journey.

Watson, B. A. [27] Diary, April 5-May 4, 1849. Begins on crossing the Mississippi River at Hannibal, Missouri, and continues to St. Joseph. Watson was a member of the same company as Biddle, *q.v.*, whose diary continues the story. Printed in the form of a letter of May 4 in the Springfield *Illinois Journal*, May 29, 1849. Two additional letters of May 20 and June 11, printed in the *Journal* for June 7 and August 9, 1849, give further details of the journey, as far as Fort Laramie.

Watson, William J. [50] Diary, May 8-September 13, 1849. Begins on leaving St. Joseph. Printed as *Journal of an Overland Trip to Oregon, Made in the Year 1849 . . .* (Jacksonville, Illinois, 1851), copy in Harvard University Library.

Webster, Kimball [119] Diary, April 17-October 19, 1849. Begins on departure from Boston; includes some additional entries to January 8, 1850, and a more fragmentary record, enlarged by reminiscences, of experiences in California and the Pacific Northwest before returning east via Panama in 1854. Webster was one of the same company as Batchelder and Stuart, *q.v.* Printed as *The Gold Seekers of '49* (Manchester, New Hampshire, 1917).

Wells, Epaphroditus [69] Letters, April 1, 1849-September 14, 1851. Wells came from Downers Grove, DuPage County, Illinois; his letters describing the overland journey were written from Fort Madison, Iowa, April 1; St. Joseph, May 8; Fort Childs, May 27; Fort Laramie, June 16; Salt Lake,

July 20; and Sacramento, October 18, 1849. Six other letters were written in 1850-1851 from Sacramento, Trinity River, "Churn Creek Diggins, Chasta Co Calia," and Chasta Plains. Typed transcripts in Missouri Historical Society, Utah State Historical Society, and Bancroft Library.

Willis, Edward J. [56] Diary, May 1-September 1, 1849. A Virginian's record, beginning at Independence. Original MS. in Yale University Library.

Wistar, Isaac Jones [51] Diary, May 3-August 26, 1849. The diary is incorporated into the *Autobiography of Isaac Jones Wistar, 1827-1905* (Philadelphia, 1914, 2 vols.; republished, New York, 1937, 1 vol.), which also includes an account of his experiences in California, 1849-1857.

Wood, Joseph Warren [49] Diary, May 6, 1849-April 4, 1853. Begins at St. Joseph and continues until after his return home to Walworth, Walworth County, Wisconsin, on December 31, 1852. Original MS. in Henry E. Huntington Library; photocopy in Bancroft Library.

Young, Sheldon [71] Diary, March 18, 1849-February 5, 1850. Begins on departure from Joliet, Illinois; later describes his journey on the southern road from Salt Lake, and travels through Death Valley. Typed transcript in Henry E. Huntington Library. Most of the diary is printed in Margaret Long, *The Shadow of the Arrow* (Caldwell, Idaho, 1941), pp. 241-263; and a part in LeRoy R. and Ann W. Hafen, eds., *Journals of Forty-niners, Salt Lake to Los Angeles* (Glendale, 1954), pp. 60-66.

ADDENDA

Several diaries appeared while this book was in press, too late to be weighed in analysis or notes, though added to the chart.

Joseph Waring Berrien [7A], whose diary (March 31–August 15, 1849) is being edited by T. C. and Caryl Hinckley of Bloomington, Indiana, was a New Yorker, more recently of St. Louis, who set out from the Missouri with Gelwicks, *q.v.*, but was left behind on Raft River July 1. His diary begins on leaving St. Louis and ends the day after reaching Sacramento.

Henry W. Burton [24A], of whose diary (April 29–August 30, 1849) a photocopy is in the University of Wyoming Library, started from St. Joseph with a Dr. Knapp. His diary ends while still in the Sierra, though a table of distances indicates he went on to Johnson's Ranch, Sacramento, and San Francisco.

An eastbound Mormon journal additional to those listed on page 178 above is that of Oliver Boardman Huntington, who left Salt Lake April 14 in Allen Compton's mail party, reached Fort Laramie May 8, and says he encountered the first Forty-niners near the Forks of the Platte about May 14 or 15; he reached Kanesville May 25. Huntington's is a full record only as far as South Pass, April 26. Photocopies are in the Bancroft and Huntington libraries, and a typed transcript in the Utah State Historical Society.

INDEX